ADOLESCENT-TO-PARENT ABUSE

Current understandings in research, policy and practice

Amanda Holt

First published in Great Britain in 2013 by

The Policy Press
University of Bristol
Fourth Floor
Beacon House
Queen's Road
Bristol BS8 1QU
UK
Tel +44 (0)117 331 4054
Fax +44 (0)117 331 4093
e-mail tpp-info@bristol.ac.uk
www.policypress.co.uk

North American office:
The Policy Press
c/o The University of Chicago Press
1427 East 60th Street
Chicago, IL 60637, USA
t: +1 773 702 7700
f: +1 773-702-9756
e:sales@press.uchicago.edu
www.press.uchicago.edu

British Library Cataloguing in Publication Data
A catalogue record for this book is available from the British Library.

Library of Congress Cataloging-in-Publication Data
A catalog record for this book has been requested.

ISBN 978 1 44730 055 7 paperback
ISBN 978 1 44730 056 4 hardcover

Cover design by Robin Hawes
Front cover: image kindly supplied by www.istock.com
Printed and bound in Great Britain by TJ International, Padstow
The Policy Press uses environmentally responsible print partners

Contents

List of figures, tables and boxes   v
Acknowledgements   vi

Introduction: the problem of adolescent-to-parent abuse   1
    What is parent abuse?   1
    Problems with terminology   3
    "I didn't do anything about it at the time": problems in   4
    researching parent abuse
    The importance of this book   8
    "The time has come to do something about it": why now?   9
    Overview of chapters   11
    Summary   12

one   **Abuse in families: commonalities, connections and**   15
    contexts
    Introduction   15
    Abuse in families   15
    The emergence of family abuses as a 'social problem'   19
    The relationship between different forms of family abuse   24
    The prevalence of parent abuse: populations and   26
    sub-populations
    Summary   34

two   **Experiences of parent abuse**   37
    Introduction   37
    Abusive behaviours in the child–parent relationship   37
    The development of the 'parent abuse dynamic'   43
    The impact of parent abuse   49
    Summary   54

three   **Explaining parent abuse**   57
    Introduction   57
    From identifying 'factors' to developing explanations   57
    Intrapersonal explanations   58
    Interpersonal explanations   62
    Intrafamilial explanations: family systems of communication   68
    Structural explanations: isolation, peers and deprivation   71
    How do parents understand the causes of parent abuse?   73
    Summary   76

four	**Parents, children and power relations**	**79**
	Introduction	79
	The social construction of the child–parent relationship	79
	The reshaping of children, parents and the state	82
	Parenthood, childhood and power	85
	Gender, parenthood and power	92
	Summary	96
five	**Frontline service responses to parent abuse**	**99**
	Introduction	99
	Frontline service responses: inconsistency, perversity and a policy silence	99
	Criminal justice responses to parent abuse	100
	Local authority social services' responses to parent abuse	107
	Education and health service responses to parent abuse	111
	Voluntary and community responses to parent abuse	112
	Key recommendations for policy makers	115
	Summary	117
six	**Working with parent abuse**	**119**
	Introduction	119
	Working with parent abuse: setting the scene	119
	Group interventions	125
	Family interventions	132
	Potential prevention strategies	138
	Summary	140
seven	**Adolescent-to-parent abuse: future directions for research, policy and practice**	**143**
	Whose responsibility?	143
	Future directions for policy making	144
	Future directions for practice	147
	Future directions for research	149
	For parents and families	151
Resources		**153**
	Resources for practitioners	153
	Resources for researchers	154
	Resources for parents	154
Appendix: Adolescent-to-parent abuse: initial assessment		157
References		159
Index		183

List of figures, tables and boxes

Figures

2.1   The development of the 'parent abuse dynamic'   45
6.1   The Abuse and Respect Wheels   131

Tables

1.1   Commonalities and differences across forms of family abuse   18
        (UK)
5.1   Sources of support sought by parents experiencing parent   100
        abuse (UK)
5.2   Statutory frontline service responses to parent abuse   113
        (England and Wales)
6.1   Summary of established parent abuse intervention   123
        programmes and approaches

Boxes

1.1   The prevalence of parent abuse in the UK   28
3.1   Identifying parent abuse   60
4.1   Feminist explanations of parent abuse   94
6.1   Example of a young person's 'rap' from the Break4Change   128
        programme
6.2   What parents have found to be helpful in interventions   138
        for parent abuse

Acknowledgements

I would like to thank the following for advice, comments and information: Robin Bhairam, David Carson, John Coleman, Tim Early, Nollaig Frost, Carol Hayden, Peter Jakob, Lesley Murray, Judy Nixon and Simon Retford.

I would also like to thank the staff and students at the Institute of Criminal Justice Studies, University of Portsmouth; Karen Bowler and Laura Vickers at The Policy Press, and Rowena Mayhew, copy editor; and my friends and family for their encouragement and support throughout the writing of this book.

I would like to gratefully acknowledge the generosity of all the anonymous participants whose experiences shaped this book – without whom, the problem of parent abuse would remain unarticulated.

The problem of adolescent-to-parent abuse

"He'll scream and shout at me, awful abuse, absolutely awful abuse. He'll throw things at me, he'll punch holes in doors, he'll threaten to hit me, and this'll be all in front of my three little ones. So when it came to punching holes in the front door, screaming abuse at me at eight o'clock in the morning, I thought, 'No, the time has come to do something about it.' 'Cos one time that he was kicking off, he was throwing things at me and it ricocheted off me and hit my youngest baby, who is 21 months you know, and a shoe ricocheted off me and hit him. Well I can't have that. I didn't do anything about it at the time, but that sort of behaviour I can't have. He's done it in front of his friends, thrown big pieces of hardboard at me and garden toys and everything and I said to his friends, 'Look, I'm not a horrible mum, John is just like this.'" (Sally, mother of John, aged 15 – from *original transcript*,[1] Holt, 2009)

What is parent abuse?

Sally's experience may sound very familiar to those who have experienced, researched or worked with victimisation in the family home. But what might make Sally's experience less familiar to readers is that her perpetrator is 15 years old, and is her son. And while abuse directed towards parents from children and young people appears to be as prevalent as other forms of family abuse, experiences of it remain unarticulated. Parent abuse refers to *a pattern of behaviour that uses verbal, financial, physical or emotional means to practise power and exert control over a parent.* The parent may be a biological parent, step-parent or a parent in a legal capacity, and the son or daughter is still legally a child (ie, under 18 years) and is usually living in the family home with their parent(s). As Sally's account highlights, parent abuse is likely to involve both physical and non-physical forms of abuse, and the exercise of control is usually evidenced by the parent's inability to 'do anything about it'. Furthermore, like all forms of family abuse, it produces both short-term distress and long-term harm for the families involved: empirical research has been relatively consistent in identifying fear, guilt, shame and despair in parents and feelings of helplessness and inadequacy in the child or young person. It is also implicated in damage to physical and mental health. As in Sally's case, siblings may also be at risk of harm, and it has been found to strain relationships with other family members. It can also disrupt the employment, education and financial stability of individuals and families.

However, what makes 'parent abuse' distinctive from other forms of family abuse is that it involves a transgression of conventional notions of power relations. In cases of *child abuse, intimate partner violence, elder abuse* and even *sibling abuse*, the perpetrator is understood to have both 'cultural authority' and greater economic, political and physical power in relation to the victim. This is not necessarily the case with parent abuse and this makes understanding it and responding to it particularly difficult. The term 'abuse' generally refers to an 'abuse of power' committed by those with the *most power* against those with the *least power*. But in cases of parent abuse, what kind of power *is* being exploited by the child or young person? This conundrum highlights the limitations of current theorising around family abuse when applied to the dynamics of adolescent-to-parent abuse, and perhaps begins to explain the lack of research attention to this particular form of family abuse.

In clarifying what we mean by 'parent abuse', it is also important to clarify what parent abuse is *not*, and therefore what is beyond the scope of this book. Parent abuse goes beyond the everyday experiences of children 'hitting out' at parents, which can happen for all sorts of medical, developmental and situational reasons and is therefore outside the parameters of 'abusive behaviour'. It also goes beyond 'one-off' incidents: parent abuse involves a *pattern of behaviour* that occurs repeatedly. This is not to suggest that one-off incidents of aggression or injury are not serious, but that it is the *continual* nature of the abusive behaviours that causes such devastating effects, and these effects tend to be cumulative, rather than incident-specific. Indeed, repetition (or threats of repetition) forms an integral part of abuse, because of the control it enables and the fear it provokes.

It is also important to distinguish parent abuse from *elder abuse*, which refers to adult abuse towards another who has reached post-retirement age (and who may or may not be a parent to the perpetrator). Clearly there is still a debate to be had regarding when and if one form of family abuse transforms into another, but the shift in power dynamics as family members transition to a later life stage is likely to produce a different abusive context to the one where adolescent-to-parent abuse plays out, and we therefore need to be mindful of this distinction. Finally, this book does not consider *parricide*, the act of killing one's father or mother (although the term technically applies to the killing of any close relative). This is an extremely rare phenomenon that has been found to be unique and distinct from parent abuse in terms of its case characteristics.[2]

Problems with terminology

"The nearest we would come to is a category for 'socially unacceptable child behaviour', and that would be the one we would choose. But that would [also] include drugs and alcohol, missing from home, stealing, offending in the community, and obviously not necessarily parent abuse." (Practitioner from a Multi-agency Risk Assessment Team, England – from Holt and Retford, 2012: 3)

Another defining feature of parent abuse is that the terminology used to name it is not consistent across professions or academic disciplines. The terms we use, and the breadth of behaviours that they incorporate, are important not just for the purpose of defining research and theoretical parameters, but also because they affect parents' and young people's ability and readiness to articulate their experiences and seek help and support. It also shapes who they seek help and support from. Terminology also affects policy makers' and practitioners' readiness to respond to such help-seeking, particularly in terms of where they see the extent and limits of their professional obligations. Frizzell's (1998) analysis of parent abuse suggests that it is professionals, rather than the families themselves, who are in control of the definitional process and such control extends to the research community who exercise a great deal of power through their 'scientific authority' (Muehlenhard et al, 1992). It is important therefore to justify why this book has the title that it has.

'Adolescent-to-parent abuse' and the less-cumbersome 'parent abuse' are the most commonly used terms in the research literature, and these are the terms that are used throughout this book. I use the terms to centralise the *abusive* nature of the problematic relationship in question. I also use them as I consider it important to include non-injurious forms of abusive behaviours – such as financial, verbal and emotional abuse – which are often integral to the abusive dynamic where physically injurious forms of abuse also feature. However, it is important to acknowledge that, for some families, the notion of *abusive* and *abused* family members may be unpalatable, given the extreme forms of brutality and pathology that these terms usually connote. Therefore it may be a term that families are reluctant to identify with. Other research refers to 'child-to-parent violence' or 'adolescent-to-parent violence'. Such terms are useful in highlighting the potential criminality of the behaviour, and indeed are found most frequently in criminal justice research. However, such terms inevitably include violence that is not necessarily abusive (eg, violence against a father in an attempt to protect a mother or siblings) and exclude forms of continued psychological aggression, which can be extremely damaging nevertheless. Other less-used terms in the research literature include variants of 'teenage *aggression* towards parents', 'youth who *assault* parents', '*battered* parents', 'parents *victimised* by children' and '*filial violence*'. Other literature has gendered the parent and/or the child or young person (eg, '*male* adolescent violence towards *mothers*') to reflect both the theoretical approach of the research and its sample base.[3]

To some degree, this lack of consensus regarding terminology reflects the relative infancy in recognising that parent abuse is a problem worthy of research. It also reflects the multidimensional nature of the problem, and an uncertainty as to what its defining characteristic actually is. Yet the question of terminology is important because each term serves to frame the problem in a particular way. This has implications for how we conceptualise the problem and the methods we employ to find out about it, as well as for how policy makers and practitioners respond to it. Furthermore, the current impoverishment of language that is available to parents living with abusive children can exacerbate feelings of isolation that parent abuse already produces. Using the example of incestuous child sexual abuse, Kitzinger (2010, p 89) explains how, before cultural recognition of the problem in the 1980s, which included the naming of it, survivors struggled 'to articulate the literally unspeakable'. Thus, terminology is important because, without it, people may not come forward to either seek support or indeed participate in research.

"I didn't do anything about it at the time": problems in researching parent abuse

Researching family abuse is inherently difficult. Mainly this is because it takes place within an arena that is understood universally to be 'private', while access to research participants is further complicated because of the social isolation that is often a feature of such cases. Furthermore, victims of family abuse may, at times, deny the existence or extent of the problem. Therefore, identifying and accessing participants willing to share their experiences are difficult. However, such problems are exacerbated in cases of parent abuse – partly because of the difficulties in 'naming' the problem discussed earlier, and also because parent abuse involves a 'double stigma', featuring the widely documented stigma of experiencing violence in the home (eg, Stanko, 2003), alongside the stigma associated with parenting a 'problematic' child or young person (eg, Jackson and Mannix, 2004). Despite such difficulties, research about parent abuse has slowly emerged since the late 1970s. The majority of this research has come from Australia, Canada, New Zealand and the United States (US), but important research has also emerged from China, Germany, Hungary, Israel, Japan, Spain and, very recently, the United Kingdom (UK).

My review of this literature base (see Holt, 2012a) identified four principal methodologies that have been used to find out about parent abuse. First, there has been an examination of existing criminal justice data, which have been collected at different stages of the criminal justice process. This has produced knowledge based on what are often referred to as 'forensic samples', which includes data from parents' formal complaints to the police about their child's abusive and/or violent behaviour (eg, Evans and Warren-Sohlberg, 1988), incident and arrest data (eg, Walsh and Krienert, 2007; Strom et al, 2010), data from court proceedings (eg, Kethineni, 2004; Gebo, 2007) and sentencing data (eg, Cochran et al, 1994). While such methods have been useful in producing large datasets available for statistical analysis, they only include cases at the most severe end of the abuse spectrum – that is, those that can be conceptualised as discrete 'incidents' that constitute criminal activity (and which therefore predominantly feature *physical* abuse). As such, these methods are likely to underestimate the *prevalence* of parent abuse (which refers to the total number of cases in a given population at any one time). Indeed, they are likely to underestimate the prevalence of cases that result in criminal action because many cases do not record 'parent abuse' as a feature of the incident (eg, a case may be recorded as 'criminal damage' without any reference to the parent as victim).

Second, large-scale epidemiological surveys have produced data from the general population, known as 'community samples', which do enable the identification of general prevalence patterns. Although not primarily concerned with parent abuse, some surveys have included questions about adolescents' violent behaviour towards their parents.

Examples include analysis from the US National Survey of Youth (Agnew and Huguley, 1989), the US-based national Youth in Transition (YIT) survey of male adolescents (Peek et al, 1985; Brezina, 1999, 2000) and the Canadian-based longitudinal Quebec Longitudinal Study of Kindergarten Children (Pagani et al, 2003, 2004, 2009). This methodological approach also includes crime-specific surveys such as the US-based National Family Violence Survey, which explored a range of violent behaviour (including violence towards parents) that takes place within the family (eg, Cornell and Gelles, 1982). Even more specialised is the Child-to-Mother Violence Scale (CMVS), which was developed by Edenborough et al (2008) in Australia and which surveyed a specially selected sample of mothers who live in violent areas to assess their experiences of parent abuse. However, all such surveys tend to rely on retrospective accounts and subjective interpretations, and use narrow questions that, in the main, focus only on experiences of *physical* abuse (whether as adolescent-perpetrators or as parent-victims).

Both criminal justice data and survey data tend to rely on quantitative data that tells us little about the wider context of parent abuse, or about the ways in which it unfolds. This is because both methods tend to construct parent abuse as a static 'event' or incident, rather than as an ongoing abusive dynamic that such incidents may or may not be a part of. To address this gap, since the 1990s much qualitative work has begun to explore these issues. This has been made possible by the emergence of local intervention programmes that have produced readily available 'clinical samples' of service users who have been questioned about their experiences of both parent abuse and the programme itself (eg, Cottrell and Monk, 2004; Munday, 2009; Routt and Anderson, 2011). While rich in detail, interview data from service users is currently limited by small sample sizes (often less than 20) and unsystematic evaluation designs. It is also important to note that the findings can only reflect the experiences of those families who have already sought help and support.

A fourth principal methodology, which has also drawn on 'clinical samples', has involved researching those families who have been referred for medico-psychiatric intervention. In such cases, practitioners have produced data either qualitatively, through the use of clinical observations and case notes (eg, Harbin and Madden, 1979; Charles, 1986; Micucci, 1995; Sheehan, 1997) or quantitatively, through the analysis of large datasets derived from clinical records in an attempt to identify 'typologies' of parent abuse (eg, Laurent and Derry, 1999; Nock and Kazdin, 2002; Boxer et al, 2009). Despite the difference in method, both approaches have been used to identify potential 'causes' of parent abuse from a psychopathological perspective.

Adolescent-to-parent abuse: Current understandings in research, policy and practice draws on research produced by all of these principal methodologies, and as such research findings need to be considered in terms of the methodological limitations outlined here. As with any social research, different kinds of methods tend to yield different kinds of findings since each draws on different definitions, populations and outcome measures. The lack of consistency in what we can say with confidence has certainly been a barrier to measuring the prevalence and frequency of parent abuse, to understanding its development and maintenance, and to working out appropriate strategies for intervention at primary, secondary and tertiary levels. Nevertheless, after 30 years of research it is important to recognise that we can say *something* about parent abuse, and one of the key aims of this book is to draw together this disparate knowledge to identify commonalities within this diverse research base. However, the book also draws on original data from three small-scale qualitative studies. The first study involved interviewing parents from the south of England about their experiences of parenting a 'young offender'. During these in-depth interviews, many parents spoke to me about their own experiences of physical, emotional, financial and verbal abuse within the family home, which was perpetrated by their teenage children, and I include extracts from these interviews throughout the book (see Holt, 2009). A second study analysed accounts of parent abuse that had been posted on two UK-based online parenting support forums, and my analysis explored how such experiences were constructed in an online context (see Holt, 2011). A third study involved interviews with practitioners who worked within different frontline service organisations within one metropolitan district in the north of England. This local case study explored practitioners' attempts to respond to cases of adolescent-to-parent abuse from within their own policy frameworks and from their collective resource base (see Holt and Retford, 2012). Like much of the parent abuse research that draws on qualitative data, these research findings are drawn from relatively small samples, and I do not claim to be able to make broad generalisations from them. But I do hope that, by drawing together this original data with findings from other published research studies, consistencies across the data can be identified to provide much-needed insights into this important, yet hidden problem.

The importance of this book

One of the common findings identified in the research literature is the devastating immediate and long-term impact that parent abuse can have on individuals and families. Both in the UK and elsewhere, the lack of any national policy response has meant that practitioners from a number of agencies at the local level have had to develop programmes and interventions of their own with few resources. Many of these initiatives have produced positive effects for the families involved, and therefore a further aim of this book is to share these examples of good practice while emphasising the need for policy makers to acknowledge the problem of parent abuse and develop the national and regional policy responses that are so sorely needed.

While this book is written from a UK perspective, I have drawn heavily on the international evidence base for at least three reasons. First, countries outside the UK – notably Australia and the US – have been much quicker to recognise parent abuse as a topic worthy of research attention. And while of course there are some differences in findings across the international literature base, there are also sufficient commonalities to suggest that much can be learned and applied. Second, one of the aims of this book is to extend the debate beyond the 'individual' and the 'family' and to explore the wider political and cultural contexts of parent abuse. As highlighted earlier, understanding the role of power in child–parent interactions is key, and the power relations that operate within families need to be understood as part of a continuum of power relations that operate in wider society. And in the absence of existing comparative research into parent abuse, drawing on international perspectives enables us to consider how parent abuse is played out at a societal level, and to understand how individuals, families and communities shape and are shaped by their political, national and cultural contexts. Finally, it is becoming increasingly apparent that parent abuse transcends national borders and is a growing problem across them. Therefore, this book has been intentionally written to appeal to an international audience, and it includes research, theory and practice case examples that are sufficiently inclusive to 'ring true' to those researchers, practitioners and policy makers who work outside of the UK.

"The time has come to do something about it": why now?

Different forms of family abuse (eg, intimate partner violence, child abuse and so on) each came into being as a unique 'social problem' and the history of each of these emergences is distinct (see Chapter One). However, as Finkelhor (1983) astutely observed, the social histories of their emergence share a similar developmental process: initially, there is a denial or minimisation of its existence, with claims made as to its rarity and exceptional quality. Then, once the 'social problem' has come to public attention, analysis invariably focuses on the extreme pathology of the perpetrator and, alongside (or instead of) this, the culpability of the victim. With this in mind, it is perhaps unsurprising that the first academic paper dedicated to addressing parent abuse conceptualised the problem from a psychopathological perspective through the use of the medico-psychiatric term 'battered parent syndrome'. 'Battered parents: a new syndrome' was published in the *American Journal of Psychiatry* by Harbin and Madden (1979) and, using anecdotes based on the clinical observations of 28 families, the authors argued that dysfunctional family dynamics in the form of 'overly-permissive parenting' were the cause of such abuses. Indeed, the denial and minimisation that Finkelhor (1983) identified within the social histories of family abuse appeared to have been replicated within these families themselves, as Harbin and Madden (1979) noted how family members avoided discussing the abuse, minimised its seriousness and refused outside help.

A second influential publication was Straus et al's (1980) *Behind closed doors: Violence in the American family*. This book explored data from the comprehensive National Family Violence Survey and identified a significant degree of violence taking place in US family homes. A focused analysis of this data in relation to parent abuse found 9% of parents reporting that their children (aged 10-17) had been violent towards them at least once in the previous 12 months, with the most common forms of violence identified as 'pushed or shoved', 'slapped' and 'threw things'. Severe violence, defined as 'punching', 'kicking' or 'use of a knife or gun', had a prevalence rate of 3% over the previous year.

Research literature exploring parent abuse continued steadily throughout the 1980s, and the emergence of more practice-orientated research in the mid-1990s saw this development quicken and diversify. Two key books that drew on this practice literature were Price's (1996) *Power and compassion: Working with difficult adolescents and abused parents*, which was aimed predominantly at therapeutic practitioners, and Cottrell's (2005) *When teens abuse their parents*, which was aimed predominantly at parents. However, no further books on the topic have been published, and until now, no book has attempted to draw together findings from a range of theoretical and practice perspectives to offer a comprehensive analysis of current understandings of parent abuse in research, policy and practice.

There are a number of possible explanations as to why there has been such a silence surrounding adolescent-to-parent abuse compared to other forms of family abuse (most notably child abuse and intimate partner abuse, both of which have gripped public and political attention at different times). For one, there is no obvious campaign group (such as the women's movement) or professional organisation (such as childcare professions based in social work or education) that might enable a collective advocacy role in relation to parent abuse. And two, given that parent abuse is characterised by an inverse of traditional power relations, there is no obvious 'deserving victim'. Indeed, if anything, the past 20 years have seen an intensification of the culture of 'parent blame' in relation to troublesome and troubled young people. Across a number of Euro-American[4] jurisdictions, this has culminated in the introduction of parental responsibility laws, which have enabled courts to formally criminalise parents for the behaviour of their children.[5] However, perhaps far more pervasive has been the concomitant proliferation of parenting resources – for example, parenting classes, parenting manuals and 'transformative' parenting television programmes such as *Supernanny*. While some might consider such resources to be a welcome support for parents, such a cultural shift might also be considered to represent a more problematic form of regulation and surveillance over particularly disadvantaged parents. But irrespective of its meaning, such a heated political and cultural context makes the idea of parents *as victims* of their children appear untenable. Indeed, despite an abundance of parenting classes, books and television programmes, the problem of parent abuse rarely comes up, which only adds to the sense of isolation that is a feature of parents' experiences of parent abuse (see Chapter Three). Indeed, it is telling that when the content of parenting support resources is produced by parents themselves, such as on interactive website support forums, the problem of parent abuse, and the lack of available support, are very much in evidence (see Holt, 2011).

However, a public and political recognition of parent abuse as a social problem may not be far off. There certainly appears to be increasing research interest in the topic and Routt and Anderson (2011) suggest two reasons for this. First, researchers are increasingly recognising the role of *intergenerational transmission* in the development and commission of family violence, particularly in relation to witnessing domestic violence as a child, and alongside this is an increasing acknowledgement that parent abuse may play an important role in this cycle. Second, practitioners 'on the ground' are increasingly vocal in their need for established protocols and appropriate interventions for dealing with parent abuse, and this is forcing the pace of research and thinking. I hope that this book will contribute to this development.

Overview of chapters

This book begins by raising a number of themes, which are then developed in subsequent chapters. However, readers are also invited to dip in and out of the book, as each chapter retains a distinctive focus, which may be of particular interest to particular readers.

Chapter One develops many of the themes raised in this Introduction by situating parent abuse within the wider context of family abuse. It provides a brief overview of how child abuse, intimate partner violence, sibling abuse and elder abuse emerged as social problems in theory and in practice, and explores the similarities, differences and relationships between such family abuses and parent abuse. The chapter then explores what we know about the prevalence of parent abuse, and patterns in gender, age and other case characteristics.

Chapter Two focuses on findings from qualitative research regarding how parents experience abuse perpetrated by their children. It discusses different forms of parent abuse and examines its emergence and maintenance. It then describes the effects of abuse on parents and their families, including its impact on mental, physical and emotional health and on relationships, employment, finances and communities.

Chapter Three explores the different scientific explanations that have been put forward to explain parent abuse. These include *intra*personal explanations (which draw on the role of psychopathologies, substance use and personality and/or behavioural characteristics); *inter*personal explanations (which highlight the role of generational transmission of violence and early parenting practices); *intra*familial explanations (which discuss the role of family communication styles); and structural explanations (which explore the role of poverty, social isolation and peer influence). The chapter concludes with an exploration of how parents themselves understand the abuse and how these relate to scientific explanations.

Chapter Four adopts a sociocultural approach to explore how the organisation of power relations between parents and children may be implicated in the manifestation of particular abusive tactics within the 'parent abuse dynamic'. The chapter begins by exploring how 'parenthood' and 'childhood' have been constructed in 21st-century Euro-American cultures before discussing how shifts in the relative power of children and parents *outside* the family home might shape the power dynamics between children and parents *inside* the family home. The chapter concludes with an examination of how gender and age mediate power relations between children and parents and explores their role in the commission of parent abuse.

Chapter Five explores how frontline services respond to parent abuse, with a focus on service responses in England and Wales. It identifies the tools that are available to criminal justice agents (eg, the police, courts and youth offending services), local authority social care departments (children's and adults') and health and education practitioners. The chapter then discusses how the voluntary and community sectors can and do respond before concluding with five key recommendations for policy makers as to how the evident gaps in service responses might be addressed.

Chapter Six explores the development of local intervention work and identifies what lessons can be learned from such programmes. The chapter begins by exploring the help-seeking contexts of parent abuse, important issues in clinical assessment, and the plurality of strategies and approaches that working with parent abuse demands. The chapter then discusses a range of established group programmes and family interventions that have been developed in response to parent abuse and identifies what characteristics of such interventions make them successful. The chapter concludes with an exploration of potential prevention strategies.

Chapter Seven offers a brief overview of the key messages from the book and sets out future directions for policy makers, practitioners and researchers in tackling the problem of adolescent-to-parent abuse.

Summary

- Parent abuse involves a pattern of behaviour that uses physical and non-physical means to practise power and exert control over a parent.
- A number of terms are used in researching parent abuse, most commonly 'parent abuse', but also 'child-to-parent violence', 'aggression towards parents' and 'filial violence'.
- To date, four distinct research methods have been used to produce knowledge about parent abuse. These are secondary analyses of criminal justice data, large-scale surveys, small-scale qualitative data

produced by intervention groups with service users, and case study or typological analyses carried out by medico-psychiatric professionals.

- Over the past 30 years, there has been a gradual increase of research into parent abuse, but it is yet to achieve the status of 'social problem' in the way that other forms of family abuse have. However, due to professional recognition of its role in other social problems, this is likely to change.

Notes

[1] Throughout this book, where a source line for a direct quote states *original transcript* and then cites a publication, the quote came from the research conducted for the publication cited but was not included in the published text.

[2] A large-scale US study found that, in cases of *parricide*, offenders are more likely to be male, older and white, and are more likely to use a weapon, compared to perpetrators of *parent abuse*. Victims of parricide are more likely to be male, older, white and step-parents compared to victims of parent abuse (Walsh and Krienert, 2009). There is also evidence that offenders committing *parricide* have frequently experienced severe abuse from their parent(s) (Heide, 1992).

[3] While the term 'parent abuse' is used throughout this book to refer to the issue generically, when referring to specific research studies the terms used are those commensurate with each author's use.

[4] I use the term 'Euro-American' here in the same way Strathern (1997, p 42) uses the term to refer to 'the largely middle-class North American/ Northern European discourse of public and professional life'. As such, I use the term conceptually (rather than geographically) to highlight the culturally determined nature of the processes that are under discussion in this (and other) chapters.

[5] See, for example, the use of Parenting Orders in England and Wales (eg, Holt, 2008), the use of parental compensation and restitution measures across Australian states (eg, McMahon, 2004) and the use of parental responsibility laws across the US (eg, Harris, 2006).

ONE

Abuse in families: commonalities, connections and contexts

Introduction

This chapter aims to contextualise 'parent abuse' within a wider framework of family abuse. It begins by providing an overview of the historical context, characteristics and prevalence of different kinds of abuse in families (ie, child abuse, intimate partner violence [IPV], elder abuse and sibling abuse) before identifying their conceptual similarities, differences and connections. The chapter then explores what we know about the prevalence and personal and situational characteristics of adolescent-to-parent abuse (eg, gender, age, ethnicity and so on) before considering the role of cultural context in its emergence and identification.

Abuse in families

While there is a dominant narrative within all cultures that families are a place of safety and protection, for many families across the world this is not the case. Indeed, Gelles and Straus (1979) suggest that the unique characteristics of the family make it the most violent of all institutions. These unique characteristics that enable its violence include:

- the intensity of time that family members spend together;
- the intensity of commitment that family members must make to each other;
- the conflict-structured nature of family interactions, which have a competitive 'zero-sum game' quality to them (eg, family interactions over television channel choice, which means that, if one family member 'wins', another must 'lose');
- the differing social locations of family members, in terms of age and gender (and the roles and statuses ascribed to these social locations);
- the high degree of privacy the family enjoys away from formal controls and surveillance;

- the extensive knowledge that family members have of each others' social biographies and vulnerabilities;
- the continual life transitions that a family must undergo (eg, births, divorces, deaths), which makes it particularly stress-prone.

Family abuse can be directed towards – and perpetrated by – spouses, parents, children, siblings and grandparents, as well as extended family members. In this book, 'abuse' is understood as a pattern of interaction that has the effect of disempowering an individual. Furthermore, given its relational nature, it requires both a degree of intentionality on the part of the perpetrator and an experience of disempowerment on the part of the abused. However, identifying what constitutes 'abuse' is problematic because ideas about what is 'acceptable' and 'unacceptable' behaviour within the dynamic of 'family relationships' are both historically and culturally determined. Understanding the context of abuse is therefore critical to its identification, and perhaps the most important context is the *harm caused*. The harm caused may be immediate and/or long term and while it may produce material damage (eg, physical injuries or damage to property), the continual abuse of power can also damage an individual's dignity, independence and sense of personal agency.

In most Euro-American cultures today, abuse in families is understood to take a number of forms:

- **physical abuse** – including hitting, slapping, pushing and kicking; misuse of restraint or sanctions;
- **emotional abuse** – including verbal abuse, threats of harm or abandonment, blackmail and coercion, harassment, humiliation and intimidation, undermining of competence and self-esteem;
- **financial/material abuse** – including theft, fraud, exploitation, coercion and pressure regarding transactions; misuse/misappropriation of, demands for or damage to property, possessions, benefits and/ or money;
- **sexual abuse** – including rape, sexual assault and other sexual acts (including non-contact acts) without consent, or where the individual is unable to consent;
- **neglect** – including failure to provide access to health care, social care or education; ignoring care needs and withholding medication, nutrition or heating.

Depending on the formation of the family relationship in question, some of these forms will be more pertinent than others. For example, while neglect is likely to feature in cases where there is a dependent relationship (such as those involving a child or an older person), neglect is a less relevant form of abuse in other cases, such as *adolescent-to-parent abuse*. Similarly, financial abuse is likely to feature in cases of *elder abuse* since the older person may possess financial resources and property, but it is likely to have less salience in cases of *child abuse* or *sibling abuse*. Further, the social location (eg, gender, age) of the individuals involved will also shape forms of abuse. Thus, sexual abuse is more prevalent in cases of *IPV* and *child abuse*, in part because of the way that women and children are sexualised in dominant cultural media. Furthermore, not all of these forms of abuse may constitute a criminal offence.

However, different forms of family abuse – namely child abuse, IPV, elder abuse, sibling abuse and parent abuse – also share a number of similarities. For example, they all produce similar kinds of immediate and long-term harms (in terms of both physical and mental health problems) and frequently (although not always) feature a gendered dynamic, with 'male perpetrator → female victim' being the most common dyad. The high likelihood of *repeat victimisations* and the high frequency of *polyvictimisation*, whereby the same individual is likely to experience a number of types of abuse simultaneously (such as physical abuse and sexual abuse, for example) are also common to all forms of family abuse. There is also increasing evidence that people with disabilities are particularly vulnerable to all forms of family abuse and violence, with additional disability-specific abusive tactics directed towards them (Sullivan and Knutson, 2000; Hassouneh-Phillips and Curry, 2002).

It is important to note that differences in definitions and methods of data collection both across different forms of family abuse and within different research studies make it problematic to make definitive conclusions in terms of comparisons. Nevertheless, Table 1.1 highlights some key similarities and differences, using data from the United Kingdom (UK) as an example.

Table 1.1: Commonalities and differences across forms of family abuse (UK)

Abuse	Emergence of social problem	Advocacy organisations	Statutory responsibilities	Victimisation: lifetime prevalence	Gender of victim (prevalence)	Gender of perpetrator (ratio)	Effects of victimisation	Reference
Child abuse	1850s–1910, then 1960s	NSPCC; Barnardo's; CEOP; Save the Children; Action for Children	Local authorities and family courts	25%: Overall[a] 16%: Neglect 8%: Physical 7%: Emotional 1%: Sexual	27%: Female 23%: Male	66:33 ratio of male:female perpetrator	Physical injury; trauma-related symptoms (eg, insomnia, anxiety, guilt); suicidal ideation and attempted suicide; self-harm; delinquency (eg, violence, truancy, drug misuse)	NSPCC (2011)
Intimate partner violence	1960s–1970s	Women's Aid; Refuge	Multi-agency, including specialist police response	20.3%: Overall[b] 12.6%: Physical 12.1%: Non-physical (emotional and financial) 10.5%: Sexual	26.6%: Female 14%: Male	92:8 ratio of male:female perpetrator*	Physical injury; reproductive health problems; mental health problems (eg, depression, anxiety, post-traumatic stress disorder, self-harm); emotional problems (eg, trust in relationships); suicide attempts	Home Office (2012) *Hester et al (2006)
Elder abuse	1980s	Action on Elder Abuse	Department of Health; social services	3.4% : Overall[c] 1.2%: Financial 0.8%: Physical 0.3%: Sexual	4.3%: Female 2.3%: Male	74:26 ratio of male:female perpetrator	Emotional symptoms (eg, anger, upset); social isolation; physical injury (eg, discomfort, pain)	O'Keefe et al (2007)
Sibling abuse	1980s	None specifically, but see Child abuse	None specifically, but see Child abuse	25.2%: Overall[d] 11%: Physical* 1.7%: Sexual*	UK studies inconclusive: Wiehe (1997) suggests female victim:male perpetrator is most common dyad		Trauma-related symptoms; suicidal ideation; self-harm	NSPCC (2011) *Browne and Hamilton (1998)
Parent abuse	–	–	–	14.5%: Overall[e]	8.5%: Female 6.1%: Male	No significant difference	Emotional problems (eg, guilt, betrayal, grief); social isolation; physical and mental health problems (eg, anxiety, depression); relationship, employment and financial problems*	Browne and Hamilton (1998) *See Chapter Three

Notes:
CEOP = Child Exploitation and Online Protection Centre; NSPCC = National Society for the Prevention of Cruelty to Children.
[a] Prevalence refers to experience over lifetime of childhood abuse (including neglect) from adult family member (from sample aged 18-24 years).
[b] Prevalence refers to experience over lifetime of IPV since age of 16 years (from sample aged 16-59 years).
[c] Prevalence refers to experience of abuse (including neglect) since age of 65 years (from sample aged 66 years and over).
[d] Prevalence refers to experience over lifetime of sibling abuse (ie, by sibling aged under 18 years) in childhood (from sample aged 18-24 years).
[e] Prevalence refers to experience over lifetime of perpetrating 'violent tactics' against parent at least once (from sample of undergraduate university students).

The emergence of family abuses as a 'social problem'

The differences that do exist across forms of family abuse have much to do with how each has emerged as a distinct 'social problem' within its own socio-historical context. The consequence of this is that different groups of individuals have claimed a stake in each kind of family abuse, whether in terms of campaigning and advocacy on behalf of victims, taking professional responsibility for its management and prevention, or setting out the research parameters for its conceptualisation and theoretical analysis. To illustrate, what follows is a brief overview of how each form of family abuse emerged as a 'social problem', using the UK context as an example. Discussion focuses on how each came to be institutionalised such that it now exists within its own 'infrastructure', which underpins our understanding of and responses to that particular problem. This will serve to highlight both the possibilities and the limitations of extending the conceptual, institutional and policy-making parameters of each form of family abuse so as to incorporate the problem of parent abuse (which has not yet achieved the status of 'social problem').

The emergence of child abuse

The first form of family abuse to be recognised as a 'social problem' was child abuse. In the mid-19th century, concerns over child cruelty and neglect (and its links to subsequent delinquency) emerged within what was known (in both the UK and the US) as the 'child-saving movement'. Voluntary organisations such as the National Society for the Prevention of Cruelty to Children (NSPCC) were established, alongside legislation that gave the state powers to remove children from the family home (Parton, 2007). Ferguson (1996) traces the emergence of a *child protection discourse* from this period, whereby childcare practitioners developed a professional culture and associated practices, which operated around the notion of children being *in need of protection* from abusive and/or neglectful parents. Concerns over *child abuse* within families diminished after the end of the First World War (1914-18) and with the establishment of children's departments and the institutionalisation of social work following the Second World War (1939-45), attention shifted to *child neglect* with a focus on keeping families together.

Therefore, 'child abuse' had to be identified as a 'social problem' for a second time in the 1960s. This time it was framed as a medical issue, having been brought to attention by clinicians from the US through the notion of 'battered baby syndrome' (eg, Kempe et al, 1962). The category of 'child abuse' gradually expanded over the next decade to include abuses that were less observable: emotional abuse and sexual abuse. In the UK, a number of high-profile cases[1] forced the development of practice guidance and legislation following government inquiries. One key development included the broadening of state responsibilities to include all children deemed to be 'at risk'. Today in the UK, responsibility for taking action against child abuse lies with the state, and in particular with family courts and children's social care departments within local authorities. However, all practitioners who work with children (eg, teachers, health workers, criminal justice practitioners) have what are known as 'safeguarding responsibilities' (Parton, 2011). Yet these responsibilities extend only as far as children and young people who are at risk of *victimisation*, and child protection resources and protocol do not extend to safeguarding *adults who are at risk from children and young people*. In the UK, since the establishment of the NSPCC in 1884, numerous child advocacy, support and campaign groups have been established to work on behalf of child victimisation, including Barnardo's, Save the Children and Child Exploitation and Online Protection Centre (CEOP).

The emergence of Intimate Partner Violence

Campaigning against violence towards women in marriage formed an integral part of the first-wave feminist movement (up until the 1920s). However, it emerged much more forcefully during the second wave of feminism in the late 1960s and early 1970s. During this period, voluntary and community organisations established a number of refuges for women and children which, together with campaign groups, applied political pressure for legislative change. In the UK, the establishment of the House of Commons Select Committee on Violence in Marriage in 1974 recognised violence and sexual abuse within the 'matrimonial home' for the first time and with it the need for legislation, policy guidance and resources to respond to it. Since that time, legislation (eg, the Domestic Violence and Matrimonial Proceedings Act 1976), policy guidance (eg, Home Office, 1990), policy initiatives (eg, Multi-Agency Risk Assessment Conferences) and domestic violence delivery plans (eg, Home Office, 2006) have emerged to provide a multi-agency network of resources and working practices in the prevention and intervention of IPV. Furthermore, since 1974, definitions have broadened to include non-married as well as non-cohabiting partners (known as 'dating violence'[2]), and now include lesbian, gay, bisexual and transgender (LGBT) relationships as well as IPV perpetrated by women against men. While local resources have been developed to provide tailored support to these groups (as well as to other marginalised groups such as minority ethnic families), the recent *Call to end violence against women and girls: Action plan* (Home Office, 2011a) highlights plans to develop national policies to support such groups.

Dominant understandings of IPV have most frequently been located within a feminist discourse. As such, male violence against women is commonly conceptualised as part of a wider tapestry of patriarchal relations that underpin our current social and political systems (eg, Dobash and Dobash, 1979). Perhaps because such discourses position children as secondary *victims* of IPV (and of male violence in particular), definitions have always excluded children and adolescents as possible *perpetrators* of violence against women. Such exclusions have been achieved both explicitly through the use of the term 'between adults' in policy documents and implicitly through common reference to the nature of the relationship as one of sexual intimacy, rather than of familial intimacy. IPV support services mainly come from a network of voluntary and community organisations, which together help to provide telephone helplines, legal advocacy, therapeutic support and refuges. In the UK, national organisations include Refuge, Women's Aid, the National Domestic Violence Helpline, Men's Advice Line (for male victims) and Broken Rainbow (for LBGT victims), all of which receive government funds. Other support services operate at regional and local levels, and often depend entirely on voluntary workers and charitable donations.

The emergence of elder abuse

In the same year that Harbin and Madden (1979) published their paper on 'battered parent syndrome' (see previous chapter), findings from a survey of elder abuse in the US were published, under the title *Battered elder syndrome: An exploratory study* (Block and Sinnott, 1979). This study drew on police and social services records together with self-report data and found incident rates comparable to those of IPV and child abuse. The study was seminal in raising awareness of the problem of elder abuse, although the issue was also being raised by the medical profession in the UK from the mid-1970s (Penhale, 2008). Throughout the 1980s, attempts were made in the UK to raise the profile of elder abuse (as had been achieved in the US), through multi-agency conferences (such as the conference on elder abuse sponsored by the

British Geriatrics Society in 1988 – see Holt, 1993) and publications (eg, Eastman, 1984; Tomlin, 1989). However, it was only in the 1990s that elder abuse was recognised by UK policy makers, through the National Health Service and Community Care Act 1990 and the Social Services Inspectorate (SSI, 1992, 1993). Since that time, the Department of Health (DH, 2000, 2001, 2005) and the Association of Directors of Social Services (ADSS, 2005) have produced policy guidance on this issue. Most significant was *No secrets: The protection of vulnerable adults* (DH, 2000) which enabled a coordinated multi-agency response to elder abuse to be led by local authority social services departments. The UK campaign group Action on Elder Abuse was established in 1993, while other international organisations include the International Network for the Prevention of Elder Abuse and the US-based National Committee for the Prevention of Elder Abuse.

To date, little research has explored possible links between parent abuse and subsequent 'elder abuse'. However, this may be less surprising than first appears because the parameters of elder abuse have always been defined clearly in a way that makes it distinct from 'parent abuse'. In particular, UK government documents make reference to adult victims as those who 'may be eligible for community care services … [and] … unable to protect himself or herself' (DH, 2000, p 8). The implied vulnerability of the older person in this definition is also present in how the document sets out the spatial context of elder abuse: nursing, residential and day care settings, hospitals, custodial situations and public places are all listed alongside the family home as locations for potential abuse (DH, 2000). This makes elder abuse a distinct form of family abuse in the sense that, like child abuse, the definition also applies to abuse perpetrated by *non-family* members from *outside* the family home. This distinction makes drawing together analytical threads that underpin family abuses more complex since, in such cases, the centrality of the family may not be the key component of analysis.

The emergence of sibling abuse

Despite evidence that it is widespread and can have traumatising and injurious effects (Finkelhor et al, 2006), there has been relatively little research on sibling abuse. 'Sibling abuse' generally refers to physical, emotional and/or sexual abuse between children living in the same household, regardless of whether they are genetically related. Again, reference to it began in the early 1980s in the US, particularly with the publication of the influential National Family Violence Survey and the finding that 82% of families reported sibling violence (Straus et al, 1980).

Research since that time has been steady, although dominated by the US and Canada, with relatively little research from the UK. Research studies often combine 'sibling' and 'peer' victimisation, which can make it difficult to tease out the salience of family processes within the abusive dynamic. Furthermore, more recent research has also started making reference to sibling and peer 'bullying' when discussing behaviours that were defined previously as abusive or violent (eg, Monks et al, 2009; Naylor et al, 2011), which adds to the sense of nebulousness when attempting to identify, measure and respond to sibling abuse. It may be that it is only when abusive encounters between siblings reflect the personal characteristics of those we expect to be involved in incidents of 'family violence' that it is seen as such – hence the finding that incidents between siblings are most likely to be reported to the police when the perpetrator is aged 14 years or over, and are more likely to feature male perpetrators and female victims (Krienert and Walsh, 2011).

While the protection of children 'at risk' forms part of local authorities' child protection responsibilities (see earlier), sibling abuse has never been a priority. Indeed, there is evidence that its impact is minimised within professional discourses (Phillips et al, 2009) as well as among families themselves (Hardy, 2001; Kettry and Emery, 2006). Along with a reluctance to intrude into 'family business', Wiehe (1997) suggests that the silence is due to an overwhelming discourse of normality and, from some childcare professionals, a belief that abusive behaviours between siblings are an important component of 'growing up'. However, given the documented links between parent abuse and the contemporaneous perpetration of sibling abuse (Laurent and Derry, 1999), this is an issue that is relevant to our understanding of adolescent-to-parent abuse, and how agencies do (or should) respond.

Situating parent abuse within the infrastructures of family abuse

So, we have four different forms of family abuse that have emerged as social problems over the past 50 years. Each has its own distinct social history as to how it became recognised, each has its own advocacy and campaign groups, and each has its own policy and practitioner ownership (or dis-ownership) of responsibilities. In terms of the latter, some of these responsibilities are informed by international treaties regarding human rights abuses – for example, the United Nations' *Convention on the rights of the child* (UN, 1989) and the United Nations' *Declaration on the elimination of violence against women* (UN, 1993). It is important to understand how different forms of abuse have emerged as distinct social problems within their own socio-historical context because the way that social problems emerge shapes how each is distinctly theorised by academics, addressed by policy makers and responded to by practitioners. This is informative when we try to formulate strategies for understanding and responding to *parent abuse*, because at present it has no institutional 'infrastructure' to speak of. Furthermore, as the following chapters will illustrate, attempts to borrow from existing 'infrastructures' to enable scientific explanations (see Chapter Three), policy responses (see Chapter Five) and practitioner responses (see Chapter Six) have understandably fallen short.

What is more, existing institutional infrastructures around family abuse explicitly exclude parent abuse because of how they conceptualise their own problem:

- Conceptualisations of 'child abuse' draw on a dyad of *children at risk* from parental and/or adult perpetrators.
- Conceptualisations of 'IPV' draw on a dyad of women and children at risk from *adult* male perpetrators.
- Conceptualisations of 'elder abuse' draw on a dyad of *vulnerable* adults at risk from *caregiver perpetrators*, who may or may not be a family member.
- Conceptualisations of 'sibling abuse' draw on a dyad of *children at risk* from other child perpetrators.

The dyad under examination in cases of 'parent abuse' takes on some of the characteristics of each of these forms of abuse, but perhaps not sufficiently enough to enable the institutional mechanisms that are already in place to respond to the emerging problem of parent abuse.

The relationship between different forms of family abuse

One outcome of conceptualising family abuses as a set of self-contained social problems is that research attention has focused on examining correlations between them. Particularly consistent are findings that link witnessing domestic violence with experiencing child abuse (eg, Hester et al, 2007). There is also evidence that victimisation in childhood is linked to subsequent perpetration of sibling abuse (Tidefors et al, 2010), that sibling victimisation is linked to subsequent perpetration of dating violence (Simonelli et al, 2002; Sims et al, 2008) and that childhood victimisation is linked to IPV victimisation in adulthood (Coid et al, 2001). There is also considerable evidence of *secondary victimisation*, in that witnessing family abuse produces its own set of immediate and long-term effects, not dissimilar to those produced by primary victimisation in families (eg, Kitzmann et al, 2003).[3] Secondary victimisation might also include the children and young people whose mothers were abused as children, the effects of which continue to shape her children's lives (Noll et al, 2009).

Regarding parent abuse, its links to other forms of family abuse is one line of inquiry that is receiving increased research attention (although this may be due to the expansion of work into other forms of family abuse rather than any newfound interest in parent abuse per se). In particular, research suggests that witnessing IPV is linked to later perpetration of parent abuse (eg, Cornell and Gelles, 1982; McCloskey and Lichter, 2003; Ullman and Straus, 2003; Boxer et al, 2009; Kennedy et al, 2010) and that the perpetration of parent abuse co-occurs with parent-to-child abuse (eg, Cornell and Gelles, 1982; Hartz, 1995; Browne and Hamilton, 1998; Brezina, 1999; Ullman and Straus, 2003; Boxer et al, 2009).[4] Other research has identified links between parent abuse and contemporaneous perpetration of sibling abuse (Laurent and Derry, 1999). Furthermore, evidence suggests that young people who are abusive towards their parents are more likely to go on to behave abusively towards dating partners (eg, Mitchell, 2006; Laporte et al, 2009) and marriage partners (O'Leary et al, 2004).

However, despite the apparent fruitfulness of such lines of inquiry, it is important to treat the 'cycle of violence' theory, which underpins this research approach, with caution. The 'cycle of violence' theory suggests that earlier victimisations of family abuse can produce either later experiences of *re-victimisation* or later perpetration through the process of *intergenerational transmission*. However, such an assumption is problematic for a number of reasons, not least because the majority of people who experience family violence *do not* go on to perpetrate it (nor indeed do they continue to be victimised in adulthood). Indeed, the very dominance of this 'discourse of determinism' can serve to pathologise people who have experienced family abuse because others may expect it of them. It is also problematic because evidence suggests that any possible intergenerational transmission is mediated by gender: female victims experience later victimisation, while male victims are more likely to become perpetrators (Itzin et al, 2010) and adequate explanations of why this might be have not been forthcoming. A more detailed discussion of these findings, and the processes that might explain them, can be found in Chapter Three.

The prevalence of parent abuse: populations and sub-populations

The following section explores in greater detail what we know about adolescent-to-parent abuse from the statistical data in terms of its overall prevalence in particular populations and sub-populations. Subsequent chapters will seek to make sense of these findings.

The overall prevalence of parent abuse

As discussed in the previous chapter, researching parent abuse is hugely problematic, and measuring its overall prevalence in the general population particularly so. Analysis of forensic and clinical samples might shed light on the kinds of families who are involved in particular kinds of institutional responses to parent abuse once it becomes an identified 'case', but such samples tell us little about overall prevalence. Perhaps the most comprehensive study using this approach was carried out by Du Bois (1998), who identified all cases of 'parent battering' within one state (Baden-Württemberg) in what was then the Federal Republic of Germany. Data were obtained from all child and adolescent psychiatric departments, all child/adolescent psychiatrists working in private practice, all child guidance and family advice centres, all social service and child welfare departments, all public health departments and all juvenile courts of justice within that particular state (population 9.5 million). It identified a frequency rate of six cases per one million accumulated over a two-year period (Du Bois, 1998).

Large-scale surveys are the only appropriate way of measuring overall prevalence, as they take a random sample of people and can therefore tell us either the proportion of children/young people who report perpetrating parent abuse or the proportion of parents who report having been victims of it. Usefully they also attempt to identify parent abuse that has not been reported previously or identified as a 'case'. But because such surveys come as subsets of national epidemiological studies, they tend to be incredibly limited in what they ask about parent abuse. Nevertheless, some of the key findings from such survey data include the following:

- Based on self-reports from young people, data derived from the US-based Youth in Transition survey (1966-69) and the National Survey of Youth (1972) produced estimates of between *6.5% and 10.8% of young people 'having hit' one parent at least once* in the previous one to three years (Peek et al, 1985; Agnew and Huguley, 1989; Brezina,

1999, 2000). Excluding 'trivial incidents', in 92.4% of these cases the young person used their hand (to punch, slap, punch or scratch, for example) and *in 7.6% of these cases, the assault caused physical injury* (Agnew and Huguley, 1989).

- Based on self-reports from parents, the US-based National Family Violence Survey (1975) found that *20.2% of mothers and 14% of fathers reported being hit by their child* in the previous 12 months (Ullman and Straus, 2003).
- The Quebec Longitudinal Study of Kindergarten Children (1986-96) from Canada triangulated self-reports from both young people and their parents and found *prevalence rates for physical aggression at 13.8% towards mothers and 11% towards fathers*, and for *verbal aggression at 64% towards mothers and 56% towards fathers* in the previous six months (Pagani et al, 2004, 2009).

Although many of these surveys are now dated, they still represent the most reliable measures of prevalence that we have at present. More recent surveys that have sometimes been drawn on in the published literature to estimate prevalence rates are problematic because they had very low response rates and used non-probability sampling methods. This resulted in the reporting of some misleadingly high and misleadingly low prevalence rates. For example:

- Claims that 51% of Australian mothers have experienced adolescent-to-mother violence are based on a study that posted 6,000 questionnaires to mothers living in three local government areas that experienced high levels of family violence. Of the 1,024 (17%) that were returned, 51% described experiencing adolescent-to-mother violence (Edenborough et al, 2008).
- The often-cited statistic of 29% of US mothers having experienced physical assault was derived from the return of only 22.6% of 669 questionnaires sent out to mothers (Livingston, 1986). As in the study above, it is likely that those mothers affected by parent abuse were returning the questionnaires.
- Many claims have been made in literature reviews about the relatively low prevalence of parent abuse in France (see, for example, Bobic, 2004; Estevez and Gongora, 2009) often citing a study by Laurent and Derry (1999). However, its grandstanding statistic of a 3.4% prevalence rate was produced by examining the clinical records of 645 children and young people who were hospitalised in a psychiatric department over a nine-year period. This is unlikely to be representative of the general population.

Box 1.1: The prevalence of parent abuse in the UK

The UK in particular is poor in its measurement of parent abuse: there have been no large-scale surveys, no analysis of criminal justice data and it only featured once (in 1996) in the British Crime Survey. Police records are not helpful as there is no category code available to record 'parent abuse', and neither is it necessarily identified as 'domestic violence'. Therefore, we are left with three rather disparate estimates:

- Mirrlees-Black et al (1996) reported data from the British Crime Survey, which showed that 1.9% of domestic violence incidents involved assaults against parents, although this analysis included adult perpetrators. The same survey found that less than 4% of incidents involved school-aged children.
- Browne and Hamilton (1998) found that 14.5% of 232 psychology undergraduates at Birmingham University reported in a questionnaire to having used violent tactics against a parent, with 3.8% perpetrating 'severe violence' at least once.
- Parentline Plus (now Family Lives), the UK government-funded parenting support helpline, reported that 27% (approximately 22,500) of 'long' telephone calls (ie, over 20 minutes) received between June 2008 and June 2010 concerned parents experiencing physical and verbal aggression from their children (Parentline Plus, 2009).

Parent abuse: gender

Mothers and fathers

Whether reported by young people or their parents, the survey data discussed above suggest that mothers are more likely to be targeted by their children, both verbally and physically, compared to fathers. However, this pattern does appear to shift as the child ages, with older males (aged 17-18 years) more likely to assault fathers (Peek et al, 1985; Agnew and Huguely, 1989). Browne and Hamilton's (1998) UK survey of undergraduates also found that *more severe* forms of violence (defined as 'hitting with a fist or object, kicking, beating the other person up and threatening with a knife or weapon': 1998, p 66) were used against fathers, although an earlier US survey found that mothers were more likely to experience severe violence (Cornell and Gelles, 1982).

Such findings are supported by criminal justice data, which suggest that between 72% and 85% of offences are against mothers (Evans and Warren-Sohlberg, 1988; Cochran et al, 1994; Kethineni, 2004; Gebo, 2007; Snyder and McCurley, 2008; Ibabe and Jaureguizar, 2010; Strom et al, 2010; Routt and Anderson, 2011). There is also evidence that violence used against mothers is more *frequent* (Routt and Anderson, 2011) and that violence that targets mothers is more likely to result in police arrest than violence towards fathers (Strom et al, 2010). The disproportionate targeting of mothers is also evident in clinical data, whether from medical and psychiatric treatment centres that primarily work with the child/young person (eg, Laurent and Derry, 1999; Nock and Kazdin, 2001; Perera, 2006) or from community-based support programmes that primarily engage with parents (eg, Cottrell, 2001; O'Connor, 2007).

Criminal justice data also suggest that the young people involved disproportionately come from lone-parent families, particularly those headed by the mother (Evans and Warren-Sohlberg, 1988; Kethineni, 2004; Ibabe and Jaureguizar, 2010; Kennedy et al, 2010; Routt and Anderson, 2011). This has been found to be significant when compared to control samples of young people who are involved in the justice system for other offences. Pagani et al (2003) suggested that changes in family structure (such as divorce) act as a risk factor in mother abuse since it produces a number of stressors that are likely to precipitate parent abuse. These include family adjustment to a new status and responsibilities, alienation from the non-resident parent, increased financial hardship and reduced support from the wider family. However, while some statistical data suggest that a disproportionate number of lone parents are seeking support for parent abuse compared to what one might expect in the general population (eg, Parentline Plus, 2010), other survey data (eg, Peek et al, 1985; Agnew and Huguley, 1989) and clinical data (eg, Boxer et al, 2009) have found no significant correlation between family structure and parent abuse.

Sons and daughters

Criminal justice data suggest that perpetrators are more likely to be male, with estimates ranging from 58% to 84% (Evans and Warren-Sohlberg, 1988; Kethineni, 2004; Gebo, 2007; Walsh and Krienert, 2007; Snyder and McCurley, 2008; Ibabe and Jaureguizar, 2010; Strom et al, 2010; Routt and Anderson, 2011). However, Gebo's (2007) US comparison of juveniles who had committed violent offences against family members compared to those who committed non-familial violent offences was insightful in finding that the difference in proportion of male:female offenders was significantly smaller in cases of family offences (ie, 58:42 for family offences, compared to 82:18 for non-family offences). Furthermore, most survey data have *not* found any significant differences in the gender of perpetrators (Agnew and Huguley, 1989; Paulson et al, 1990; Ullman and Straus, 2003; Pagani et al, 2004) although one survey found males perpetrating *more* violence, and *more severe* forms of violence, than girls (Cornell and Gelles, 1982). It might be that the slightly higher proportion of male perpetrators within the criminal justice system is due to the heightened severity of their abusive behaviour, which in turn is more likely to be defined, processed and/or charged as 'criminal'. Or it may be due to a *perception* that male perpetration of parent abuse is more severe and/or criminal than female perpetration. Interestingly, recent research suggests that any apparent 'gender gap' in arrests for parent abuse-related offences is narrowing (Strom et al, 2010).

Gender may also play a role in mediating the use of weapons in parent abuse. Some US research suggests that girls are more likely to use weapons (Charles, 1986; Gebo, 2007), despite the disproportionate use of weapons by boys more generally (Snyder and Sickmund, 1999). Some of this discrepancy might be explained by type of weapon, with more recent findings suggesting that females are significantly *less* likely to use physical weapons (eg, guns) than males, but are *more* likely to use personal weapons (eg, hands, feet) (Walsh and Krienert, 2007; Strom et al, 2010). However, given the difference in gun control laws in the US compared to most other countries, it is clearly problematic to attempt to apply these findings to other national contexts.

Parent abuse: age

The mean age of parent abuse *offenders within the criminal justice system* is 15 (Kethineni, 2004; Gebo, 2007; Walsh and Krienert, 2007). As Gebo (2007) found in her control sample of non-familial offenders in the US, this is the mean age for juvenile offenders generally, and is similar to that found in England and Wales (Youth Justice Board/Ministry of Justice, 2011). Again as with general youth offending, there is evidence that female offenders of parent abuse are slightly younger than males (Kethineni, 2004; Walsh and Krienert, 2007), as are their (parents-as) victims (Walsh and Krienert, 2007). The only non-US criminal justice data have come from Spain, where one study that examined court reports of violence against parents found that the majority of offenders (39.7%) were aged 17 years (Romero et al, 2005). However, this statistic perhaps tells us more about the particular juvenile justice practices within different countries, and the age at which it is deemed appropriate for criminal justice agents to get involved, rather than the mean age of perpetration per se (eg, the age of criminal responsibility in Spain is

16 years, compared to 10 years in England and Wales). Non-criminal justice studies (ie, using community and clinical samples) slightly vary in terms of their identified 'age of onset' and 'peak age of abuse', but overall the mode age of onset seems to be around 12-14 years, with peak age of abuse a couple of years later, followed by a steady decline after the age of 18. These findings suggest that the abuse starts some time before interventions, criminal justice or otherwise, take place. Indeed, in some qualitative studies, parents reported experiencing 'problematic' behaviour towards them from their child as young as five years, but only identified it as 'abusive' in the teenage years (Cottrell, 2001; Howard and Rottem, 2008; Parentline Plus, 2010; Biehal, 2012).

Studies that have drawn on clinical data, criminal justice data and survey data tend to have identified a mean age for parents at approximately 41-50 years (Laurent and Derry, 1999; Stewart et al, 2006; Walsh and Krienert, 2007). Given that this is the mean age range for parents of teenagers in Europe and North America, this is of little surprise. However, the finding that younger mothers are more resourceful in accessing institutional support services (Stewart et al, 2007; Nugent, 2011) suggests intriguing ways in which such contexts shape help-seeking behaviours in relation to parent abuse. This is an important issue to which we return in Chapters Two and Six.

Parent abuse: ethnicity, religiosity and social class

Some data suggest that the majority of perpetrators and victims are white Caucasian (Charles, 1986; Agnew and Huguley, 1989; Snyder and McCurley, 2008), although one study that analysed police reports of parent abuse-related incidents did identify a disproportionate number of minority ethnic families involved (Evans and Warren-Sohlberg, 1988). There is also evidence of gender mediation here, with one study finding white females more likely to be violent towards a parent than black females (Kennedy et al, 2010). An intriguing Hawaiian survey by Hartz (1995) found that European American teenagers were significantly more likely to respond to parent aggression with counter-aggression, compared to the three other ethnic groups that were studied (Japanese, Filipino and Polynesian). However, other studies have found no significant relationship between ethnicity and violence towards parents (eg, Cornell and Gelles, 1982; Gebo, 2007). Yet despite the lack of conclusive data, ethnicity and race relations are clearly important in shaping experiences of parent abuse – particularly in terms of help-seeking behaviours in families and the possibility of institutional responses that are experienced as discriminatory.

Of surveys that explored religiosity, significant correlations were identified between reduced physical assault and increased religiosity within the child or in the family home (Peek et al, 1985; Paulson et al, 1990; Elliot et al, 2011). In particular, Paulson et al (1990) found that Hispanic young people were significantly less likely to assault parents and suggested that this might be because Hispanic parenting styles emphasise 'religiously-sanctioned paternal authority' (1990, p 130).

Research has found little *statistically significant* correlation between parent abuse and social class identifiers (eg, income, education, occupation), whether through surveys (eg, Peek et al, 1985; Agnew and Huguley, 1989; Paulson et al, 1990; Stewart et al, 2006), criminal justice data (eg, Ibabe and Jaureguizar, 2010) or clinical data (eg, Boxer et al, 2009). There are two exceptions: first, a US large-scale survey (Cornell and Gelles, 1982) identified a relationship between the severity of parent abuse and a father's occupation and family income (with 'clerical workers' and 'middle-income families' at greatest risk). Second, a clinical study found that adolescents (who were referred to a US outpatient treatment centre for troubled adolescents) who engaged in 'parent-directed physical aggression' were significantly more likely to be from two-parent European American families of higher economic status than a control group (Nock and Kazdin, 2002). However, we need to be mindful that, certainly in the latter study, such differences may reflect the characteristics of families who seek help through medical routes rather than the characteristics of parent abuse per se. This is something that qualitative data, discussed in the following chapter, can shed light on.

Parent abuse: case characteristics

Compared to adolescents who commit other types of offences, criminal justice data suggest that offenders who commit parent abuse-related crimes experience significantly more behavioural and/or attendance problems in school (Routt and Anderson, 2011). They also experience more learning difficulties (Ibabe and Jaureguizar, 2010). More than half have used substances prior to their offences (Kethineni, 2004), significantly cocaine (Ibabe and Jaureguizar, 2010). They are also significantly more likely to have been diagnosed with a mental health problem (Routt and Anderson, 2011), have previously been hospitalised for psychiatric reasons (Kennedy et al, 2011), have previously received psychological treatment (Ibabe and Jaureguizar, 2010) and have previously attempted suicide (Kennedy et al, 2011). There is also evidence of gang involvement (Kethineni, 2004; Kennedy et al, 2010).

Regarding previous offences, the data are mixed: some analyses suggest significantly fewer or no previous offences compared to those who commit other types of offences (Cornell and Gelles, 1982; Gebo, 2007; Ibabe and Jaureguizar, 2010). Other studies have found previous offences for violence (Kethineni, 2004; Kennedy et al, 2010) or delinquency (Evans and Warren-Sohlberg, 1988). However, Pagani's longitudinal survey, which used a community sample, also identified high levels of substance use and histories of classroom violence as significant predictors for aggression towards mothers (2004) and fathers (2009). This lends support to the salience of these particular case characteristics. Similarly, community surveys have also found correlations between truancy (eg, Paulson et al, 1990) and exclusion from school (eg, Cornell and Gelles, 1982) with physical assaults on parents.

Parent abuse: nationality and culture

Much of the literature concerning the prevalence of parent abuse needs to be understood within its North American context. Given the methodological problems with studies that have used non-probability samples of homogenous and unrepresentative populations, it is impossible to say with any certainty what prevalence rates might be in other countries, although the emerging literature base from Australia, France, Germany, Hungary, New Zealand, Spain and the UK suggests that parent abuse is a problem across many Euro-American cultures. Further afield, a number of research publications concerning parent abuse have emerged from Japan (Inamura, 1980; Kumagai, 1981; Honjo, 1988). Indeed, Kozu (1999) claims that *filial violence*[6] was the first form of family abuse to receive public attention back in the 1970s, with the social problems of IPV, elder abuse and child abuse emerging in response to its publicity. Nevertheless, the basic characteristics appear to be similar to those found elsewhere: male violence perpetrated primarily against mothers, with the child's modal age between 15 and 16 years (Inamura, 1980). Other intriguing findings from Japan suggest that, in cases of male perpetration, fathers are frequently absent (physically or emotionally) from the family home, and that perpetrators are often the eldest children, or lone children, in families that are relatively economically privileged (Kumagai, 1981). In contrast, Segal (1999) reflects on the absence of any discussion of filial violence in India, whether in the media, research literature or by the families themselves with whom she has researched. Segal (1999) suggests that, while it is possible that parent abuse does not happen in India, its silence in Indian discourse may be due to particular cultural practices concerning the management of family problems and disclosure. Indeed, the existence of so-called 'culture-bound' categories of family abuse, such as 'daughter-in-law abuse' (eg, Gangoli and Rew, 2011; Raj et al, 2011), highlights the extent to which family abuse is shaped by its cultural context, in terms of both how it is enabled within particular familial power relations and how it is identified as a 'social problem' from the outset.

Summary

- Child abuse, IPV, elder abuse and sibling abuse are all well recognised in research, policy and practice and share a number of commonalities. These include the gendered nature of abuse, its immediate and long-term effects, and the frequency of *repeat victimisation* and *polyvictimisation*. Parent abuse shares these characteristics, although it is also unique in ways that make existing policy and practice frameworks – which have been formulated in response to distinct forms of family abuse – inadequate to respond to it.
- Evidence suggests that parent abuse is linked to other forms of family abuse, notably experiencing child abuse, witnessing IPV between parents, contemporaneous perpetration of sibling abuse and subsequent perpetration of dating violence.
- Methodological problems make the estimation of overall prevalence of parent abuse problematic, but large-scale US surveys estimate that 6-10% of young people have hit parents at least once in the previous one to three years.
- The most common relationship dyad found in parent abuse is 'son → mother', although survey data suggest fewer gender differences in son/daughter perpetration.
- Age of onset is approximately 12-14 years, with peak age a year or two after then. The average age of parent abuse-related offending within the criminal justice system is 15 years.
- Evidence is inconclusive regarding social class, ethnicity and previous offending. However, data do suggest links between perpetration and school problems, substance use, mental health problems and gang involvement.
- Parent abuse is documented across Euro-American cultures – particularly Australasia, Europe and North America, as well as Israel and Japan. Its absence has been noted in India, perhaps highlighting the importance of cultural context in both the enablement of parent abuse within families and its recognition as a social problem.

Notes

[1] Key examples include the deaths of Maria Caldwell in 1973 and Victoria Climbié in 2000.

[2] And within this category, 'adolescent-to-adolescent dating violence' is increasingly recognised in policy and research as a distinct form of dating violence (Barter et al, 2009).

[3] Indeed, witnessing IPV in childhood is now recognised as a form of psychological abuse by the UK government (DSCF, 2010, p 4).

[4] Note that some of this research includes 'corporal punishment', which is not always considered to be 'child abuse', particularly at the time that many of these studies were conducted.

[5] Note that some of this research includes 'corporal punishment' which is not always considered to be 'child abuse', particularly at the time that many of these studies were conducted.

[6] The term 'filial violence' generally refers to child-perpetrated violence against any family member, although this is usually the parent (Kozu, 1999).

TWO

Experiences of parent abuse

Introduction

The previous chapter examined the *quantitative* data derived from criminal justice records, medical records and surveys, and highlighted the salience of gender, age and particular case characteristics that feature in parent abuse. However, this quantitative data needs to be understood in context, and this chapter draws on *qualitative* data derived from original and other published research to offer insights into how parents conceptualise and understand their lived experiences of 'parent abuse'. For example, how do parents describe the different forms that 'abuse' can take (ie, verbal, economic, physical and emotional abuse)? How do parents understand its emergence and escalation in interactions? How do parents manage the tapestry of contradictory emotions that parent abuse produces? The chapter concludes by examining the immediate and long-term impact of parent abuse, for both parents and other family members.

Abusive behaviours in the child–parent relationship

As previously discussed, family abuse can take a number of forms (ie, physical, emotional, financial and sexual abuse, and neglect) and some of these forms are more pertinent than others depending on which family members are involved. Thus, the ways in which 'the child–parent relationship' is organised and practised in particular contexts shapes what particular forms of parent abuse can be made possible. This section explores parents' accounts of living with abuse from their children, identifies the forms of abuse[1] that are pertinent in cases of adolescent-to-parent abuse and discusses how the organisation and practice of the child–parent relationship enables particular abusive tactics to manifest in everyday interactions.

Verbal abuse

While often categorised as a type of 'emotional abuse' in the family abuse literature, *verbal abuse* requires its own consideration in cases of parent abuse because of (a) its relative frequency compared to other forms of parent abuse and (b) its emergence as the first form of abuse to manifest in the development of a 'parent abuse dynamic'. Furthermore, parents describe verbal abuse in ways that suggest that they think of it as distinct. For parents, verbal abuse constitutes:

- yelling or screaming at the parent ("in my face", as one parent has described);
- using derogatory and insulting names;
- swearing and using other offensive language.

Of course, what is often considered 'everyday teenage behaviour' may, from time to time, involve similar behaviours that serve to challenge the hierarchy of power within the child–parent relationship. It is therefore important to recognise that it is the *pattern* of verbal aggression – in particular, the way in which it operates alongside other forms of abusive behaviour – and its *impact* that makes it abusive. Thus, we need to take into account the *context* of the verbal abuse and what it symbolises: that is, a complete breakdown of the hierarchy of power that underpins normative constructions of the child–parent relationship.

The content of abusive comments often denigrates the parental role by undermining or criticising the parent's ability to nurture and care for her/his children. It may also denigrate other characteristics of the parent, such as their intelligence or appearance (Price, 1996). The denigration of parenting abilities is also used as an abusive tactic by perpetrators of intimate partner violence (IPV) (Bancroft and Silverman, 2002). Indeed, some mothers have commented on how their child's verbal abuse 'echoes' that previously experienced from an abusive ex-partner, as one mother explained: 'It's disturbing for me when I recognise it … that sometimes I feel I am living in the relationship with my ex-husband. It disturbs me enormously' (mother, Australia – from Howard and Rottem, 2008, p 43). In some cases, there may be a sexual undertone to the content of a child's verbal abuse and this may be very explicit, as in the extract below:

> … it's just disgusting, but to a point where it just became so normal that that's how they [her two sons] would talk to me every day. They'd be like that from the minute you wake up to the time they go to bed. The derogatory things that come out of my boys' mouths is a major concern … not just calling me 'slut' and 'whore' and things like that, really disgusting things that they've told me to do with my friend

> Amanda because they hate her ... they've gone and told me
> to do sexual things. (Mother, Australia – from Howard and
> Rottem, 2008, p 38)

One reason why such comments have such abusive power is because references pertaining to the sexuality of a parent – and particularly to a 'deviant' sexuality – transgress the normative boundaries of what defines parental authority. While evidence (eg, Stewart et al, 2006) suggests that sexual abuse is extremely rare in parent abuse and does not form a part of the tapestry of parent abuse in the way that other forms of abuse work together, it should not be discounted completely from any discussions of parent abuse. As the above extract demonstrates, it may well exist 'on the edges' of parent abuse, and might play a significant role in its threat, if not in its practice.

Economic abuse

As with verbal abuse, economic abuse emerges early on in the development of a parent abuse dynamic and is a relatively frequent form of abuse. From parents' accounts, economic abuse constitutes:

- damaging property (eg, kicking in doors and walls, breaking windows);
- damaging furniture and possessions (eg, throwing or smashing up chairs, tables and/or other objects);
- generating fines and other costs outside the home for which the parent is financially liable;
- theft of possessions or money;
- demanding money or goods from the parent(s).

In their discussion of abusive tactics used in IPV, Adams et al (2008, p 564) defines 'economic abuse' as 'behaviours that control a woman's ability to acquire, use and maintain economic resources, thus threatening her economic security and potential for self-sufficiency'. Some of the tactics used by male partners to curtail a woman's economic position are specific to an IPV context – for example, failing to show up to care for children when a partner needs to work or refusing to put a partner's name on house deeds. However, other tactics used in IPV may also apply to other abusive family contexts, including the 'child–parent' context – for example, the theft of money or possessions, preventing sleep or harassing victims during the working day.

Yet there are other abusive tactics that are specific to adolescent-to-parent abuse because the way the child–parent relationship is organised and practised gives particular behaviours an abusive power. For example, one feature of the child–parent relationship is that parents either own their own home and possessions or are in some way responsible for them. Parents are also financially liable for the costs generated by their children's behaviour. This legal characteristic of family life in Euro-American cultures enables the child to act abusively in ways that would not be possible within other relationship contexts.

I asked one mother about her son's forthcoming court appearance for criminal damage and what had led to her pressing charges against him:

> "Because I don't own my own home – it's a rented house and obviously he can't go around doing that [ie, damaging the property] and he does things like that quite frequently at home. I've never pressed charges on him before but I thought, 'No, he's got to learn that he cannot do it at home.' So my partner went as the appropriate adult, and his answer to it was – this is my son –'I wish my Mum owned her own house because I could smash up what I wanted.'" (Mother, England – from *original transcript*, Holt, 2009)

While of course this mother's experience may not be representative of all parents' experiences, it does highlight how the economic context of family life shapes the options available for parents to respond to parent abuse, as well as the ways in which young people can exercise power. In cases such as this, where the parent is a tenant in social housing, criminal damage to property has to be reported otherwise the tenant is made liable for any damage. And given that parents who live in rented accommodation are likely to have less disposable income to make good any damage caused, options are more limited for less advantaged parents. Such cases reflect wider issues concerning how social inequalities shape parents' experiences of and responses to parent abuse. This includes the extent to which families have access to resources that can make the effects and consequences of parent abuse less visible to the outside world.[2]

The organisation and practice of the child–parent relationship enable particular abusive tactics in other ways as well. For example, alongside the parent's responsibility to provide a home for their child is the increasing cultural pressure to provide for their child materially and emotionally. Such a pressure appears to be exploited by children and young people who make demands on their parents, which may become particularly powerful when accompanied by threats of violence or by the emotional manipulation of parents' feelings of inadequacy. Children accusing their parents of being 'bad parents' and of not fulfilling their 'responsibilities' have been documented in parents' accounts of parent abuse (Cottrell, 2001).

Physical abuse

Physical abuse is perhaps the most identifiable form of abuse and its manifestation often marks the point when parents become aware of the seriousness of the abusive dynamic between themselves and their child. From parents' accounts, physical abuse includes:

- hitting;
- punching;
- slapping;
- pushing;

- kicking;
- spitting;
- throwing objects at parents.

Some of these actions may constitute both economic and physical abuse, since a parent's possessions may be used (and damaged) to simultaneously injure parents. Furthermore, for many parents, violence towards property symbolises the threat that *they might be next* (Jackson, 2003; Edenborough et al, 2008). This highlights how a seemingly static 'incident' (such as 'criminal damage') forms part of a wider tapestry of abuse, which may have more meaning than perhaps first appears.

> "He has punched and kicked me while on holiday, kicked holes in most of my doors, smashed a TV and now my other two children are getting scared of him. We had another incident last night after I told him to get off the Xbox as I could see he was getting wound up, he kicked a hole in his bedroom door and I thought he was going to punch me, but he just started shoving me down the hall." (Parent, UK – from *original transcript*, Holt 2011)

Across the qualitative research, parents consistently comment on the relative size of their child-as-perpetrator. In particular, mothers highlight concerns about their growing son's increasing physical presence and their own ability to 'manage' him (Jackson, 2003; Eckstein, 2004; Holt, 2009; Hunter et al, 2010). This is interesting in relation to Agnew and Huguley's (1989) finding that the size of the young person is irrelevant to the likelihood of parent abuse. However, it is *size differential* (rather than absolute size) that is likely to be of relevance here. Particularly within a son–mother relationship, rapid shifts in size and strength during the teenage years can create a sudden shift in the power dynamic between parent and child, which may be accompanied by a mother's equally sudden recognition of her own vulnerability:

> "He picked me up the first time and threw me across his bedroom, and then I was actually scared of him." (Mother, England – from *original transcript*, Holt, 2009)

> We would always get caught up in fights … they'd be physical fights between me and him … it got to the point where he got bigger than me and I thought, "I can't get involved in this anymore, he's going to kill me." (Mother, Australia – from Howard and Rottem, 2008, p 37)

Emotional abuse

Parents often report that emotional abuse is the most difficult form of abuse to come to terms with, something that victims of IPV have also reported (eg, Follingstad et al, 1990). Emotional abuse often goes beyond verbal abuse in the sense that there is an underlying psychological dynamic at play, which may not be obvious at a superficial level. Indeed, emotional abuse may be exercised with a smile and a kind voice, rather than using overt aggression. From parents' accounts, emotional abuse includes:

- intimidating and undermining the parent;
- attempting to make the parent feel unstable or 'crazy';
- threatening to harm the parent or others (including siblings and pets);
- threatening to harm themselves (eg, suicide or self-harm);
- withholding affection or ignoring the parent (eg, 'silent treatment');
- running away from home;
- lying to the parent.

Again, it is important to stress that many of these behaviours may constitute 'one-off' incidents engaged in by the majority of children and young people at some time or another; it is the *pattern* and *consistency* of the behaviours, and the damage they cause, that makes them abusive: 'Our daughter was very quick to tell is how lousy we were as individuals and as parents. That is unbelievably hard to hear on a regular basis, and it certainly affected our feelings about ourselves' (Mother, Canada – from Cottrell, 2005, p 12).

Abuse is an ongoing social process that works to control even the most mundane aspects of parents' day-to-day lives. For example, one mother reported how her son would monitor her telephone calls, steal her car keys and lock her in the car. She described life with him:

> [He'd be] with me 24 hours a day and I couldn't even get to make a call … if he'd go and have a shower, I'd have two minutes, stolen moments so quick to make a call … I'd sit down and he'd sit next to me. I'd get up, he'd be behind me. I'd go to the toilet, he'd be behind me. (Mother, Australia – from Howard and Rottem, 2008, p 38)

Yet again, it is clear to see that it is the context of the 'child–parent relationship', in terms of how it is organised and practised, that enables the child to exercise power in particular ways. For example, a common abusive tactic involves a child threatening to 'call the authorities' and make an allegation of child abuse (Price, 1996; Cottrell, 2001; Cottrell and Monk, 2004). Such threats are powerful because family services are configured in ways that assume that it is the *child* (rather than the *parent*) who is at risk of family abuse (see Chapter Five) and both parents and children are aware of the potential consequences of such allegations. Furthermore, such threats may have particular potency in cases where a parent had previously harmed or used force on their child (Cottrell and Monk, 2004).

The development of the 'parent abuse dynamic'

The previous section considered different forms of parent abuse – verbal, economic, physical and emotional abuse – separately to illustrate how particular abusive tactics are enabled within the context of the child–parent relationship. However, such distinctions may be misleading because different forms of abusive behaviour work together to form an overall pattern of parent abuse, and the effects of *polyvictimisation* are all the more powerful because of this. Such distinctions may also be misleading because forms of parent abuse blur where they intersect, such that verbal abuse may have sexually abusive undertones, and the use of objects and possessions may be used to produce both physically and economically damaging outcomes. Nevertheless, it is analytically useful to keep hold of these different forms when considering the emergence and development of the 'parent abuse dynamic', since evidence suggests that each form emerges singularly, beginning with verbal abuse.

The onset of parent abuse

Jackson's (2003) in-depth interviews with six mothers who were experiencing parent abuse revealed that mothers noticed a perceptible shift in the dynamic of the child–parent relationship. Previously described as 'affectionate and relatively uncomplicated', relationships with their child became 'strained, fragile and fraught with tension' (2003, p 324) as mothers slowly became fearful and concerned for their personal safety within their own homes. As one mother commented: 'He would do things like elbow me out of the way if I walked past him, whereas before he would have moved aside for me' (Mother, Australia – from Jackson, 2003, p 325).

In Eckstein's (2004) study, as well as many others (Cottrell, 2001; Jackson, 2003; Haw, 2010), there are striking similarities in parents' narratives describing the onset of parent abuse: it emerges gradually, starting with less-severe forms of *verbal abuse*, before increasing in intensity over a period of months. It then develops into *physical abuse* and/or *emotional abuse*. Figure 2.1 illustrates this process.

In Eckstein's (2004) study, parents rated the *seriousness* of different forms of abuse and unanimously parents rated *verbal abuse* as 'least serious' and *emotional abuse* as 'most serious'. Although less physically injurious, it appears that what was so distressing was not the actual physical assault, but the knowledge that such assaults *came from their child*, as one mother explained: 'It wasn't that it bothered me that I would wake up dead, but it bothered me that he would do that to me' (Mother, US – from Eckstein, 2004, p 376). Such findings are illuminating, but it is important to recognise that ratings of severity, as with definitions of abuse, are likely to be culturally specific. Thus, the meanings that we ascribe to the experience of being attacked by one's child are shaped by the meanings we attach to the child–parent relationship, which are historically and culturally determined. This is an issue to which we return in Chapter Four.

Research suggests that the emergence of a 'parent abuse dynamic' is characterised by an initial sense of *disbelief* that someone who they bore and brought up could behave like that towards them (Cottrell, 2001; Jackson, 2003; Cottrell and Monk, 2004; Galvani, 2010). This in itself highlights how our understandings of the child–parent relationship shape our experiences of abuse within it: the disbelief is brought about because such abusive behaviours conflict with normative ideas about

Figure 2.1: The development of the 'parent abuse dynamic'

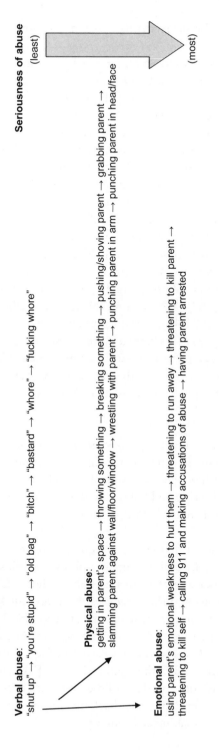

Seriousness of abuse
(least)
(most)

Verbal abuse:
"shut up" → "you're stupid" → "old bag" → "bitch" → "bastard" → "whore" → "fucking whore"

Physical abuse:
getting in parent's space → throwing something → breaking something → pushing/shoving parent → grabbing parent → slamming parent against wall/floor/window → wrestling with parent → punching parent in arm → punching parent in head/face

Emotional abuse:
using parent's emotional weakness to hurt them → threatening to hurt them → threatening to run away → threatening to kill parent → threatening to kill self → calling 911 and making accusations of abuse → having parent arrested

Source: Developed from Eckstein (2004)

how growing children should *protect* their parents, as both they and their parents age.

And because abusive behaviours emerge gradually, for some time they are likely to go unarticulated as a problem, if not entirely unnoticed, by the parent. However, once *physically* abusive behaviours emerge, which is arguably the least ambiguous form of abuse, most parents do recognise the problem as a serious one. Furthermore, once parents experience physical abuse from their child, their child's verbal threats, which may accompany it, are much more powerful in producing fear because the parent now has evidence that the child will enact those threats. As one mother explained: 'Once he started physically abusing us, [then] when he would make threats to kill us and things like that it carried with it a whole new weight ... and so the threats that he was using in the emotional abuse all of a sudden became real to me' (Mother, US – from Eckstein, 2004, p 375).

In tracing the escalation of abusive interactions, a number of studies (eg, Price, 1996; Eckstein, 2002; Jackson, 2003; Doran, 2007; Haw, 2010) have identified the role of 'asking patterns' in precipitating verbal abuse towards parents (which may then escalate into other forms of abuse). 'Asking patterns' involve the young person asking the parent for something (eg, to borrow the car or to stay out all night) and a parent's refusal precipitates an abusive incident, as the following account illustrates:

> This morning because I wouldn't take her to school and buy her some tobacco she flew into a rage, threw everything off my sideboard, smashed a glass and ripped a towel rail off the wall, constantly swearing and telling me she f★★★ing hated me. (Parent, UK – Parentline Plus, 2010, p 11)

Eckstein (2002) further identified a role for 'requesting patterns', which involve the parent asking the child/young person for something (eg, a request for information or to partake in a household chore). Although 'requesting patterns' escalated into *verbal abuse* far more quickly than did 'asking patterns' (often within a matter of seconds), Eckstein (2002) noticed that 'requesting patterns' did not produce an escalation beyond *verbal abuse* into *physical or emotional abuse*, perhaps because the young person was less invested in the conflict. Indeed, Eckstein found that 'requesting patterns' soon produced little abuse at all, as parents attempted to contain the abuse by either backing away from repeating their requests or avoiding making any requests at all.

The maintenance, management and cessation of parent abuse

Eckstein (2004) closely examined the impact of a parent's behaviour on the development of the parent abuse dynamic. Initially, parents attempt to challenge the abusive behaviours by, for example, arguing back or imposing sanctions on their child. But as the young person continues to refuse to recognise parental authority by ignoring their rules and guidelines, parents change their communication styles to avoid further abuse. Eckstein (2004) suggests that this change in communication style produces changes in the interactional dynamics of power, such that parental authority is diminished further and parental control is lost. The result is that any form of discipline is now impossible. The overwhelming powerlessness in parents is evident from Eckstein's (2004) analysis, which found that young people eventually control every abusive interaction with their parent(s). Thus, *verbal abuse* would only stop when the parent gave in to the young person's demands; *physical abuse* would only stop when the parent or young person left the house or when the police were called; *emotional abuse* would only stop when the young person grew tired or distracted.

This process of initially attempting to control the abuse through challenging it and then, when such attempts fail, retreating into acceptance, has been found in other empirical studies (Howard and Rottem, 2008; Hunter et al, 2010; Holt, 2011). As two parents commented:

> I was always trying to change things, but whatever I did was ineffective. He brought me to the point where I was literally speechless. I would walk off shaking my head thinking 'I have no control here at all. Nothing.' (Mother, Australia – Anglicare Victoria, 2001, p 1)

> "Today has been horrendous and I am now wishing I was dead. I am too soft with him and he always gets his own way. Today he has kicked, thumped and battered me. Today I had to get out of the house so I did, he proceeded to lock the door behind me. All I did was sit over in the local park, cried, thought, cried, thought and cried some more." (Parent, UK – from *original transcript*, Holt, 2011)

In my own analysis of parents' experiences posted in online support forums, parents reported trying a number of strategies to *change* the abusive situation. Such strategies included physical retaliation, self-defence, reasoning with the child, use of sanctions (eg, grounding the child or blocking telephone calls) and asking the child to leave home. Once these strategies were found to have no effect, parents resigned themselves to merely *cope with*, rather than *change*, the situation.[3] One way of coping was to merely look forward to their child's 18th birthday, when the child would no longer be their parents' legal responsibility and could therefore be asked to leave home. Other parents anticipated that this transitional age would mark the point when their child would 'morph back into a person', as one parent described it (Holt, 2011, p 459). Other reported coping strategies include parents locking themselves in the bedroom at night (Jackson, 2003), living and eating in the bedroom (Paterson et al, 2002) and leaving for work two hours early every morning to avoid confrontations (Haw, 2010). In relation to her abusive 16-year-old son, one mother describes her avoidance strategy:

> I can't sit in the same room as him. So I basically go and sit … if he's in here, I go … me and John [her younger child] go upstairs and sit in the bedroom and watch telly or whatever. We shouldn't have to live like that, but it's easier on me, otherwise I'll end up cracking up. (Mother, England – from Hunter et al, 2010, p 270)

Another mother described how she slept in her clothes and parked her car facing down on her driveway, ready for a quick escape: 'I could tell by the way he looked at me that something was going to happen, and that I would have to be ready to get away' (Mother, Australia – from Sheehan, 1997, p 83).

The aftermath of abusive encounters tends to vary among families. For some parents, there is a period of extreme remorse and promises of change (Howard and Rottem, 2008) – something that is also common in IPV and is described as the 'honeymoon period' in IPV literature (eg, Pagelow, 1982). For other parents, there is 'a profound lack of remorse', with young people continuing to justify their abusive behaviour (Cottrell and Monk, 2004, p 1085; see also Holt, 2011).

And further down the line? In a series of life history interviews with 60 mothers who had experienced parent abuse, Stewart et al (2007) followed up 48 mothers some five years later. Some of the young people had since moved away from home and severed all ties with their mother, and this produced its own emotional strains. In other cases, the children (now adults) continued to live with their mothers, or had moved back home having already left. In other cases, the mothers' children would return home sporadically. In such cases where contact continued, so did the abuse.

The impact of parent abuse

Emotional impact

Research suggests that experiencing parent abuse produces a range of somewhat conflicting emotions. In many ways it is both the strength of these emotions, and the tensions between them, that make parent abuse so difficult for parents to cope with. The initial *disbelief* appears to be exacerbated by the fact that many parents have not heard of parent abuse and are unprepared for it (Jackson, 2003). Other parents are confused as to whether their child's behaviour *is* abusive and/or violent (Paterson et al, 2002; Gallagher, 2004a).[4] *Denial* of the seriousness of the problem has also been identified in some studies (Jackson, 2003; Cottrell and Monk, 2004) and by some therapeutic practitioners who have worked with parent abuse (Harbin and Madden, 1979; Charles, 1986). The combination of disbelief and denial goes some way to explaining the delay in parents' acknowledgement of the problem and attempts to seek help. Empirical studies that have examined parents' accounts suggest that the emotional landscape of parent abuse is characterised by the following:

- **Fear** – Parents' fear for their own safety is very profound: 'I thought he was going to kill me,' one mother explained (Haw, 2010, p 69). Such fears extend to other family members, particularly siblings (Holt, 2009, 2011; Munday, 2009). Parents' accounts continually refer to 'walking on eggshells' (Paterson et al, 2002; Howard and Rottem, 2008; Haw, 2010; Tew and Nixon, 2010) in describing their state of permanent self-surveillance in an attempt to avoid 'triggering' an abusive incident. Furthermore, some parents fear violent retribution from their child should they seek help (Cottrell and Monk, 2004).
- **Concern and worry** – Fear can extend beyond safety fears into a more general anxiety about the impact and consequences of the abuse. Parents fear that siblings may learn to imitate the abusive behaviours, or respond through depressive symptoms or 'acting out' (Cottrell, 2001). Parents also fear that the abusive young person may come to harm, for example by carrying out their threats to self-harm or kill themselves. Parents also fear that their child may become embroiled in the criminal justice system (Cottrell and Monk, 2004; Edenborough et al, 2008) or that they may behave abusively and

violently towards their own future partners (Howard and Rottem, 2008). Such worries and concerns shape the options that parents think are available to them and also provide an enabling context for the child or young person to exercise power over them.

• **Betrayal** – Parents have reported feeling unable to leave the child/ young person unsupervised, and dread coming home if the young person is left alone. Thus, there is a loss of trust and sense of betrayal for the parent (Cottrell, 2001; Jackson, 2003). This sense of betrayal is also evident in the disbelief experienced by parents at the onset of parent abuse.

• **Self-blame and shame** – Feelings of failure as a mother/father/ parent can lead to self-blame and a sense of responsibility to put things right because of their role as both adult and parent (Paterson et al, 2002; Jackson, 2003; Cottrell and Monk, 2004; Doran, 2007; Howard and Rottem, 2008). Such feelings can be reinforced by young people telling the parent that their abusive behaviour *is* their parent's fault. Self-blame is felt particularly strongly when the abuse seems targeted towards only them: children are rarely abusive towards *every*one, and the parent often recognises this (Paterson et al, 2002). However, feelings of self-blame are not straightforward, and some research has found parental resistance to self-blame, at least in their public accounts of the abuse (O'Connor, 2007; Holt, 2011). However, the 'parent-blame culture' that permeates parents' lives enables a fear that they will be blamed publically if the abuse becomes known (Doran, 2007; Howard and Rottem, 2008). This can perpetuate a strong sense of shame in parents (Haw, 2010) and can contribute to their reluctance to seek help.

• **Resentment** – If only one parent is the target of abuse then this can produce resentment towards the other parent (Edenborough et al, 2008). Resentment may be particularly strong if the other parent also lives in the family home, appears disengaged from what is happening or is seen to be 'taking sides' (Stewart et al, 2007; Haw, 2010).

• **Loss and grief** – If the child/young person is removed from the family home as a result of the abuse, experiences of loss and grief can impact on all the family. This may feel particularly severe for lone parents who have no other children (Cottrell, 2001). Parents may also experience the loss of, and grieve for, an idealised future for their family that will never be realised (Paterson et al, 2002; Howard and Rottem, 2008).

• **Hopelessness and despair** – Once a number of options have been explored in an attempt to end the abuse, parents frequently sense that nothing can be done to alleviate the abuse. The biological, legal and cultural bond between child and parent may reinforce this sense that the situation is interminable (Haw, 2010; Holt, 2011). *Polyvictimisation* is known to reduce an individual's resilience in overcoming the effects of family abuse (Sabina and Straus, 2008; Turner et al, 2010) and the centrality of *polyvictimisation* to parent abuse makes evidence of hopelessness and despair unsurprising.

Despite presenting this as a 'list' of emotions, it is important to recognise that the emotional terrain of parent abuse is not straightforward. One consistent theme in the data is that emotional experiences are ambiguous and operate around particular emotional tensions. For example, my own research found that *guilt* was a common feature of parents' accounts (Holt, 2011). But this was not because parents felt that they were to blame: it was because the feelings they had for their child transgressed what parents 'should' feel for their child. That is, the 'unconditional love' espoused by the ethic of 'good parenthood' had been replaced with a dislike or hatred towards their child and a yearning for their child to leave the family home. As described by one parent, this resulted in feelings of 'pain, guilt and anguish' (Holt, 2011, p 457). Again, such findings highlight how experiences of parent abuse are shaped by our understandings of the normative 'child–parent relationship' and what we perceive to be transgressions of this relationship. Another example of this is the *resentment* produced by parent abuse, which comes about through a perceived imbalance between parental love received and parental responsibilities shouldered. Such an imbalance transgresses the 'reciprocality' that is assumed to be an essential part of the child–parent relationship. Similarly, the *loss and grief* experienced when a child is forced to 'flee the family nest' transgresses the normative developmental transitions that frame our expectations of when and how a young person should shift from the role of 'child' to the role of 'adult'.

Impact on personal life, family life and community life

Both in my own and other research (see, for example, O'Connor, 2007; Howard and Rottem, 2008; Munday, 2009; Haw, 2010; Hunter et al, 2010), parents report that young people are also involved in abusive behaviours towards their siblings – physically, emotionally, verbally and economically. While research suggests that both experiencing sibling abuse and witnessing family abuse is linked to later relationship problems (see Chapter One), sibling abuse that is perpetuated alongside parent abuse can have more immediate effects. For example, siblings who are old enough may physically withdraw from the family home, which can exacerbate the isolation already felt among parents. One lone father I spoke to described such a consequence:

> "She's [his daughter] deciding to spend a lot of time at her friends. She's phoning me nearly every day now, 'Do you mind if I stay at my friend Jenny's again tonight? And go to school with her in the morning?' He [his son] is affecting her life as well now, which I don't think is right. This is her home as well. Why should she be pushed out? The way I see it, it's as if he's trying to take over the place. I mean, the way he speaks to me and everything. He even hits her and that. I've spoken to social services about this but … all of a sudden, they've just gone quiet, as if they don't want to know any more. I'm basically left on my own, that's how I feel." (Father, England – from *original transcript*, Holt, 2009)

For siblings who are too young to withdraw from the family home, the abused parent may risk their own safety to protect their other children, as one lone mother explained:

> "If we go back to Year 7 or Year 8, it was every single day, several times a day, it would either be me or the girls and I'd have to sort of like, step in and get between him and the girls. The girls would be behind me so I would sort of like get most of it but at the moment that seems to have settled down an awful lot. I mean at the moment he might square up to me but I just sort of stand my ground and he knows that I will get the better of him. Again, whether that's something that he's learned over time that if I have to use dirty tactics to rugby tackle him to the floor and sit on him, then that's what I'll do." (Mother, England – from *original transcript*, Holt, 2009)

For parents who live with a partner, parent abuse can lead to conflicts over what the causes are and how to deal with it (Cottrell, 2001; Haw, 2010). In some cases, parental roles prescribed by gender mean that mothers feel that the problem is left for them to deal with (Holt, 2009; Haw, 2010) and research has found that mothers who *lack* partner engagement or support find it difficult to effect change (Stewart et al, 2007). Lone mothers have commented on how the absence of partner support makes them both more vulnerable targets and less resourced in finding solutions (Jackson, 2003; Edenborough et al, 2008). Quantitative data suggest that in two-parent families, mothers are more likely to be targeted, while mothers report that the abuse is most severe when they are alone with the child (Edenborough et al, 2008; Howard and Rottem, 2008).

However, the impact of parent abuse goes beyond the family home and seeps into wider relationships with family and community. Abuse is sometimes directed at extended family members (Jackson, 2003; Howard and Rottem, 2008) who, in some cases, distance themselves from both the young person in question and his/her parent, further exacerbating parental isolation (Holt, 2009). Some parents have commented that they feel that other family members are manipulated by their child into believing that the abuse is the parent's fault (Cottrell, 2001; Howard and Rottem, 2008). Other parents have reported a distancing from neighbours (Jackson, 2003) and parents have spoken to me about how their relationships with new partners had ended because their partner could not deal with their child's abusive behaviour. Parents also report withdrawing from social activities and relationships because of concerns about the abuse (Howard and Rottem, 2008).

Both the emotional impact of parent abuse and its effect on other family members can have a knock-on effect on other aspects of a parent's life. Parents have reported how the abuse can exacerbate existing health problems as well as create new problems (Cottrell, 2001; O'Connor, 2007). This includes mental health problems such as clinical distress, anxiety and depression (Paterson et al, 2002; O'Connor, 2007; Howard and Rottem, 2008; Parentline Plus, 2010). In some cases parents have turned to prescribed medication or self-medication (eg, using drugs or alcohol) (Cottrell, 2001; Haw, 2010). The stress and anxiety produced by parent abuse can affect concentration at work, while receiving telephone calls at work and needing to take time out to attend court and/or counselling sessions can be disruptive to a parent's employment (Cottrell, 2001; Howard and Rottem, 2008; Holt, 2009). There are also related financial costs, such as the payment of court fines and replacing stolen and damaged items. There may also be costs involved in seeking help, such as counselling (Cottrell, 2001), which may need to be sought privately given the current lack of any public provision of support in many places.

Summary

• Parent abuse can take a number of forms, including verbal abuse, economic abuse, physical abuse and emotional abuse. Most commonly, verbal abuse is the first to emerge and, over time, other forms of abuse may manifest.
• The social and political context of child–parent relationships, in terms of how such relationships are understood, organised and practised, shapes the particular form of abusive tactics that can emerge. It also shapes (and limits) the possible ways in which parents can respond to the abuse.
• Parents' responses to abusive encounters change over time. While initially parents may challenge or resist the abuse, it may soon become 'normalised' and parents will focus instead on containing or avoiding the abuse.
• The emotional impact of the abuse is complex, but frequently involves fear, concern, betrayal, self-blame, resentment, loss and despair. The emotional landscape of abuse is underpinned by tensions as emotions are often in conflict with each other.
• The impact of parent abuse also extends to other family members and to the wider community. It also impacts on parents' physical and mental health, employment and finances.

Notes

[1] Parent abuse has been conceptualised within different categories in some literature. For example, Stewart et al (2007) contrast *acting out abuse* (which includes verbal, physical, domineering and obstructive abuse) with *psychological abuse* (which includes manipulative behaviour, severing relations and betrayal of trust). But these categories do correspond with the more common categories described here (which, of course, overlap to some degree).

[2] The son's comment in this extract is also illustrative of how children and young people appear to actively select which object or possession to damage, something that has been found in other parental accounts (eg, Haw, 2010). This suggests that young people display at least some degree of intentionality (and therefore control) over their abusive behaviours.

[3] It is telling that, in a web-survey concerning experiences of parent abuse, when asked 'What discipline technique works best for you?' the option that scored the highest response by far (43%) was 'nothing works' (Parentline Plus, 2010, p 19).

[4] Such confusion clearly has methodological implications for any research that aims to measure the prevalence of parent abuse. As Paterson et al (2002) comment, it is only after parents engage in intervention programmes that they come to define particular behaviours as 'violent' or 'abusive'. This makes intervention evaluations that rely on pre- and post-programme measures of abuse problematic (see Chapter Six for further discussion).

THREE

Explaining parent abuse

Introduction

This chapter examines the theoretical explanations that have so far been put forward by researchers to explain parent abuse. The chapter includes explanations that draw on the roles of psychopathologies, personality/ behavioural traits, substance misuse, the learning of violence through observation, parenting practices, family communication patterns and the role of social isolation, peers and deprivation. Throughout the discussion, the chapter assesses the current evidence that supports each explanation and offers a critique of its limitations. The chapter concludes with a brief overview of how *parents* understand their own experiences of parent abuse, and reflects on how empirically based theoretical models, which carry the power of 'scientific authority', are intrinsically linked to parents' own explanations of what is happening to them.

From identifying 'factors' to developing explanations

Despite the relative infancy of research exploring parent abuse, theoretical models have, in the main, been refreshingly resistant to single-factor causes. Given the complexity of the problem and the number of correlational factors so far identified (see Chapter One), many researchers have emphasised the need to combine a range of explanations. Most comprehensive has been Cottrell and Monk's (2004) 'nested ecological model', which identified substance misuse, mental health issues, parenting styles, peer influence, poverty and the socialisation of male power among the factors that contribute to the commission of parent abuse. However, it is important to move beyond the identification of factors that appear more or less frequently in cases of parent abuse to explain *how* each contributory factor is implicated. This requires a more fundamental analysis. For example, some contributory factors, such as mental health disorders and personality traits, constitute *intrapersonal explanations* in that they locate the cause wholly within the child or young person. Other factors, such as parenting practices or previous exposure to family violence, constitute *interpersonal explanations* in that they locate the cause of parent abuse within the child–parent dyad. Yet other contributory factors, such as family communication styles, constitute *intrafamilial explanations*, which locate the cause as not within one or two individuals but in the space between family members. Fourth, contributory factors such as poverty and social isolation constitute *structural explanations*, in that they locate causes within wider social and economic systems of power that structure the lives of families and communities. Finally, factors such as the dominant societal norms that devalue motherhood and tolerate violence constitute *sociocultural explanations*.

Identifying, discussing and evaluating these different forms of explanation is important for at least two reasons. First, these explanations provide the theoretical foundation for prevention and intervention practices, and they inform policy makers and practitioners of where resources should be best placed to enable their success. Second, the explanations – which are based on findings from empirically based research studies – form the basis of, but are not equal to, 'common-sense understandings' of parent abuse. Common-sense understandings circulate culturally and find their way into everyday discussions about family abuse and violence and the way that they implicitly attribute blame and responsibility shapes how people *respond to* parent abuse. These implications need to be acknowledged.

While particular explanations may have salience in particular cases, no one theory is likely to be adequate in 'explaining' parent abuse. However, it is important to first understand how simple processes contribute to an abusive dynamic before we can convincingly offer a robust, integrated explanation for a problem that is so complex. What follows is a review of the range of explanations that have so far been offered by those with 'scientific authority' to explain parent abuse.[1]

Intrapersonal explanations

Psychopathologies

Intrapersonal explanations for parent abuse locate the cause of the problem entirely within the individual perpetrator of the abuse – that is, within the child or young person. Such theories are premised on the notion that violent and abusive behaviours are pathological, and are therefore caused by individual 'abnormalities' such as mental illness, personality disorders, the effects of substance misuse or other assumed psychological deficits. Clinical methods tend to inform this theoretical perspective, using observations, clinical interviews and case notes from families who have sought (or been referred for) medical or psychiatric treatment. As such, these theories tend to be based on data from cases of physical abuse and/or abuse that is considered to be at the most severe end of the spectrum, often where abuse is presented alongside other behavioural, medical or developmental problems. A handful of studies have focused on the relationship between parent abuse and a specific clinical 'syndrome' such as Tourette's syndrome (eg, Pretorius, 1992; DeLange and Olivier, 2004) or attention deficit hyperactivity disorder (ADHD) (eg, Ghanizadeh and Jafari, 2010). However, more common are studies that have analysed case records to develop parent abuse 'typologies'. Key findings include the following:

- A sample of 22 adolescent 'parent batterers' in France were identified as having significantly high levels of mental disorders (according to classifications in the *Diagnostic and statistical manual of mental disorders*, DSM–III–R:APA, 1987), including 'borderline personality disorder' and 'conduct disorder'. High levels of depression were identified in their mothers (Laurent and Derry, 1999).
- A study of 32 adolescent 'parent batterers' in Sri Lanka found that obsessive-compulsive disorder was the most common single diagnosis (using DSM–IV: APA, 1994), with a prevalence rate of 25%, compared to a prevalence rate of 6.8% in a control sample (Perera, 2006).
- A study from the US analysed data from 74 families who were subjected to 12 quantitative checklists – including the Parent-Directed Aggression Inventory, Research Diagnostic Interview, Interview for Anti-social Behaviour, Health Resources Inventory, Parenting Stress Index, Child Behaviour Checklist and the often-used Conflict Tactics Scale.[2] Compared to a control group, it found that adolescents who aggressed against their parents scored a higher number of 'oppositional symptoms' (using DSM–III–R) and 'possessed' poorer adaptability and frustration tolerance. Their parents scored highly for 'parenting stress' (Nock and Kazdin, 2002).

Outside of these clinical studies, reference to psychopathologies features in almost all of the parent abuse literature in some form. The presence of mental health and behavioural problems such as ADHD and post-traumatic stress disorder (PTSD) have been quantified in both forensic samples (eg, Evans and Warren-Sohlberg, 1988) and in small service-user samples (O'Connor, 2007; Parentline Plus, 2010), although in the latter case, these were quantified from parents' qualitative reports, which were not necessarily based on clinical diagnoses.

In terms of substance use in young people, it has been linked to abuse against parents in both criminal justice data (Kethenini, 2004; Ibabe and Jaureguizar, 2010) and community samples (Pagani et al, 2004, 2009). However, rather than having a direct role in terms of the 'effects' of substances on brain and behaviour, it has been suggested that its role is more indirect in that a young person's use of substances can instigate conflicts between parent and child that result in parent abuse (Pelletier and Coutu, 1992). In particular, research suggests that both 'asking patterns' instigated by the young person (eg, making demands for money) and 'requesting patterns' instigated by the parent (eg, parents' attempts to monitor the situation) become more frequent when a young person is using substances and when a parent is attempting to manage this stressful change in circumstances. As will be explored later in this chapter, many parents' accounts of their experiences of parent abuse reflect this analysis.

Box 3.1: Identifying parent abuse

A range of instruments have been developed in an attempt to quantify 'parent abuse' for the purposes of identifying links with other quantifiable variables. These instruments include the following:

- **Parent-Directed Aggression Inventory** (Kazdin, 1998) – This inventory identifies seven physical abuse items, each of which is rated on a five-point scale in terms of frequency and severity. The inventory also includes other items such as the gender and number of recipients, age of onset and possible motivation.
- **Conflict Tactics Scale (CTS)** (Straus, 1979), or the **Revised CTS (CTS2)** (Straus et al, 1996) – This scale measures violence among *all* family members, and includes measures of physical aggression, psychological aggression and injury for each member rated on a six-point scale for frequency in the past year.
- **Violent Behaviour Questionnaire** (Paterson et al, 2002) – This questionnaire measures parent abuse across five categories (verbal, physical, social-emotional, property and life threats) using 22 descriptors, each of which is rated on a seven-point scale ranging from 'not a problem' to 'a severe problem'. It also includes 20 parent strategies used to manage the abuse, which are rated for effectiveness on a seven-point scale.
- **Child-to-Mother Violence Scale** (Edenborough et al, 2011) – This scale measures the frequency of different abusive behaviours and triggers for abuse (eg, drugs/alcohol, enforcing house rules), each on a four-point scale. Questions are also asked about the mother's actions following the abuse

and support networks accessed. Open-ended questions are included to allow additional clarification and detail.

Personality, behavioural and cognitive 'traits' and 'deficits'

The development of typologies has not been restricted to clinical samples undergoing medico–psychiatric treatment. Surveys undertaken by non–clinicians have also produced typologies by identifying and quantifying personality, cognitive and/or behavioural characteristics in young people and correlating this with engagement in parent abuse. This has enabled the production of profiles of children and young people identified as 'at risk' of perpetrating parent abuse. One example is Elliott et al's (2011) identification of 'mattering' as a key risk factor in adolescent-perpetrated family violence. Mattering is defined as 'the extent to which people believe they make a difference in the world around them' (2011, p 1007), particularly 'mattering' to one's family. 'Mattering' is measured by the total score of an individual's strength of agreement to a 15–item index (eg, 'In my family's social gatherings, no one recognises me'). In their analysis, Elliott et al (2011) found that 'mattering', mediated by self–esteem and attitude to family violence, was an important protective factor against adolescent engagement in family violence (this study did not specifically focus on violence towards *parents*, although parents constituted the majority of victims). By way of explanation, Elliot et al (2011) postulate that failing to 'matter' produces low self-esteem in young people and a corresponding sense that there is 'little to lose' by violently lashing out. The shame and frustration that is inherent in 'not-mattering' makes violence appear an attractive method of conflict resolution and of restoring a positive self-concept.

However, this explanation is only one of many possible ways of making sense of this data, and we cannot be sure that it is valid when the evidence consists only of a series of correlation coefficients. This is a limitation in all such studies that attempt to identify psychological *processes* through *static* and *de-contextualised* measures (such as rating scales). Similar methods have been used to identify 'deviant beliefs' (Agnew and Huguley, 1989), 'low self-esteem' (Paulson et al, 1990), 'demandingness' (Nock and Kazdin, 2002), 'antisocial personality traits' (Castañeda et al, 2012) and 'personal autonomy' (Ibabe and Jaureguizar, 2010) as possible causes of parent abuse. However, detail regarding the process and context of parent abuse is lacking. Furthermore, the extent to which these attitudinal or behavioural checklists *explain* or merely *describe* problematic behaviours and/or their effects is questionable.

But a more fundamental problem with such explanations is the assumption that parent abuse, or indeed family violence in general, is in any way 'abnormal' or atypical. As discussed in Chapter One, the family is a particularly violence-enabling institution and violence within it is not statistically 'abnormal'. But if we accept this, then the need for a theory that explains violence and abuse in terms of an 'abnormality' becomes redundant. However, when talking about children, there may still be an emotional and political need to construct their abusive behaviour – particularly towards their parents – in terms of an inherent psychological or personality 'deficit'. Any alternative conceptualisation, which may in some way serve to normalise parent abuse, would fundamentally challenge our dominant understandings of what the child–parent relationship is. However, while labels of pathology (whether invoking notions of psychiatric 'problems' or personality 'deficits') may bring certain rewards, such as relief from parental blame and access to resources, they can also be incredibly disempowering in their construction of the child or young person as inherently damaged and therefore as fundamentally unchangeable.

Interpersonal explanations

Social learning theory and the generational transmission of violence

Social learning theory evolved from the classic 'Bobo doll' laboratory experiments performed by Bandura et al (1961). In these experiments, children observed adults behaving aggressively (or non-aggressively) towards a large inflatable 'Bobo doll'. After this observation period, it was found that the children imitated those same behaviours towards the 'Bobo doll' that they had observed the adults engaging in, a process known as 'modelling'. Additional variables found to be significant in shaping imitative behaviour included the similarity of the adult 'model' to the observing child, the gender of the child and, in a later experiment, whether the adult 'model' was rewarded or punished for their aggressive behaviour towards the 'Bobo doll' (Bandura, 1965). The principle of operant conditioning is very important in social learning theory. It involves learning through processes of *positive reinforcement* (ie, using rewards), *negative reinforcement* (ie, the removal of an aversive experience) and *punishment* (ie, the application of an aversive experience). Thus, if the observer sees aggression continually rewarded, or at least not sanctioned, they will learn that it is both acceptable and effective. Rewards may be material (eg, money, possessions) or emotional (eg, feeling valued or powerful). Using this theoretical framework, parent abuse has been explained in terms of the performance of a pattern of behaviours that have been learned through observing other abusive family interactions.

As outlined in Chapter One, there is certainly evidence of significant correlations between the observation of abuse perpetrated by parents (whether targeted towards each other or towards their children) and the subsequent, or contemporaneous, perpetration of parent abuse. However, as discussed earlier, evidence of a correlation tells us little about process and most of the studies that have explored an apparent *intergenerational transmission of violence* have moved on from focusing purely on simplistic 'observation → response' processes to consider more complex sociological and psychological processes. For example, Brezina (1999) identified links between parent-to-child abuse and child-to-parent abuse and suggested that parent abuse serves an adaptive, problem-solving function by reducing experiences of negative and/ or abusive treatment from the parent towards the child. Thus, it is an instrumental act that removes an aversive stimulus, and thus constitutes a form of *negative reinforcement*. Alternatively, Cottrell and Monk (2004) applied a psychoanalytic perspective to suggest that young people may be violent towards a non-abusing parent as a means of 'symbolically' disclosing their own experiences of victimisation at the hands of a violent parent. They also suggested that parent abuse may be a means of expressing anger and resentment at having not been protected by the non-abusing parent from such victimisation. Other research within the family violence field has suggested that early experiences of abuse, whether as witnesses or as direct victims, can produce impaired cognitive and emotional functioning (including PTSD), so that abuse and violence become an accepted form of conflict resolution (Carlson, 2000).

However, the application of social learning principles to explain parent abuse is simplistic in a number of ways, not least because of their fundamental basis in laboratory research that involved much younger children observing 'violence' in the context of a fun game that did not produce injury. It is also simplistic to assume that response directly follows observation: in cases of parent abuse, the observation of family abuse may be ongoing. Furthermore, in cases where an abusive parent has left the family home and physical abuse between parents ends, non-physical forms of abuse may continue. Non-resident parents may also collude in, encourage or 'groom' their child's abusive behaviours towards the resident parent (or vice versa) (Itzin et al, 2010). As such, the generational transmission of *values and attitudes* may be as relevant as the reproduction of *behaviours*. It is also worth noting that, in cases where there is a link between parent-to-child abuse and child-to-parent abuse, these behaviours are likely to be mutually reinforcing, and abuse or violence towards a parent may well increase levels of parent-to-child abuse in response. The previous chapter also identified how inter-parental conflict can be exacerbated by experiences of parent abuse.

An additional complexity concerns the role of gender, which has been found to mediate social learning processes. For example, Ullman and Straus's (2003) survey found that witnessing inter-parental violence is only significantly correlated with *mother abuse* – not with *father abuse*. Further, clinical studies have found that only *son*-to-mother abuse is significantly correlated with witnessing inter-parental violence – but *daughter*-to-mother abuse is not (Carlson, 1990; Langhinrichsen-Rohling and Neidig, 1995; Boxer et al, 2009). Such findings lend support to the idea that children learn that the mother is the 'appropriate victim' by observing her victimisation at the hands of their father, and directly replicate it. Yet other survey research has found that the highest rates of child-to-mother violence is in families where inter-parental violence involved *mothers hitting fathers*, or both parents hitting each other (Ullman and Straus, 2003). Clearly, then, the gendering of such processes is likely to be incredibly complex, and involve observations of values and ideals that are not just transmitted in the family home, but are also transmitted culturally. This issue is developed in the next chapter.

So, as with the intrapersonal explanations described above, explanations that focus on the generational transmission of violence can only account for some cases of parent abuse, and even then never in their entirety. The majority of young people who grow up in violent or abusive households *do not* go on to replicate such behavioural patterns. Similarly, both the qualitative and quantitative evidence base highlights the many cases of parent abuse that take place in households that have *not* previously experienced (or claimed to experience) family abuse. However, the cultural dominance of this model in common-sense understandings of family abuse is likely to shape parents' experiences of and responses to such abuse. For example, Eckstein (2004) highlighted how parents quickly 'back off' and relinquish control during abusive interactions with their child for fear of being seen to be exacerbating the abuse themselves. The dominance of a scientific theory that implicitly blames parents may also dissuade parents from publicly acknowledging the problem and seeking help. It may also shape parents' interpretation of that help if it is not offered in a sensitive and non-judgemental way (see Baker, 2009, for a discussion of how assumptions about 'cycles of violence' are implicated in domestic violence support service responses).

This point is particularly pertinent in situations where previous inter-parental violence means that parent abuse constitutes *re-victimisation* for the parent. There are also wider problems with a theory that focuses only on the normalisation of violence *within the family* and therefore ignores the normalisation (and *gender*isation) of violence and abuse that permeates powerfully at the social and cultural levels.

Parenting practices

The idea that parenting practices can explain children and young people's abuse towards their parents is perhaps the most dominant explanation of parent abuse, both scientifically and in terms of common-sense understandings. Here, the seminal research base is anchored in the psychoanalytic and clinical approach of John Bowlby. His influential 'attachment theory' suggests that a child's earliest relationship provides the child with an 'internal working model' on which they base their expectations for all future relationships (Bowlby, 1969). This internal working model includes the infant's self-concept as well as their concept of significant others. Explicit in this idea is the exhortation that parents – particularly mothers – must nurture that first relationship through 'responsive parenting', or what Winnicott (1953) termed 'good enough mothering'. Too little attention or too much attention paid to an infant is assumed to produce overly powerful children who come to dominate their parents through an overdeveloped sense of entitlement and an underdeveloped sense of responsibility. In relation to parent abuse, two particular concepts have been made relevant in the research literature: *quality of attachment* and *parenting style*.

'Quality of attachment' and parent abuse

Bowlby (1969, p 194) described attachment as a 'lasting psychological connectedness between human beings' and it is this connectedness that fosters the development of security, trust and empathy. Drawing on concepts from *ethology*, Bowlby suggested that attachment is an instinctive biological mechanism that ensures a species' survival, but if early attachment to a caregiver does not form then emotional problems can follow as the child develops. In the United States (US), Ainsworth went on to identify and measure 'attachment' by setting up an experimental scenario she termed the 'strange situation' (Ainsworth and Bell, 1970; Ainsworth et al, 1978). This involved acting out a scenario where the primary caregiver and their child play together before the caregiver leaves the room and, in the interim, leaves the child with a stranger. A few minutes later, the caregiver returns and the child's reaction to this 'strange situation' is observed. The child's reaction is interpreted as an indication of the type of attachment relationship they have with their primary caregiver and three distinct forms of attachment were identified: *secure attachment, avoidant-insecure* and *ambivalent-insecure*, with the majority of child–parent relationships falling into the first category. Subsequent studies have tested Bowlby's assumptions about the consequences of poor early attachment by tracing the developmental pathways of these three different groups, with some studies finding correlations between *avoidant-insecure* infants at 18 months and increased risks of problem behaviour in later childhood and adolescence (Sroufe et al, 1999; Fagot and Kavanagh, 1990), particularly for boys and aggressive behaviour (Renken et al, 1989).

Building on this research, some large-scale quantitative surveys have identified correlations between parent abuse and 'quality of attachment'. The latter has been assessed using a number of indicators, including the extent to which young people *feel close to and accepted* by parents (Agnew and Huguley, 1989), *feel emotionally rewarded* in their interactions with parents (Paulson et al, 1990) and *feel in agreement* with their parents (Peek et al, 1985). Significantly, these studies measure 'attachment' along a single quantitative scale, rather than using a category system as the original theory might suggest. As a consequence, such attempts to identify links between attachment and parent abuse remain underdeveloped. There are also conceptual problems with such models, such as the likely two-way nature of attachment patterns, since 'difficult' infants may elicit particular caregiving responses from their parents. Thus, the measures used in the parent abuse literature may be measuring merely one particular antecedent of poor child–parent attachments, rather than any consequence of them. Furthermore, other factors are likely to moderate any relationship between 'attachment' and parent abuse. This includes early experiences of abuse or neglect, which have been found to be linked to both attachment quality and subsequent levels of aggression in childhood (Finzi et al, 2001).

'Parenting style' and parent abuse

The notion of 'parenting style' is based primarily on Baumrind's (1966, 1967) influential empirical research from a sample of 100 US schoolchildren. Using observations and interviews with parents, Baumrind analysed 'childrearing style' along four dimensions: disciplinary strategies, warmth, communication styles and expectations of maturity. Baumrind identified three consistent styles: authoritarian, authoritative and permissive. An *authoritarian style* is characterised by forceful discipline and non-negotiable rules, where behaviour is controlled through punishment and child autonomy is curbed. In contrast, an *authoritative style* is characterised by the use of consistent and rational rules that are explained to the child, as are the consequences if the rules are broken. Discipline is achieved through rewarding 'good behaviour' and encouraging self-control (rather than obedience). Finally, a *permissive style* is characterised by unconditional acceptance of the child who is encouraged to be autonomous, with little discipline and few rules imposed unless reached by consultation with the child.

Given how central the notion of 'power' is to Baumrind's typology, it is unsurprising that it soon featured in explanations of parent abuse, particularly within the therapeutic literature. Harbin and Madden (1979) were the first to identify a link, suggesting that *permissive styles* encourage children to develop independence prematurely – a process they termed 'parentification'. They described such family situations as ones where parents have 'abdicated the executive position' and, by way of illustration, described a case where a son had broken his mother's back and kicked her in the face. Responding to the question of whether their son's behaviour was right or wrong, both parents replied: 'it was neither right nor wrong, Doctor...' (Harbin and Madden, 1979, p 1289). Harbin and Madden (1979) went on to explain that abuse towards parents constitutes a child's inappropriate response to a responsibility that they are not yet capable of managing. Other qualitative literature that attempts to explain parent abuse in terms of 'permissive parenting' includes Charles' (1986, p 353) notion of 'overly-reasonable, democratic families' who 'over-intellectualise' the dynamics of authoritative parenting and Gallagher's (2004a, p 9) notion of 'over-entitled' children whose parents 'have taken democratic parenting ideals too far'. All of these studies have suggested links between such parenting practices and the social class and educational level of the parents, although such links remain unquantified.

More recent research has suggested that authoritarian *and* permissive parenting (or an oscillation between the two) is a product of 'parental helplessness'. The notion of 'parental helplessness' refers to a parent's perception that they have less power than their child, which may indeed reflect the actuality of some parents' lives. Weinblatt and Omer (2008) suggest that 'parental helplessness' is common in parents of children with severe behavioural problems. They also suggest that authoritarian and permissive parental responses can escalate the commission of parent abuse, either through 'reciprocal escalation' (in which violence begets violence) or through 'complementary escalation' (where parental submission increases a child's demands and threats). However, it is important to note that inconsistent parenting can be a feature of mothers living with intimate partner violence, who are strict when their abusive partner is present and permissive when not (Holden and Ritchie, 1991). This suggests that family context is an important mediating factor in shaping parenting practices, and an examination of how different forms of family abuse shape each other may be a fruitful area for further research.

As with 'attachment', numerous questionnaires have been developed to measure 'parenting style', and research has identified links between 'permissive' parenting styles and higher levels of parent abuse (Paulson et al, 1990) and between 'inconsistent parenting' and parental assault (Peek et al, 1985; Jablonski, 2007). A correlation has also been identified between a lack of positive reinforcement for good behaviour in parenting practices and increased adolescent-to-parent aggression (Jablonski, 2007). However, as with quality of attachment, it may be that particular parenting practices, whether permissive or otherwise, are a *response* to a child's difficult or violent behaviour, rather than a *cause* of it. Indeed, it is very difficult to parent a child authoritatively while feeling intimidated and fearful of them and what is essentially a coping strategy may be frequently misunderstood as indicative of 'pathological parenting'. It is a concern that in both scientific and common-sense understandings of parent abuse, parents who predominantly display 'permissive styles' are soon labelled as the all-encompassing and deviant 'permissive parent'. The de-contextualised nature of this construction is unfair and inaccurate, since many parents who experience abuse from one child do not have problems with their other children, and the child in question may be well behaved in other contexts outside the family home.

Intrafamilial explanations: family systems of communication

While the interpersonal explanations discussed above move beyond 'individuals' to focus on 'dyads', the theoretical lens is nevertheless an individualistic one, in that it focuses on how each individual *impacts on* the other. As such, solutions tend to focus on change within each individual, such that parents must change their parenting style, and children and young people must develop secure attachment bonds. In contrast, intrafamilial explanations explore the interactional space between individuals. This approach centralises 'the family' as the unit of analysis. Intrafamilial explanations of parent abuse suggest that particular sequences of family interaction enable and maintain 'problematic relations', of which violence is one example. Intervention must therefore involve working with the whole family in identifying problematic forms of communication and in suggesting alternatives.

In relation to parent abuse, Micucci (1995) used a single case study to illustrate the ways in which family communications can serve to maintain and even escalate parent abuse, even if family members are attempting to achieve the opposite. He identified a number of characteristics of families where adolescent-to-parent abuse is a feature:

- **Family relationships organise around the violence** – This refers to the way that *all* family interactions focus on (what they understand to be) 'the problem'. In an attempt to reduce or contain the abuse, parents may neglect other aspects of their lives. This includes the neglect of other family members as well as social activities and relationships.
- **Families agree that the young person is 'the problem' of the family** – Such agreement results in family members ignoring their own role in eliciting or maintaining the abusive interactions. In turn, this shapes family members' assumptions about the purpose of intervention and how the young person's 'problem' will be identified and solved.
- **Families attend only to evidence that confirms their beliefs regarding who is and is not 'the problem'** – For example, family members only pay attention to confirmatory evidence that the young person is 'the aggressor', or that the parent(s) is 'controlling'. Alternative suggestions regarding other, more positive roles are defended against. If family members do not agree, then much time and effort are spent trying to persuade the others of their opinion. Disagreement can be quite common: for example, Micucci (1995) intriguingly suggests that, in two-parent families, the parent who is more involved with the child tends to construct them as helpless and in need of *protection*, while the less-involved parent tends to construct the child as wilful and in need of *control*.
- **Families *conditionally* accept each other and the situation** – Unspoken 'rules' shape what (and who) is 'acceptable' and this imposes tight limitations on 'acceptable' behaviours. However, the lack of articulation of such rules makes them difficult to challenge, and problem behaviours (such as violence) may be one way for family members to communicate their resistance to such rules.

Micucci (1995, p 155) cites a young person's account of his abusive behaviour to illustrate how parent abuse might act as a method of communication: 'That dude [his father] thinks he's always right. The only way to get through to him is to show him not to mess with me' (male adolescent, US). Eckstein's (2004) analysis of the communication patterns observed in parents' accounts of abuse highlights how parents and their child(ren) are locked in an abusive communication dynamic, which they both unwittingly maintain. As discussed in the previous chapter, Eckstein (2004) found that the development of a 'parent abuse dynamic' is gradual, starting with *verbal abuse* and moving on to *physical abuse* and/or *emotional abuse*. And while parents might initially challenge the abuse, the communicative patterns are such that young people fail to engage with such challenges. This results in parents having to find alternative ways of interacting with their child, which in some cases involves accepting the abusive behaviour as 'normal'. While this alters the relationship dynamics in terms of power and parental authority, it also enables parents to manage the trauma that accompanies it. As one mother commented: 'You can't see a way out of it and you learn to live with it' (mother, Australia – from Haw, 2010, p 82). For many parents, when parent abuse becomes normalised, it serves as a method of communication, which conveys particular meanings. For example, in Eckstein's (2004) research, when an abusive interaction stopped at *verbal abuse* and did not escalate into *physical abuse* or *emotional abuse*, many parents interpreted this as 'winning'. Another example from Eckstein's research is the construction of a 'hierarchy of abuse', which parents used (a) to measure how much their child loved them (for example, an abusive encounter that did not escalate beyond *verbal abuse* was interpreted as indicative of a child's greater love) and (b) to indicate the depth of their love for their child (for example, by enduring particularly severe levels of abuse).

Such *intrafamilial explanations* construct family members as part of a dynamic process, rather than as passive recipients of abuse and as such it could be considered as an implicitly empowering approach. Such explanations also avoid blaming one particular family member, which enables the exploration of how each family *interaction* contributes to an abusive outcome. Nevertheless, the implication that there exist 'dysfunctional' communication patterns in families does allow whole families to feel blamed, regardless of how it is framed by practitioners. Furthermore, the avoidance of individual blame might also be considered to be a problem because it avoids any question of *who* is responsible for the abuse and violence and *who* should be made accountable. As discussed in Chapter Six, while this may appear to be an academic question at the theoretical level, it can quickly become a pressing issue in the treatment room when those same theories are drawn on to develop intervention strategies.

Structural explanations: isolation, peers and deprivation

Structural explanations for parent abuse highlight the contribution of factors from *outside* the family unit. This includes peers and associates, education and schools, social isolation, poverty and social deprivation. They are 'structural' in the sense that they are shaped by multiple and interlocking 'systems' of power (such as gender, 'race' and social class), which organise social life. Such systems both enable and limit access to opportunities and resources, producing particular social and economic advantages for some while disadvantaging others. It is important to examine these structural processes because they shape constructions of family abuse and people's responses to it. Thus, what might look like the same problem of 'parent abuse' may produce dissimilar outcomes across different structural contexts, whether for victims, perpetrators or practitioners.

For example, the previous chapter identified parental social isolation as one 'effect' of parent abuse as friends, family and neighbours distance themselves from the abusive young person and/or their family. However, Cottrell (2001) suggests that parent abuse might also be *enabled* by a parent and their children's social isolation – illustrated by one young person's response as to why she abused her mother: 'because I have no one else', she replied (Cottrell, 2001, p 10). We also know that aggressive young people tend to be friends with other aggressive young people (Deptula and Cohen, 2004) and that young people who assault their parents associate with peers who do the same (Kratcoski, 1985; Agnew and Huguley, 1989). Thus, one way of explaining parent abuse is through the role of peer associations, which are structured by social class, gender, age and ethnicity and which enable an attitude of acceptance of parent abuse among young people. However, one interesting finding is that assaults on parents are much more likely to be committed alone compared to other kinds of assault, which are more likely to take place with co-offenders (Snyder and McCurley, 2008). Again, this indicates that the role of peer associates is likely to be particularly complex in understanding the commission of parent abuse.

Ethnicity may be another structural factor that shapes experiences of, and responses to, parent abuse. A recent study found that young black people are particularly at risk of adverse outcomes following the commission of parent abuse and the subsequent breakdown of the child–parent relationship. Such adverse outcomes include homelessness, mental health problems and alcohol misuse, and the researchers suggested that, although particular parenting practices found in black families serve as a protective factor against parent abuse, when adolescent violence undermines these parenting practices, there are few other protective factors available to insulate young black people from its consequences (Haber and Toro, 2009). The link between parent abuse and subsequent risk of homelessness for young people has also been suggested by Howard and Rottem (2008) in their interviews with mothers who experienced parent abuse and whose children subsequently left home.

Undoubtedly, social isolation, peer association and adverse outcomes are shaped by wider structural forces, but such processes become harder to define and measure as they become more distant from the focus of inquiry. So far, little research has explored how parent abuse can be explained in terms of influences that are external to the family unit, or how social class, gender or 'race' might mediate such influences. However, what we do know is that structural factors, such as poverty and parental stress, are implicated in those more immediate factors that have been identified in this chapter, such as parenting practices (Kotchick and Forehand, 2002) and mental health problems in young people (Samaan, 2000). Furthermore, some identified factors, such as substance use in young people, often co-exist alongside others (such as mental health problems) and may well be symptomatic of yet other contributory factors (such as previous experiences of family abuse) (Simpson and Miller, 2002).

In considering structural explanations of parent abuse, it is important to acknowledge that many of the antecedents (or 'risk factors') of parent abuse are those that have been implicated in youth offending *outside* the family home: family disruption and conflict, substance use, mental health and behavioural problems, school and educational issues, and peers involved in similar behaviours (Farrington et al, 2012). Indeed, as discussed in Chapter Five, parent abuse often only becomes known to others through a young person's involvement with youth offending services. However, as highlighted in Chapter One, while some research has identified links between parent abuse and youth offending (Kethineni, 2004; Kennedy et al, 2010), other research has found no such links (Gebo, 2007; Ibabe and Jaureguizar, 2010). We should therefore be wary of over-relying on criminal justice data to find out about the causes of parent abuse as it may be representative of only a small sub-group of cases of parent abuse. It may be that far more parent abuse is taking place undetected in families where there is no history of youth offending.

How do parents understand the causes of parent abuse?

All of the theories discussed in this chapter are derived from research data and carry the weight of scientific authority with them. However, a handful of studies have explored how *parents themselves* explain the cause of their child's abusive behaviours. As I have argued elsewhere (see Holt, 2011), this is a tricky terrain for parents to negotiate, since the most dominant explanation in scientific and common-sense discourse is that the roots of violent and abusive behaviour lie in the perpetrator's own childhood – perhaps through witnessing violence between parents or through damaged attachment bonds with the mother, for example (eg, Kalmus, 1984; Skuja and Halford, 2004). While such explanations have been offered by survivors of IPV when asked to identify the causes of their partner's violence (eg, Boonzaier, 2008), such options are clearly problematic when parents are asked to explain the causes of adolescent-to-parent abuse.

Indeed, the research literature has found no consistent pattern in parents' own explanations of parent abuse and parents tend to offer a range of explanations at the individual, family, structural and sociocultural levels. In one survey, 38.5% of parents were at a loss to provide any explanation at all (Parentline Plus, 2010). Of those studies that have asked parents to explain the abuse, the most commonly cited explanations are the following:

- **Mental illness or psychological problems** – Parents draw on evidence of clinical diagnoses to support such explanations for the abuse, which range from ADHD and conduct disorder to more extreme disorders such as psychosis and schizophrenia (Cottrell, 2001; Doran, 2007; Stewart et al, 2007; Haw, 2010).
- **Substance use** – Parents have suggested that substance use influences the *severity* of abuse, rather than the commission of abuse itself (Cottrell, 2001; Jackson, 2003; Cottrell and Monk, 2004; Haw, 2010). Other parents have blamed substance use for precipitating challenging interactions, which then lead to abuse when, for example, parents refuse their child's demands for money (Jackson, 2003).
- **Previous family abuse** – Mothers have drawn on assumed links between previous abusive behaviour perpetrated by the child's father,

whether targeted towards the mother and/or her children, and their child's abuse towards them. The links are explained by mothers in terms of (a) the child emulating the father, (b) the child having been traumatised by witnessing family abuse or (c) the child blaming the mother for not protecting them, which is often accompanied by a mother's guilt that she could have done more to protect her child (Paterson et al, 2002; Stewart et al, 2007; Howard and Rottem, 2008; Haw, 2010; Hunter et al, 2010).

- **Family disruption** – Lone parents have identified the onset of parent abuse as occurring shortly after the date of parental separation (Cottrell and Monk, 2004). This has been explained in terms of (a) the ensuing *family disruption* and (b) the child's resentment towards the resident parent because of their role in instigating the separation (Haw, 2010).
- **The influence of peer groups** – Parents have identified 'the wrong crowd' or other influential people or social groups as unduly influencing their child's behaviour (Cottrell and Monk, 2004; Stewart et al, 2007).
- **Gendered power imbalances** – Mothers have identified gender inequalities as a potential cause, often in conjunction with other explanations. The problem has been identified as operating both within the family home (eg, the sexist attitudes of fathers, who children have modelled themselves on) and outside the home (eg, the cultural messages about gender roles and the inequalities of power between men and women) (Cottrell and Monk, 2004; Stewart et al, 2007).

Very few empirical studies have questioned young people about their role in parent abuse. Those that have (Cottrell and Monk, 2004; Biehal, 2012) found that many of those explanations offered by parents were mirrored in young people's explanations, such as the role of past family abuse:

> I started beating my Mom up when I was eight … so I think [the violence] came from that, like through the sexual abuse and stuff … I was trying to let her know maybe that I needed her to listen to me … that I was being hurt by my dad. (Female adolescent, Canada – from Cottrell and Monk, 2004, p 1083)

> My stepfather caused it because he was battering me and winding me up. He left ages ago but it still has an effect. (Male adolescent, UK – from Biehal, 2012, p 254)

... and the influence of gendered roles, whether in terms of the young person's compliance with them or resistance to them:

> You kind of look up to your Dad. If he's rough, you are too. (Male adolescent, Canada – from Cottrell and Monk, 2004, p 1081)

> Well everyone thinks I'm supposed to be so perfect and nice, and I don't want to be like that so I'm going to totally go opposite. (Female adolescent, Canada – from Cottrell and Monk, 2004, p 1081)

It is important to acknowledge that both parents' and young people's explanations as to how they understand the causes of parent abuse should not be used as evidence per se as to 'the causes of parent abuse', despite some research studies attempting to do so. Both parents and young people need to navigate around discourses of blame and responsibility in their provision of explanatory accounts of why parent abuse happens, and this discursive context is likely to shape the particular narratives offered. Nevertheless, an understanding of how families account for abusive behaviours is useful for two reasons. First, it is useful because parents' understandings of parent abuse shape how they respond to it, particularly in terms of help-seeking behaviours. For example, Stewart et al (2007) found that if mothers understood the cause of the abuse as related to a 'pathology' (eg, a child's mental health problem), then those mothers would respond sympathetically and in a protective capacity, perhaps by seeking support from schools or health professionals. Indeed, Edenborough et al (2008) notes how mothers whose children had been given a clinical diagnosis were particularly proactive in seeking support for abusive behaviours. In contrast, mothers who explained the abuse in terms of their child's personality or an innate temperament tended to implement strategies (or attempt to) without seeking outside support (Stewart et al, 2007). Thus, it appears that parental attributions in relation to parent abuse, in terms of how *blameworthy* the child is and how *changeable* the cause is, shape parental responses.

But understanding how families explain their child's abuse is also useful because those 'common-sense understandings' that circulate culturally – and which are derived in part from scientific explanations – tell us something important about the way in which 'child–parent relationships' are constructed in any given historical and cultural context. This in turn is likely to shape the way we construct abuses of this relationship (whether perpetrated by the parent or by the child) and the way that we respond to such abuses. The following chapter explores further the ways in which child–parent relationships are the product of cultural and historical contexts and how these contexts shape the exercise and abuse of power within the family home.

Summary

- A number of scientific theories have been put forward to explain parent abuse, and they differ in their focus of inquiry – from the intrapersonal level, the interpersonal level, the intrafamilial level to the wider structural and sociocultural levels of inquiry.
- *Intrapersonal explanations* suggest that psychopathologies (such as clinical disorders), substance use and personality traits in the young person contribute to parent abuse. Such explanations operate within a deficit model, and suggest that the problem (and solution) lies with the child or young person.
- *Interpersonal explanations* suggest that the observational learning of violence in the family home, and problematic parenting practices, contribute to parent abuse. Such explanations also operate within a deficit model, but suggest that the problem (and solution) lies primarily with the parent(s).
- *Intrafamilial explanations* suggest that communication patterns within families contribute to the development and maintenance of parent abuse. Such explanations suggest that the problem (and solution) lies with no one individual but requires an awareness of and change in family communication practices.
- *Structural explanations* suggest that factors outside the family, such as poverty, schools and peer groups, shape experiences of family life, including parent abuse. That these factors are shaped by systems of power such as gender, social class and 'race' is important in understanding the different contexts that shape parent abuse and responses to it.
- Parents' explanations of parent abuse draw on a number of 'common-sense' understandings, which are derived from scientific theories. The most frequently cited by parents are mental health and psychological problems, substance use, previous abuse, family disruption, influential peers and gender inequalities.

Notes

[1] It is perhaps worth noting that, while there are many theoretical models that have the *potential* for explaining parent abuse (eg, psychoanalysis, perceived control theory), only those that have been researched directly in relation to parent abuse are reviewed in this chapter.

[2] For a critique of the Conflict Tactics Scale, see Yllo (1988).

FOUR

Parents, children and power relations

Introduction

The idea that all interactions, including abusive ones, are culturally and historically situated is a key theme in this book. This chapter focuses specifically on this issue by exploring the ways that power is organised through particular social structures and is complicit in how parent abuse is practised, experienced and responded to. The chapter begins by discussing how notions of 'parenthood', including ideas about its emotional terrain, are currently constructed in Euro-American cultures. The chapter then examines how the organisation of power relations between children and parents *outside the family home* might shape the interactional dynamics *within the family home*. Gender and age are important systems on which these power relations are organised and their role in adolescent-to-parent abuse is given particular attention in this chapter.

The social construction of the child–parent relationship

A male and a female together provide the biological basis for a child and, in those child–parent relationships where this biological basis remains, parenthood involves an 'embodied, visceral experience' (Miller, 2005, p 108). However, this corporal aspect of parenthood is not equal for mothers and fathers: as Strathern (2011, p 255) observes, the visibility of motherhood through the birth process itself means that '[motherhood] is constituted in her connection with the child, where fatherhood is constituted in his relationship to the mother'. Furthermore, the *salience* that different cultures ascribe to biology in defining family relationships differs across contexts. For example, in Euro-American cultures today, scientific 'facts' about sexual procreation are central to parentage (Strathern, 2005). This gives a certain clarity to the defining parameters of parenthood, with the legal rights (and responsibilities) of ownership assigned to two (or even one) individuals in their entirety. However, such an individualistic approach has been contested by many feminist thinkers who, in highlighting how such assignations have enabled women to become subjected to particular forms of regulation, have suggested alternative ways of constructing and assigning 'parenthood'. For example, Rich (1976) suggests the concept of a 'mothering continuum' while hooks (1984) promotes the term 'childrearing' (rather than 'parenting').[1] Such suggestions have aimed to highlight the fluidity of the parenting role and the childcare work of those who are not 'blood parents' – for example teachers, social workers and babysitters. In many *non*-Euro-American cultures, many community members – including other children – take responsibility for the care and supervision of children (Rogoff, 2003). Indeed, the problematic application of Ainsworth's 'strange situation' (Ainsworth and Bell, 1970; Ainsworth et al, 1978) (see Chapter Three) to many non-Euro-American cultures serves as a reminder of how scientific frameworks for researching 'child development' are cultural and historical artefacts, which do not produce knowledge that can be applied universally.

Constructing the child–parent bond: individualisation and emotionalisation

Cultural and historical contexts not only shape the extent to which notions of parenthood are individualised or collectivised; they also shape the meanings that we ascribe to it. For example, Zelizer (1985) describes how the child–parent bond has become increasingly imbued with discourses of *emotional* investment since the beginning of the 20th century, a process she terms 'the sacralization of the child' (1985, p 22). This has resulted in children being valued exclusively in emotional terms. In contrast, in many *non*-Euro-American cultures, the child–parent bond is imbued with a number of meanings that do not centralise emotion, and instead centre on the importance of family honour, ethnic or religious affiliation and/or paternal authority, for example (Ambert, 1994).

It has been argued that the centrality of emotion in current Euro-American constructions of the child–parent bond has been enabled by the advance of *developmental psychology*, which has its roots in the child-saving movement of the 19th century (see Chapter One). Rose (1989, p 156) argued that developmental psychology, as a sub-discipline of psychology, served to reconstruct parenting as a 'labour of love' by ensuring that 'the mundane tasks of mothering [were] rewritten as emanations of a natural and essential state of love'. This rewriting is implicit in many of the child development theories put forward to explain problematic adolescent behaviour, particularly in terms of the role of inadequate parenting practices and the absence of love (see Chapter Three). A kind of *psychological determinism* forms the spine of these scientific explanations, all of which are based on the premise of a passive and power*less* 'vulnerable child' and an active and power*ful* 'god-like parent'. Yet there two problems with such a conceptualisation. First, it enables the perceived problems of children and young people to be contained and packaged within a 'parent–child dyad' that ignores the structural and interactional context of such problems (Burman, 2008). This allows individual parents to be wholly and solely blamed. Such blame is likely to be felt particularly acutely in Euro-American cultures where the notion of 'parenthood' is both individualised and infused with an emotional imperative. Second, the spread of psychological determinism from 'scientific theories' of child development to culturally circulated 'common-sense understandings' has provided children and young people with the means to challenge parental authority and gain control. Price (1996) documents many examples of young people accusing their parents of not loving them or of neglecting them as a tactic of emotional abuse.

Constructing parental roles

In her anthropological work, Goody (1982) identified five parental roles that are common to all societies and which have been institutionalised to a greater or lesser degree. These involve:

- bearing and begetting a child;
- endowing a child with civil and kinship status;
- nurturing a child (eg, feeding and caring for the child);
- training a child (eg, education, initiation rituals);
- sponsoring a child into adulthood (eg, providing resources such as financial support for home or marriage).

Despite the universality of these roles, there are nevertheless historical and cultural variations in who performs them. In current Euro-American cultures, these parental roles are highly gendered and are likely to be performed by only two, or perhaps one, individual. Yet these roles are important in giving meaning to parents' experiences, and when parents are experiencing parent abuse, the sheer weight of all of these different roles is likely to produce a particularly distressing web of meaning. For example, in the parental accounts of abuse described in Chapter Two, many mothers described a profound disturbance over the abuse being perpetrated by someone who was born of them, such that what was understood as *a physical part of them* (in terms of shared biological make-up) had *turned against them*. The dominance of evolutionary discourses, and particularly the notion of kin selection, undoubtedly contributes to the sense of *unnaturalness* that such mothers have described in relation to their experiences of parent abuse. Similarly, the cultural importance placed on the parental role of 'nurturer' (and the psychological determinism that frames it) is likely to damage the parent's identity when a child is violent or abusive towards the nurturer, for what must such abusive behaviour say about a parent's ability to parent? Similarly, the parental role of sponsoring a child into adult citizenship is undoubtedly challenged if a parent seeks social support and, by doing so, raises public attention to the abusive behaviour of their charge. In many cases, the abusive behaviour may constitute criminal behaviour, and a parent's search for support may well result in prosecution and a criminal record for the adolescent who is transitioning into adulthood. However, in thinking about how constructions of parenthood shape experiences of adolescent-to-parent abuse, it is important to recognise that the meanings and the roles we ascribe to parenthood are different for mothers and fathers, in both nature and degree. For example, there is much evidence to suggest that both parental blame and the weight of parental roles is directed onto, and felt by, mothers much more forcefully. Thus, the gendering of parenthood produces a gendering of experiences of parent abuse in terms of what the abuse means for the parent. This is an issue to which this chapter returns.

The reshaping of children, parents and the state

Children's rights and parental responsibilities

In current Euro-American cultures, both the position of the family unit in relation to other institutions, and the position of family members in relation to each other, are in constant flux. In terms of the latter, it has been suggested that child–parent power relations have significantly shifted: where once power operated hierarchically through notions of 'parental authority', current child–parent power relations are characterised by notions of 'democracy' and 'egalitarianism' (Giddens, 1991; Beck, 1992). It is certainly the case that children were once considered to be the *property* of their parents (or rather, of their father) and as such were not considered as beings in their own right. Consequently, children had no 'rights' of their own and parents had very few 'responsibilities' towards them. However, the 'child-saving movement' brought new concerns with child welfare, in turn instigating a large amount of legislation in a relatively short space of time. In the United Kingdom (UK), this legislation introduced specialised responses to juvenile offending (Youthful Offenders Act 1854), compulsory education (Elementary Education Act 1870), age of consent laws (Criminal Law Amendment Act 1885) and child labour laws (Factory Act 1933). In many ways, such institutional activity served to *legalise, socialise, politicise* (and, with the advent of developmental psychology, *psychologise*) childhood into being (Hendrick, 1997). One outcome of these legislative changes was the segregation of children from adults in ways previously unimaginable, enabling children to be identified as a unique group for the very first time.

Since this time, children and young people have accrued their own set of rights. This has culminated in the United Nations' *Convention on the rights of the child* (UNCRC) (UN, 1989), an international agreement introduced in 1989 to establish special protection measures for all persons under the age of 18 years. These measures must be evident in all government policy making and they include rights to an education, healthcare and protection from exploitation and harm. However, the emergence of children's rights has taken place within a landscape where dominant understandings of 'childhood' are characterised by the notion of it being a *natural* and *universal* period of 'becoming'. Within this discourse of 'childhood innocence', children are constructed as a work in progress who must be protected, nurtured and invested in until they achieve the goal of 'being', that is, adulthood (Jenks, 1982; Qvortrup, 1994; James et al, 1998).

However, in response to the advent of children's rights, there has been a corresponding increase in the number of obligations imposed on parents to ensure that their children's rights are upheld. For example, in England and Wales, the Children Act 1989 enshrined many of the children's rights set out in the UNCRC. In doing this, a new legal concept of *parental responsibility* was created, which, in its legal codification, served to subsume the notion of *parental rights*: '"parental responsibility" means all the rights, duties, powers, responsibilities and authority which by law a parent of a child has in relation to the child and his [sic] property' (section 3.1). One outcome of this development was the enabling of parents to be subject to greater state surveillance and regulation due to its facilitation of greater parental accountability (Reece, 2009). However, research suggests that some parents are subject to greater surveillance and regulation than others, with gender, social class and ethnicity appearing to be important systems of power that shape the kinds of parents who are particularly surveyed and regulated (Phoenix and Woollett, 1991; Gillies, 2005; Holt, 2008).

From self-governing to governed: families in conflict

Alongside the political and legal reshaping of parental responsibilities and children's rights, the position of the family unit in relation to the state has also shifted. Prior to industrialisation and consequent population growth in the 1800s, in the UK and elsewhere the family was 'sovereign' and was considered to be a private sphere immune from state intervention. As such, the state would only step in *in loco parentis* when there was no 'family' available – for example in cases of neglect and child cruelty (Pinchbeck and Hewitt, 1969). While in some respects this sovereignty remains encoded (for example, in article 8 of the European Court of Human Rights), increasing aspects of family life have been opened up for scrutiny, and today parents are governed by the state rather than considered as autonomous governances in and of themselves. Thus, as Donzelot (1979, p 92) astutely observed, across Euro-American cultures there has been a profound shift from early practices of 'government *of* family' to modern practices of 'government *through* the family' as today's families are made increasingly responsible for policing their own members.

Such political, legal and cultural shifts in the conceptualisation of both parenthood and childhood have produced particular tensions for both parents and children. For example, while the discourse of 'children's rights' has been relatively dominant in recent years, the discourse of 'childhood innocence' has had greater longevity and has enabled the continuing protection of the status of childhood. One outcome of this is that children remain the single most regulated group of individuals (James and James, 2001). They still have relatively few legal rights compared to adults – for example, they cannot vote, sit on a jury, leave school, consent to sexual relations, work full time or claim benefits. Furthermore, laws prescribe how children must spend their time (eg, in education and employment), how they must be monitored (eg, through health vaccinations and national assessment tests in schools) and even how they must use public space (eg, their prohibition from public houses and betting shops). These tensions are even more apparent with older children who, upon reaching their teenage years, are likely to find themselves regulated in many ways like children while also being granted greater freedoms and responsibilities, perhaps the most salient of which in the present discussion is criminal responsibility.[2]

For both children and adolescents, then, their rights are partial and are frequently in conflict with particular forms of regulation over their lives. And with many Euro-American legislatures responsibilising parents into exercising that regulation (most explicitly through the use of parental responsibility laws), this conflict is essentially played out between parents and their children. For parents, the rights that are afforded to them are frequently in conflict with their parental responsibilities, which can quickly work to undermine parental authority – particularly when those responsibilities are enforced. Furthermore, both traditional notions of 'parental authority' and more recent notions of 'parental responsibility' may both be in conflict with recent moves to empower children and young people by enabling them to exercise agency over their own lives, articulated within a discourse of children's rights. There is some evidence that, at least for parents, such conflicts lie at the heart of the parent abuse dynamic:

> Jonathan couldn't understand that he was still a kid and he has to abide by my rules. To him, he's no, you know, that "I'm fifte, fourteen, I can do what I want, I can have a key to the house and I can come in when I want", you know, it were that what we was always arguing on, and the way he spoke to me. I mean, he'd even hit me once. (Mother, UK – from Tew and Nixon, 2010, p 584)

Parenthood, childhood and power

The previous sections highlighted the ways in which notions of 'parenthood' and 'childhood' are not universal, but are the product of their social, historical and political contexts. In Euro-American cultures, the legal, political and scientific status of both children and parents has shifted considerably over the past hundred years and this section explores how their current positioning – in relation to both each other and the state – shapes how power relations play out *between* parent and child. While Finkelhor (1983) was right to observe that power is central to all forms of family abuse, it is important to recognise that power operates societally as well as within families, and that those systems of power that shape wider social structures bleed into the family home and shape the power dynamics between family members (for example, see Archer's, 2006, finding that women's violence against men increases in cultures where women have greater political and economic power). Therefore, to get to the heart of abuses of power within the child–parent relationship, we need to ask some probing questions about the nature of that relationship: What kind of power relations does it 'normally' operate upon? And how do such operations enable a young person to act abusively towards their parent(s) in particular contexts at particular times?

Analysing power in child–parent relations

To provide a framework for the analysis of power, this chapter draws on Foucault's (1975, 1976) conceptualisation of power as a *process*, that is, power as something that is *exercised* throughout a range of social networks – these include media networks, legal networks, state networks and family networks (Foucault, 1980). Such a conceptualisation is in contrast to more 'common-sense understandings' of power, which conceptualise it as a *thing* that is 'owned' by an individual (or an organisation) and that is used to 'oppress' another in a rather mechanistic way. Instead, I am conceptualising power as always relational and as characterised by localised and specific *tactics* that operate between individuals in their everyday interactions. However, this is not to suggest that relations of power are somehow 'free-floating' and devoid of any institutional or material anchoring. Power is organised through a series of intersecting systems, such as gender, 'race', social class and age, and these systems operate across a range of social arenas (eg, in the workplace, in the family, in leisure spaces and so on). These systems of power produce both penalty and privilege (through practices of racism or heterosexism, for example), which produce specific material effects on people's lives (such as poverty). Different systems of power produce different social locations, which intersect and modify the effects of each other, such that a disabled lone mother might be penalised and privileged in all sorts of ways that differ from that of an older black father. In some social arenas (for example, in the family home), an individual may be able to exercise relatively more power than in other social arenas, in terms of the advantages and disadvantages that they are afforded. However, some individuals are *continually* afforded particular advantages while others are *continually* disadvantaged by the consistent use of *tactics* exercised both interactionally and institutionally. This may, over time, constitute an abuse of power.

However, I would suggest that one of the reasons that adolescent-to-parent abuse appears inconceivable to many is because we conceptualise the issue from a rather crude 'common-sense understanding' of power. From this perspective, it seems incomprehensible that children and young people are in a position to consistently exercise power over their parents in a way that is abusive, given all the advantages that adults are afforded in relation to their children across so many social arenas. However, a more nuanced analysis suggests that, certainly from a current Euro–American context:

- we are overestimating the extent to which parents *can* exercise power in relation to children;
- we are underestimating the extent to which children are able to exercise their own particular forms of power that are afforded to them.

A closer examination of this issue requires us to explore different 'domains of power', which are organised in more complex ways among children and parents than perhaps one might first think. In the brief analysis that follows, I argue that in terms of *economic power, political power, physical power, knowledge and resources, legal power* and *social status*, parents may not be in a position to exercise any more power than their children are. In some contexts, they may exercise less – particularly in the family home where power relations are arguably less surveyed and regulated than in other social arenas, and where particular adult 'advantages' may mean very little.

Domains of power in children's and parents' lives

Economic power and political power

Parents certainly have the potential for greater *economic power* in relation to their children, given current child labour laws in Euro–American cultures. However, for poor parents, particularly lone mothers who have been particularly disadvantaged through an increasing 'feminisation of poverty' (see Pearce, 1978), this difference may be minimal. Furthermore, for some parents, a large proportion of this economic power may be specifically constructed as money 'for' the child (eg, child support benefit), which can enable children to logically (if not legitimately) demand this money from their parent(s) as 'rightfully theirs'. Similarly, a clear distinction in the differences in *political power* between parents and children is institutionalised through the legislation of a legal voting age. Yet in practice increased feelings of political alienation and cynicism within the adult population across many Euro–American democracies (see, for example, Bromley et al, 2004; Southwell, 2008) suggests this particular entitlement to 'power' means very little outside of the family home, and much less inside. (Notwithstanding that, in some countries, a mother's political power remains as non-existent as her children's.)

Physical power

As Chapter Two identified, parents who are victimised by their children recognise that their once-dominant *physical power* can soon diminish as their child's strength and size rapidly increase during adolescence. This was particularly noted by mothers in relation to their sons. Furthermore, parents who have a physical disability may seldom have experienced greater physical power in relation to their child. But beyond the materiality of physical strength, 'physical power' should also be understood in terms of how it is constructed and practised within the child–parent relationship. The possibility of 'fighting back' and physically retaliating – which may be seen as justifiable when a victim is positioned as physically weaker than their perpetrator – has far greater social and legal ramifications when a victim is positioned as physically stronger, as a parent usually is in relation to their child. Indeed, parents have been found to be reluctant to touch their child during conflict exchanges due to a fear of it being misinterpreted as child abuse (Eckstein, 2004). This can result in parents performing the role of 'peacemaker' in place of 'disciplinarian' in their attempts to limit their victimisation. Furthermore, children can (and do) exploit their own constructed vulnerability by threatening to contact the authorities and make claims of child abuse against their parents (see Chapter Two).

Knowledge and resources

Parents are also commonly assumed to 'possess' and exercise greater *knowledge* than their children. However, not all forms of knowledge are considered legitimate and a parent with little formal schooling may exercise relatively little power through 'knowledge' in relation to their child. A related domain is power exercised through access to *resources*. But again, while it may be commonly assumed that parents have greater access to support services, information and social support compared to their child, this may become less so as the child grows older. It is also a questionable assumption in families where parents do not speak the host language and are reliant on their children to 'broker' for them, or where parents are socially and physically isolated through disability or mental health problems. Furthermore, the social isolation that is characteristic of families where abuse features (whether as an antecedent or a consequence of the abuse) is likely to limit both a child's and their parents' access to resources. However, it may be that it is the *parents* who are particularly disempowered since they face social sanctions regardless of whether they seek out resources, do nothing or actively withdraw from potential sources of support, since any of these actions may be interpreted as the mark of a 'failing parent'. It is likely that both parents and their children recognise the limits of their own and each others' resource power and this recognition may play a role in the maintenance of parent abuse. For example, as identified in Chapter Two, some parents do claim that children and young people have more resources and support available to them, something that can manifest in feelings of resentment. As parents explained:

> "I have asked police to take him away to scare him but that was a no-go. I begged the doctors and authorities – where's the help? Because I can't get any. But you can guarantee they would be here if we were showing unnecessary violence towards him." (Parent, UK – from *original transcript*, Holt, 2011)

> "When I was struggling, I'd get the Yellow Pages or the directory, and for parents there was probably a choice of five numbers of helplines. If Luke [her son] wanted help there would be the choice of a hundred." (Mother, England – from *original transcript*, Holt, 2009)

Legal power

Research that has explored parents' experiences of adolescent-to-parent abuse has also highlighted parents' awareness of the legal power that their children can exercise, both in comparison to them and, more disconcertingly for the parent, *over* them (Eckstein, 2004). In my own research, parents frequently drew on a discourse of children's rights to argue that their own rights (as well as those of other adult authority figures) have retrenched as children's rights have increased. As one mother explained:

> "I'm not blaming this government, but I think most of the governments before, they've decided to give the children so many rights, parents haven't got any. I mean, I can't go to the police and say, 'My son is mentally abusing me', 'cos you'll just get told, 'Well you're a bad parent'. But if a child goes to the police and says, 'My mother, my father, my brother or sister is mentally abusing me,' then these big cogs get into play and this poor child has got to be looked after, do you know what I mean? And they know the rules – they

> know ... the children are so, especially the ones that are misbehaving, they know that the police can't put their hand on their shoulder because they'll shout, 'Abuse!'" (Mother, England – from *original transcript*, Holt, 2009)

Given that the rights of children and the rights of parents have long been in conflict (eg, in child protection decisions), such arguments are perhaps unsurprising. Recent moves towards codifying children's rights *outside* the family home (which is what the UNCRC is primarily concerned with) appear to have shifted the dynamics that operate *within* it. There is certainly evidence that parents and children position their 'rights' in opposition to each other, resulting in interactional dynamics that reflect a 'zero sum game' whereby, for one to win, another must lose.

Not only do parents conceptualise their perceived *powerlessness* in this way (as evidenced by the extract above): the qualitative data suggests that children conceptualise their *powerfulness* in this same way by, for example, drawing on the same children's rights discourse to instil fear in, or at least to question the authority of, their parents. For example, as discussed in Chapter Two, children's threats to 'call the authorities' and make accusations against parents – what Price (1996, p 17) terms 'the hammer of the 90s' – is an abusive tactic frequently engaged in by children and young people. In some cases, these threats are realised, and parents have reported spending nights in police cells and false charges of child abuse being brought against them as a result of their child's accusations (Eckstein, 2004). Eckstein (2004) suggests that such threats are so powerful precisely because parents (and children) know the damage that such accusations can have on a parent's employment, family relations and social interactions.

The social status of 'parenthood', 'childhood' and 'adolescence'

Because the *social status* of 'parenthood' and 'childhood' encompasses all the domains of power discussed above, it is consequently also subject to shifting and interacting political, legal, social, medical, psychological and cultural contexts. This chapter has already argued that the status of 'parenthood' has diminished as a result of increased state intervention into family life and the consequent degradation of 'parental authority'. However, this has been compounded further by the rise in 'parenting expertise' over the past 20 years (Hayes, 2006; Holt, 2008; Furedi, 2009). Parenting expertise exercises power through a range of social networks, particularly through media networks (eg, through 'transformative' television programmes such as *Supernanny* and the proliferation of parenting books and websites) and state networks (eg, through government-sanctioned 'parenting academies' and court-ordered parenting programmes). But an increasing professionalisation of parenting may have come at the cost of challenging traditional notions of *parental authority* since it implies that parents do not necessarily know best, and that many parents may be making things worse.

In contrast, the status of 'childhood' has been elevated. Children's current status as an *investment for the future* (Lister, 2008) certainly affords them a particular protected status although, as discussed earlier, with protection comes many institutional and interactional practices that are inherently disempowering. However, 'adolescence' is subject to a very particular kind of 'status ambiguity' (Coleman, 2010, p 13). Indeed, the very notion of 'adolescence' is conceptualised within a wider developmental trajectory as a transitional 'stage' between 'childhood' and 'adulthood'. Thus, adolescents are subject to an impermanency where they must wait on the borders between childhood and adulthood – a position from which it is difficult to exercise acceptable tactics of power.

This ambiguity reflects particular unresolved ambivalences concerning how we conceptualise adolescents, and at the heart of these ambivalences is a set of competing discourses. Lesko (1996) identifies four competing professionalised discourses, each of which attempts to construct adolescents in particular ways:

- **medical/social science discourses** – which construct adolescents as hormone-led, identity-seeking and universally conforming with peers;
- **discourses of deviancy** – which construct adolescents as a serious social problem and prone to violence, pregnancy, underage sex and unemployment;
- **therapeutic discourses** – which construct adolescents as victims of abuse, dysfunctional families and addiction;
- **discourses of agency** – which are closely aligned with *children's rights discourses* and which construct adolescents as active social actors in their own right.

Like children, adolescents tend to be positioned not as 'beings' in their own right (unless drawing on *discourses of agency*), but as 'becomings' who may threaten the social order once they have *become*. However, adolescents' closer proximity to adulthood means that they pose a greater potential threat than children might do.

The 'status ambiguity' inherent in the notion of adolescence also challenges the assumption that families comprise two straightforward and polarised categories: *adults* = parents + over 18, and *children* = children of parents + under 18. Nevertheless, this is how power relations between parents and their children are commonly understood – that is, parents are assumed to 'have power' and children/adolescents are assumed to 'not have power'. This assumption shapes the ways in which we have organised ourselves institutionally to respond to abuse within the child–parent relationship, to the extent that statutory organisations are configured entirely around the notion that children are in *need of protection from* adults. Yet such configurations serve to hide the complex and intricate ways in which power is organised within child–parent relations and which, in some contexts, can become abusive.

Gender, parenthood and power

This chapter has already identified how the gendering of the 'corporal' aspect of the child–parent bond and the gendering of parental roles and parental blame are implicated in shaping the meanings of adolescent-to-parent abuse. The importance of gender in understanding parent abuse is also underscored by the overwhelmingly consistent finding that parent abuse is much more likely to be targeted towards mothers (see Chapter One). To explore these issues further, this section examines the ways that gender organises power relations within the family home and explores how this might further shape experiences of and responses to adolescent-to-parent abuse.

Masculinity, femininity and 'ideals' of violence

The gendered division of labour, both inside and outside the family home, means that mothers spend more time with their children than fathers and are more likely to be the resident parent in lone-parent households – thus increasing their availability as a target for abuse. Mothers may also be more frequently targeted because they are physically more vulnerable than fathers, particularly in relation to perpetrating sons. They may also be less likely to defend themselves, not only because of physical disadvantage, but also because norms of 'femininity' and 'masculinity' shape how family members engage with each other, and this includes physical engagement. Such norms are also implicated in the way that women are constructed culturally as 'ideal victims' of violence, particularly in relation to men as 'ideal perpetrators' (Christie, 1986; Madriz, 1997). This may make the victimisation of mothers more acceptable (similarly, discourses of childhood innocence may contribute to making the perpetration of violence *by children* seem inconceivable). Related to the cultural acceptance of violence towards women is a wider acceptance of the use of violence more generally, particularly in young people, which may explain cultural and subcultural differences in the perpetration of parent abuse. One study identified a role for certain cultural media preferences (eg, violent films, 'gangsta rap') in the perpetration of parent abuse (Spillane-Grieco, 2000), which, while methodologically flawed in its conflation of variables and limited sample, hints at the potential role of artefacts within youth culture in normalising violence.

The cultural acceptance of particular 'ideals' of violence is disseminated and reproduced institutionally through a range of social networks – for example, through the mainstream media, educational institutions and legal practices. However, such ideals may also be reproduced within the family home. As we know, a mother's vulnerability to adolescent-to-parent abuse is likely to increase if she has already been a victim of family abuse (see Chapter One) and one outcome of children witnessing their mother's victimisation may be their own acceptance of her role as 'victim'. This role may also become accepted by the mother herself. For example, one mother who was experiencing abuse from her son explained how her previous attempts to de-escalate violence perpetrated by her then-husband shaped her behaviour in the family home:

> I learned to shut down and not talk back and not stand up for my rights. I was thinking in order to save the peace to not fight in front of my children … if I spoke up for myself, it would like, in his own mind, provoke him. (Mother, Australia – from Howard and Rottem, 2008, p 28)

If mothers have previously been abused (whether from ex/partners or as children), then their authority and confidence in parenting can be undermined (Banyard, 1997; Levendosky et al, 2000). This may make them particularly vulnerable to parent abuse. Derived from social learning theory, Walker (1978) developed the concept of *learned helplessness* to explain the effects of domestic violence victimisation, and practitioners who have worked with parent abuse have claimed that victimised parents can take on the 'characteristics' of an abuse victim, such as powerlessness, depression and helplessness, making it more difficult for parents to change the situation (Harbin and Madden, 1979; Price, 1996; Gallagher, 2004a). Indeed, this process forms an integral part of the abusive dynamic, and is in part what enables the abuse to continue: the perpetrator recognises the diminishment of power and authority in the victim and loses respect for them, which in turn enables the justification of further abuse. As the following quote shows, parents also recognise this: 'I can't deal with her [her daughter] when I have become so stressed with her behaviour myself. I feel broken because of her' (Parent, UK – from Parentline Plus, 2010, p 15). Such effects are likely to be compounded in cases where mothers have already experienced abuse from their ex/partners, something that was also recognised by some of the mothers who I spoke to. As one mother explained to me:

> "I want to get back my strength as a parent, be more confident in my parenting. My son sees me as a weak parent – he's seen me being attacked, he's attacked me, he's seen me going into a snivelling mess. I want to get back where he looks at me and says, 'Yes, this is a strong parent.'" (Mother, England – from *original transcript*, Holt, 2009)

There are other ways in which gendered norms of parenthood shape the dynamics of parent abuse. For example, in two-parent households, power is often organised in a way that delegates maternal authority, with a father having 'ultimate authority' as 'man of the house' – often symbolised by the 'wait until your father gets home' narrative (Tew and Nixon, 2010, p 584). Thus, parent abuse may be one outcome of a teenage son inserting himself into the position of 'man of the house' after a vacancy has been left by his father. This role may come with an assumed right to exercise power over 'his' wife and children and 'take charge', as prescribed by the normative patriarchal relations that structure family life (Gallagher, 2004a; Tew and Nixon, 2010). While this vacant role may have come about because of a father's physical absence, it may also be the result of the symbolic absence of a 'father figure', perhaps because of unemployment, disability or through a questionable status as 'father' (eg, as a step-parent). In such cases, it may be the father who is vulnerable to parent abuse as his son practises what he considers a more legitimate performance of masculinity.

Motherhood, fatherhood, responsibility and blame

The greater status and authority of fathers *inside* the family home reflect the greater status and authority bestowed to men *outside* the family home. This can be seen most clearly when examining the status of lone parents, whereby lone fathers with custody of their children often enjoy the status of hero, since they are considered to fulfil both their 'breadwinner' and 'childrearing' roles. In contrast, lone mothers are often assumed to fulfil neither of these roles, and are considered to be both a 'benefit scrounger' and a 'bad mother'. Indeed, mother-blaming appears to be a persistent and pernicious feature of motherhood. This is apparent in both 'scientific theories' of child development (for a discussion, see Caplan and Hall-McCorquodale, 1985a, 1985b) and in culturally circulated 'common-sense understandings', particularly in relation to youth offending and the assumed culpability of both 'single mothers' (Mann and Roseneil, 1994) and 'working-class mothers' (Griffin, 1993). Expectations of mothers are high, from both within the family (ie, children) and outside it (eg, policy makers, service providers), and it has been argued that the ethic of 'good motherhood' demands much more stringent standards than those demanded by the ethic of 'good fatherhood' (Hester and Eriksson, 2001; Wallbank, 2001). In turn, mothers experience greater guilt and blame for the behaviour of their children than do fathers (Jackson and Mannix, 2004) and, when experiencing parent abuse, feel that, as the mother, the responsibility lies with them to stop the abuse (Jackson, 2003).

While the status of motherhood affords particular benefits (eg, legal rights and financial benefits, and perhaps decision-making power in some aspects of domestic life), it is also a status that carries the primary burden of responsibility for childhood and its consequences. This is institutionalised in a number of ways. For example, in England and Wales the legal assignation of parental responsibility automatically falls to the mother but not necessarily the father. A second example might be the disproportionate issuing of Parenting Orders to mothers by the youth courts when a child offends, by a ratio of 8:2 (Lindfield, 2001). This includes the issuing of Parenting Orders against mothers whose children are offending against them (Holt, 2009). Parental responsibility is difficult to relinquish and this produces an additional difficulty for parents – and particularly for mothers – who wish to leave the family home because their child is behaving abusively towards them. For example, one mother described abuse from her daughter as like 'reliving the nightmare I had experienced with her father ... but you cannot divorce your children' (Mother, Australia – from Haw, 2010, p 81). As discussed in Chapter Two, mothers who experience adolescent-to-parent abuse recognise such inequalities and it is likely that the resentment they so often describe is, to some extent, a consequence of bearing the dual burden of victimisation *and* victim-blame.

Box 4.1: Feminist explanations of parent abuse

It is important to acknowledge that while gender certainly mediates power relations between child and parent, it is not the *only* mediating system of power that is implicated in the 'parent abuse dynamic'. Some researchers have explicitly foregrounded gender in their explanations of parent abuse by adopting a feminist perspective (eg, Downey, 1997; Edenborough et al, 2008; Stewart et al, 2007). However, such an approach is problematic, particularly when applied to children and young people. First, while the evidence is fairly robust regarding mothers as the predominant victims of parent abuse (notwithstanding the greater likelihood of fathers under-reporting the problem), the evidence regarding male perpetrators is much less so. Indeed, as Chapter One highlighted, most community surveys have found no difference in the gender of perpetrating children. Furthermore, research so far has only explored gender as an individual 'variable' in quantitative comparisons of frequency of abuse and forms of abuse. As this chapter has demonstrated, we need a much more contextual approach that analyses gender at interactional and structural levels before we can start to understand how gender might be implicated in the commission of parent abuse. As Hakim (2011) points out, a continual challenge for any feminist analysis of violence is the question of how to avoid slipping into simplistic binaries of *good woman/bad man* or *female victim/male perpetrator*. Attempts to analyse adolescent-to-parent abuse must also respond to the question of how to include the additional *child/adult* dimension without slipping into simplistic binaries of *good mother/bad son*.

Summary

- The child–parent relationship is socially constructed. The meanings we ascribe to it and the ways in which we behave within it are shaped by historical, political, psychological, legal and cultural contexts. This has implications for how parents come to experience adolescent-to-parent abuse.
- Political, legal and cultural shifts over the past 150 years have resulted in the reshaping of relations between the family and the state, as well as between parents and their children. The power dynamics within the child–parent relationship, including the 'parent abuse dynamic', reflect these shifts.
- Attempts to understand power relations in terms of parents as *powerful* and children as *powerless* are simplistic and ignore more subtle differences in parents', children's and adolescents' political and economic power, physicality, knowledge and resource power and legal power. They also ignore the subtle shifts in the changing social

status of childhood, parenthood and adolescence. Ignoring these subtleties risks ignoring the abuses of power that can be perpetrated by children and young people against their parents.

• *Gender* and *age* appear to be important mediating 'systems of power', which shape power relations between parents and their children, and as such are particularly implicated in adolescent-to-parent abuse. While gender is (usually) constant, the role of age as a mediator is more fluid: as child and parent age, the organisation of their economic power, political power, physical power, knowledge and resources, legal power and social status changes with them. This produces changes in the power dynamic between them.

Notes

[1] It is interesting to note that, in her analysis of parenting practices (see previous chapter), it is 'childrearing styles', rather than 'parenting styles', that Baumrind (1966, 1967) refers to. Since that time, researchers in this field have reconstructed the concept of 'childrearing' into the more individualistic notion of 'parenting'.

[2] The age of criminal responsibility varies across nations, from six years in some states in the United States to 18 years in Belgium. However, across most Euro-American jurisdictions there is an ambiguity, since *both parents and their children* can be made accountable and responsible for a child's crimes through the use of some form of parental responsibility order.

FIVE

Frontline service responses to parent abuse

Introduction

This chapter discusses the ways in which existing policy and legislative frameworks shape frontline service responses to parent abuse, and how families experience these responses. Discussion focuses on *criminal justice responses* (focusing on the police, the judiciary and youth offending services), *local authority social service responses* (focusing on children's social care and adult social care) and *education and health service responses*. The chapter also explores how voluntary and community organisations have attempted to respond to parent abuse, using examples from domestic violence support, victim support and parenting organisations. Analysis suggests that while these organisations are unequipped to respond to parent abuse within their existing policy frameworks, there is nevertheless potential for them to respond in more innovative and creative ways. Based on this analysis, the chapter concludes with five suggested recommendations for change.

Because a coherent policy analysis needs to be grounded within a specific set of organisational structures, this chapter focuses specifically on England and Wales. However, where relevant, international data are drawn on both to identify consistencies across juridical and international borders and to highlight particular innovations in policy development that might usefully translate across borders.

Frontline service responses: inconsistency, perversity and a policy silence

The ambiguity and secrecy that surrounds the problem of parent abuse has no doubt contributed to its silence in public policy across Euro-American borders. In England and Wales, practitioners working within a range of statutory, voluntary and community agencies have observed an increase in reported cases of parent abuse and a lack of professional guidance in how to respond to this. This has left practitioners struggling to 'make do' within the parameters of existing policy frameworks

(Galvani, 2010; Misch et al, 2011; Holt and Retford, 2012; Nixon, 2012). One outcome of this is that practitioners both across and within particular frontline services use different languages and conceptual frameworks to understand 'parent abuse', resulting in inconsistent 'ad-hoc' agency responses to parent abuse and perverse outcomes for families (see Holt and Retford, 2012).

If parents do attempt to seek formal help for adolescent-to-parent abuse, evidence suggests that it is sought from a range of agencies, often at the same time. For example, in a web-survey based in the United Kingdom (UK) (Parentline Plus, 2010), 56% of parents said that they had sought outside help for parent abuse (Table 5.1 lists the sources of support sought). However, parents struggle to find the support that they hoped for, and the discussion that follows explores why.

Criminal justice responses to parent abuse

It has been powerfully argued that, since the 1990s, England and Wales has experienced a creeping 'criminalisation of social policy' with regard to young people (Crawford, 1997, p 228). In crude terms, this refers

Table 5.1: Sources of support sought by parents experiencing parent abuse (UK)

Who did you seek help from?		
Answer options	**Response (%)**	**Response count (total = 129)**
School	62.0	80
General practitioner	57.4	74
CAMHS (Child and Adolescent Mental Health Services)	37.2	48
Friends and family	30.2	39
Social services	22.5	29
Educational psychologist	19.4	25
Police	16.3	21
Other (please specify)[a]	16.3	21
Parentline Plus	15.5	20
Behaviour therapist	13.2	17
Psychiatrist	9.3	12
Other voluntary organisations	9.3	12
Other doctor	5.4	7

Note: [a] The most common response was health visitor.
Source: Parentline Plus (2010, p 20)

to the shift towards the troubled and troublesome behaviour of young people being predominantly positioned within a criminal justice framework. One clear example of such policy shifts is the introduction of local youth offending services in 1998, which were set up to coordinate and take responsibility for family intervention work, even in cases where children and young people were only deemed to be 'at risk' of offending. One outcome of these changes is that parent abuse has become more readily visible among this population, with parent abuse appearing in criminal justice workers' caseloads more frequently than in other frontline service workers' caseloads. A second outcome is that the problem of parent abuse is most frequently constructed within a discourse of 'delinquency', resulting in criminal justice solutions being most frequently used to respond to it. Evidence suggests that this situation is not unique to England and Wales (Downey, 1997) and such developments do raise a more fundamental question about whether criminal justice responses to parent abuse are ultimately in the best interests of a child and their family. As discussed in this section, the evidence so far suggests perhaps not.

Police responses

Parent abuse may come to police attention either through direct contact from parents (for example, to report a violent incident) or through referral from other services. For parents who contact the police, conflicts over its potential ramifications make it 'the most difficult decision of their lives', according to Routt and Anderson (2011, p 10), who interviewed parents from the United States (US) about their experiences. Evidence also suggests that there is a disparity between what parents expect from the police and what tools are available for the police to respond to such expectations. Parents often report that they contact the police because they want to send a message to their child that their behaviour is unacceptable – perhaps through the police giving their child 'a good talking to'. While research suggests that, in some cases, police involvement does act as an effective deterrent in this way (Edenborough et al, 2008; Holt, 2009, 2011), in other cases parents have felt that the abuse was not taken seriously by the police (Cottrell, 2001; Edenborough et al, 2008; Haw, 2010; Holt, 2011).

Parents have also reported feeling blamed by the police, resulting in a reluctance to make any further contact with them (Cottrell and Monk, 2004; Haw, 2010). Fear can also be a barrier to seeking police support: parents fear retribution from their child, or that they themselves may be charged with an offence – a fear that is often exacerbated by their child's threats that they will make a formal complaint against them. They also fear being subjected to institutionalised discrimination based on 'race', sexuality or social class (Cottrell, 2001), or that reporting their child's abusive behaviour to the police may confirm racist, sexist or ageist stereotypes. All of these issues appear unspecific to any one jurisdiction, with similar concerns reported across Australasia, Europe and North America.

This chasm between parental expectations and police capabilities is powerfully highlighted in a comment made by one detective inspector from a Public Protection Investigation Unit in England:

> We see incidents where [parents] call the police. Something has happened and this child, the teenager has smashed the house up ... or actually assaulted them. And when the police get there and the parents realise that [their child] will be arrested – very quickly they don't want that to happen. Very quickly what they want is some alternative solution. I don't know what their expectations are or what the police can do. They're after help and when they realise that the only help is to arrest [the young person] and take them away, that's not what they want to happen in most cases. (Detective inspector, Public Protection Investigation Unit, England – from Holt and Retford, 2012, p 7)

In England and Wales, individual police forces do not utilise a specific 'category code' to monitor incidents that involve parent abuse and there is no existing police guidance on how to respond to such incidents. In cases of child abuse, intimate partner violence (IPV) and elder abuse, clear protocols and referral tools are available to the police, such as notification to child protection services in cases of suspected child abuse or referral to a monthly Multi-Agency Risk Assessment Conference (MARAC)[1] in cases of IPV. However, incidents involving parent abuse may be recorded under a range of codes, such as 'domestic incident', 'family violence' or 'child protection', and some incident records make no reference to the abusive nature of the incident (for example, it may be recorded as 'criminal damage'). While there is anecdotal evidence that MARACs have been used in very serious cases of assault against parents, the actions available to a MARAC are very limited when the 'perpetrator' is under 18 years of age because it is difficult to meaningfully safeguard the victim (which is the aim of a MARAC) when the 'perpetrator' is living in the same home as the 'victim' and lives under their care.

Of course, if the young person is over 10 years old, then the police can arrest them for a criminal offence – the most likely being common assault, criminal damage, actual bodily harm, grievous bodily harm and/ or attempted murder (indeed, 'positive action' policies may limit police officers' sense that they can use discretion in such cases[2]). However, there is evidence that police officers offer informal advice on an ad-hoc basis, the most common advice being that families should contact social services (Holt and Retford, 2012) or seek intensive family support (Nixon, 2012). This in itself suggests that criminal justice agents conceptualise the problem of parent abuse within a discourse of 'family violence', rather than within a discourse of 'delinquency' or 'criminality'. If neither an arrest nor a referral is made, there will be no official 'case' and no 'lead contact'. The next time a parent contacts the police for help, the process will begin again, with different personnel offering a different level of service and different advice.

Judicial responses

Prosecutors are unlikely to force a parent to act as a witness against their child, so if a parent does not wish to press charges following arrest, then the case is likely to be dropped. In England and Wales, specialist domestic violence courts have been set up to support victims who are (or have been) involved in an intimate or family relationship with the perpetrator, but these are not available in cases where the perpetrator is under 18 years of age. However, Buel (2002) reports of an example in Santa Clara County, San José, US where a juvenile delinquency domestic/family violence court has been set up to respond to young people who are violent in the family home. A range of tools have been made available, including a Juvenile Delinquency Protection Order for victims (which works in a similar way to most states' adult domestic violence protection orders), a Juvenile Batterer's Intervention Program for perpetrators and a multi-agency response to supervision and assessment. This includes an in-depth investigation of the young person's home life, where particular attention is paid to any evidence of past or current family violence. Evaluation has found some success with this project, with reduced recidivism for first-time offenders and those who complied with the conditions of the probation (compared to a control group) (Uekert et al, 2006).

Such specialist courts suggest an important way forward for dealing with incidents involving parent abuse. Without them, existing sentencing frameworks may be inadequate to deal with the complexity of the problem, resulting in perverse outcomes. For example, my own research in England has found that, on occasion, parents themselves have ended up being criminalised for their own victimisation by being issued with a Parenting Order. These are court orders issued to the parents of 'young offenders' to enable them to both 'take responsibility' for their child's offences and receive 'parenting support' (usually in the form of a group parenting programme) to prevent their child's further offending (see Holt, 2009). If a parent breaches the order, they can be convicted and imprisoned. Furthermore, in cases where young people are convicted and sentenced, the legal principle of 'parental responsibility' means that parents are liable for any financial element of the sentence. In this way, one might argue that the judicial system contributes to the further economic abuse of a parent, who may become indebted by the fines and court costs generated by their son's or daughter's behaviour. The perverse outcomes that can follow are illustrated by one recent case that involved a young person refusing to pay his fine for assaulting his mother. The mother was therefore made responsible for the payment of the fine, resulting in bailiffs harassing her at her home. The mother reported that she would never contact the police again (Holt and Retford, 2012).

Outside England and Wales, similar perverse outcomes have been reported. In Canada, Cottrell (2001) reports cases of court orders that were issued against young people for incidents involving parent abuse being left to their parent(s) to enforce. This made life extremely difficult for the parents who had to continue living with their child in the interim between charge and court hearing, and resulted in them feeling less in control than ever. Parents have also complained that juvenile courts fail to communicate to their child the seriousness of the offence (Doran, 2007). Such complaints may be grounded in findings from a US study, which found that, compared to a sample of 60 young people who were convicted for non-familial violent offences, young people who were convicted for violent offences against the family were sentenced more leniently by the courts (Gebo, 2007). Such judicial practices may explain Eckstein's (2004) finding that parents' increased knowledge and experience of the judicial system resulted in them having less faith in it to protect them from parent abuse. Thus, for many parents, the criminal courts serve only to introduce an adversarial dynamic into already-strained child–parent relations, which may exacerbate, rather than alleviate, a difficult home life.

Youth offending service responses

In England and Wales, the majority of cases involving parent abuse are identified by youth offending services through their work with an offender's family following a court order. With no existing identification tool, most cases are picked up through observation or parent disclosure, as one practitioner explains:

> "I do have cases which involve physical violence, [but most] are very verbally aggressive towards their parents – lots of threats or damaging property, as a means to try and get what they want to coerce parents to doing what they want. That's what I think with most, possibly even a bit more, that a lot of the young people with their parents, when you dig deeper and you're speaking to the families and you note when you do the home visits the way they speak to the parents. And then you explore that a little bit more with the parents. They're swearing [at parents], they're slamming doors, they're breaking stuff and never being challenged about anything." (Youth offending service worker, England – from *original transcript*, Holt and Retford, 2012)

However, if we examine the operational framework of youth offending services, we can see that there are a number of problems regarding their capacity to respond effectively to such cases. At a fundamental level, juvenile justice systems are based on the assumption that young people offend *outside* the family home, and the range of sentences and conditions available to youth courts reflect this assumption. For example, in England and Wales, the Anti-Social Behaviour Order (ASBO) may be a useful pre-court disposal when dealing with parent abuse since it has the power to prohibit certain behaviours. However, ASBOs are specifically for use with those 'not of the same household' (Crime and Disorder Act 1998, c 37, section 1a) and therefore cannot be applied in such cases. This is despite parent abuse sharing many characteristics of 'antisocial behaviour' in terms of its production of persistent social and personal harm. Furthermore, a range of post-sentence interventions are available for young people that perform a range of functions, including *deterrence* (eg, a fine), *reparation* (eg, community reparation), *rehabilitation* (eg, Offending Behaviour Programme) and/or *control* (eg, home curfew). However, few of these are appropriate for incidents that involve parent abuse.

Coupled with the assumption that victims of youth offending are situated *outside of the family*, juvenile justice systems tend to operate under the assumption that the root of offending is situated *within the family*. In England and Wales, both government rhetoric and policy documentation invoke notions of a 'parenting deficit' to explain the problem of youth crime (Goldson and Jamieson, 2002) and Parenting Orders arguably represent the culmination of such invocations. As a result, Parenting Orders – and the parenting intervention programmes that parents are impelled to participate in as a condition of them – are experienced by parents as a 'punishment' for being a 'bad parent' (see Holt, 2010a, 2010b). However, the main problem with using juvenile justice parenting programmes to prevent parent abuse is that such programmes are premised on some questionable assumptions about the power dynamics between young people and their parents. For example, these programmes (like the psychological theories on which they are based) assume that family life constitutes a self-contained dyad of the *agentic parent* and *determined child*. Such assumptions are particularly evident in the dominant cognitive-behavioural programmes (ie, Triple P, Incredible Years), which operate on the social learning principle that *(parental) action produces consequence* (Stephenson et al, 2011). As discussed in Chapter Four, child–parent power dynamics are less absolute than this, particularly in families where parent abuse features. Furthermore, in such programmes it is the *parent* who is problematised and who is therefore positioned as the transformative agent who must change. It is difficult to think of any other situation where the victim of a crime is made responsible for changing the interpersonal dynamic between themselves and the perpetrator in order to stop the abuse. For example, one mother I spoke to had been given a Parenting Order following incidents involving her son's violence towards her. She explained how the 'parenting support' was presented to her by her youth offending service parenting practitioner:

> "I know Neil [the parenting practitioner] said something about they're gonna teach me not to be scared of David [her son]. 'Cos that's the bit that worries me 'cos David knows he can do whatever and I won't do nothing. I won't stop him, sort of thing, 'cos I'm scared of what he'll do to me … that is my main issue, trying not to be scared of David. That's what needs to be sorted. 'Cos I mean, it's like I said to him, 'cos they asked me if I'd ground David, does he stick to that, I said 'no, he'll climb out a window' or, and he says 'well if you stand in front of your door, and he's coming

> towards you, what would you do?', I said I'd move. I said in fact I wouldn't even stand in front of the door. That I'd just let him go." (Mother, England – from *original transcript*, Holt, 2009)

Such parenting programmes also take no account of the effects of parent abuse on the parent themselves. As Chapter Two identified, one common effect of parent abuse is the overwhelming sense of powerlessness and hopelessness experienced by parents, which can result in parental practices of compliance and withdrawal, which serve to maintain the parent abuse dynamic. Unfortunately, such practices may be interpreted as further evidence of a 'parenting deficit' rather than coping or survival strategies engaged in by a parent who is experiencing long-term abuse and violence.

Local authority social services' responses to parent abuse

In England and Wales, responsibility for safeguarding children and adults lies with local authorities. It is their responsibility to coordinate a multi-agency response to ensure that individuals 'at risk' can access the services and resources that they need. Within this remit, local authority social services departments are broadly divided into *children's social care* and *adult social care*. But as discussed in this section, both of these services are currently configured in ways that make it difficult for them to respond to parent abuse in any meaningful way.

Children's social care responses

Criminal justice agencies struggle to accommodate the problem of parent abuse because they are premised on the notion that parents are *responsible* for youth offending. In contrast, children's social care departments struggle to respond because they operate on the principle that children and young people are *vulnerable* and are in need of safeguarding from potential (adult) perpetrators of abuse and violence – particularly adults who bear caregiving responsibilities. Research suggests that children's social care practitioners (such as social workers) find it difficult to reconcile such principles with cases where family abuse features *a child* perpetrating violence against an *adult victim* (Holt and Retford, 2012; Nixon, 2012). As one social worker explained in Nixon's (2012) research:

> I think we are so focused on the child, which is a good thing because that's our job and we are taught at a very early stage in our career that it's the package around the child, it's the best outcome for children, it's about the child, but then what do you do when that child is the perpetrator? That's very difficult to deal with and it doesn't sit comfortably and it makes you a bit torn in all directions. (Senior social worker, England – from Nixon, 2012, p 231)

As discussed in Chapter One, the child and their needs are central to social care policy and practice; indeed, the whole institution of social care was set up to enable the state to step in *in loco parentis* should the child's caregivers be found to be abusive towards the child or neglectful of their needs. This operational framework is evident in social care practitioners' lack of familiarity with the term 'parent abuse' and their reluctance to use the term when talking about children, preferring terms such as 'challenging behaviour' or 'poor parenting' (Hunter et al, 2010; Holt and Retford, 2012; Nixon, 2012). The perverse outcomes that can result from such professional orientations are powerfully highlighted in a case recounted to Nixon (2012) where a mother who had threatened to leave the family home due to violence from her son was threatened by social services with prosecution for child abandonment.

Continuing pressure on time and resources in social care departments means that the thresholds for triggering a social care response are inevitably high and are inconsistently applied across local authorities (White et al, 2009). This is particularly the case when parents *request* intervention, as opposed to those who are *referred* for intervention (Biehal, 2012). As stipulated by the Children Act 1989, there are two levels of threshold that need to be met to instigate an intervention from children's social care departments. At the highest threshold, there must be a risk of 'significant harm', relevant in cases where there is 'ill treatment or impairment of health or development' (Children Act 1989, section 47). In such cases, a Care Order or a Supervision Order may be made when a child is 'beyond parental control' (a term that one could argue epitomises the parent abuse dynamic). In some cases of parent abuse, the child her/himself may be experiencing ongoing child abuse and a child protection response may be forthcoming. A child protection response may also be triggered if a child is sexually abusing their parent, although such cases are very rare. But in most other cases of parent abuse, the perpetrating child is unlikely to pass this threshold. If siblings are also being victimised, they may reach the necessary harm threshold, but as discussed in Chapter One, sibling abuse is often not identified as such, in part due to professional discourses that normalise such behaviours.

At the second, lower threshold, a local authority might be compelled to act when a child is 'in need', considered as such if the child is at risk from not achieving or maintaining 'a reasonable standard of health or development' (Children Act 1989, section 17). In such instances, a range of family support services should be provided, which might include respite care, financial support, transport assistance and advice and counselling. However, the little evidence that exists suggests that parents experiencing parent abuse who make direct and repeated requests for such help do not receive these services (Parentline Plus, 2008; Holt, 2009, 2011; Hunter et al, 2010; Nixon, 2012). Indeed, some of the parents I interviewed told me that they *wanted* their child taken into care, and had requested this, because the abuse had got so bad and they could think of no alternative option. On the other hand, just as some parents may not want to contact the police for fear of their child being criminalised, parents may be reluctant to contact social services for fear that their child (and her/his siblings) will be taken into care. Such fears have been documented in relation to parents' fears of social care involvement in cases of IPV (Stanley et al, 2009) and suspected child abuse (Cleaver and Freeman, 1995).

Given that some research has established links between parent abuse and earlier experiences of child abuse and/or witnessing IPV (see Chapter One), it is entirely feasible that young people involved in parent abuse are already known to children's social care departments. However, there are concerns about making assumptions about 'cycles of violence' and identifying children as 'at risk' of later perpetration because it encourages both practitioners and children themselves to view their future in this way (Humphreys and Mullender, 2004; LaPierre, 2008). Yet, as Wilcox (2012) points out, *underplaying* this potential link may also be problematic, since it may send the message that parent abuse is a rare response to witnessing or experiencing domestic violence. As discussed in Chapter Two, in explaining the causes of parent abuse, many parents assumed there to be a link with past domestic violence: therefore, silencing any articulation of it may serve to further isolate parents. It might also limit thinking about how children's social care services could usefully be involved in the identification of families who are experiencing parent abuse.

Adult social care responses

In England and Wales, the policy document *Safeguarding adults* suggests that 'all citizens should have access to relevant services for addressing issues of abuse and neglect' (ADSS, 2005, p 4). The document cites article 2 (*Right to Life*), article 3 (*Freedom from Torture*) and article 8 (*Right to Family Life*) from the Human Rights Act 1998 in support of this access. However, the policy guidance that follows makes it clear that only adults considered 'at risk' are qualified to receive the multi-agency response that is set out in the document. 'At risk' adults are defined as those who 'may be eligible for community care services ... [and] ... unable to protect himself or herself' (DH, 2000, p 8). The document itself justifies this narrow definition by stating that:

> If *all* adults were able to effectively access support to live safer lives at the time they needed it, there would be no need for policies and procedures aimed at addressing the needs of specific groups of people. However ... some groups of adults experience a higher prevalence of abuse and neglect than the general population and they are also not easily able to access services to enable them to live safer lives. (ADSS, 2005, p 4, emphasis in original)

Chapter One highlighted the extent to which elder abuse is a problem and the provision of a locally based, multi-agency response to older adults who are 'at risk' of such abuse is, of course, welcome. This definition of 'at risk' is also likely to apply to adults with physical, sensory and mental impairments and learning disabilities and so parents who experience such impairments and disabilities and who are experiencing abuse from their children are also likely to be included in this definition. However, in an institutional context where resources are tight and thresholds are high, all other parents are likely to be excluded – even if they are also 'not easily able to access services'. And despite the acknowledgement that practitioners also have a public duty to those adults *not* covered by this definition (ADSS, 2005, p 5), there is no policy guidance covering responses to adults who are *not* normatively constructed as 'at risk'. Thus, this public duty is not being met in practice.

Education and health service responses to parent abuse

In the Parentline Plus (2010) study described at the beginning of this chapter, schools, general practitioners and mental health services were the organisations most frequently contacted by UK parents in their attempts to get help for adolescent-to-parent abuse. With this in mind, the lack of any national policy regarding how education and health services might respond to parent abuse is particularly surprising, as is the paucity of research regarding how such cases are routinely dealt with by practitioners who work within these organisations. In England and Wales, when education and health practitioners come into contact with troubled children and young people, their responses are directed by the procedural guidance produced by their *Local Children's Safeguarding Board* (LSCB). This is a local multi-agency team that develops and manages local responses to children's safeguarding.

To take one example, the London Children's Safeguarding Board guidance recognises that 'children of both genders can direct physical, sexual or emotional violence towards their parents, siblings and/or partner' (London CSB, 2010, section 5.20.2). While the rest of this practice guidance is oriented (and worded) towards 'other children' as the potential victims, referral and assessment are recommended when there is an allegation or suspicion of physical and/or emotional abuse or harm towards 'another child *or adult*' (section 5.20.6, emphasis added). The guidance states that practitioner responses should involve discussion with the organisation's manager and nominated safeguarding children's adviser, after which a common assessment (using the Common Assessment Framework [CAF]) may take place. Following a common assessment, which may involve the identification of a 'lead professional' and the delivery of a CAF 'Action Plan', a decision will be made about whether to refer the case on to the local authority children's social care department. Similar guidance is recommended in London Children's Safeguarding Board's *Safeguarding children affected by gang activity and/or serious youth violence for child practitioners*, which points out that children and young people who perpetrate violence may need to be recognised as 'both a victim and a perpetrator' (London CSB, 2009, p 15). Thus, the practice guidance suggests a two-pronged approach where professionals must assess and support the child's welfare and wellbeing at the same time as responding 'in a criminal justice capacity' (section 6.1.2). However, this document fails to identify violence against parents in the home as a particular issue, where responding 'in a criminal justice capacity' may be particularly complex.

Each LSCB also provides guidance for education and health practitioners when there is suspected domestic violence in the home, and this may also be applicable in cases of adolescent-to-parent abuse. For example, *Safeguarding children abused through domestic violence* (London SCB, 2008) does acknowledge that children can direct violence or abuse towards parents and suggests that such behaviour 'may have its roots in early emotional harm, for which the child will need support and treatment' (section 17.2.1). Thus, the guidance suggests that practitioners assess the risk both to the mother and to each child in the family home before deciding whether to refer the case on to their local authority's children's social care department for further assessment. Contact may also be made with the mother (if the violence is disclosed by another person) and safety plans can be developed. However, further action is likely to then be the responsibility of the local authority social services department, with the same problems around meeting 'thresholds' (discussed earlier) likely to arise.

Table 5.2 summarises statutory frontline service responses to parent abuse.

Voluntary and community responses to parent abuse

Victim support services' responses

As discussed in Chapter One, following public recognition of IPV as a social problem in the 1970s, a number of domestic violence support organisations were set up in response and many of them continue to perform important work today. Alongside these services, *Victim Support* is a UK-wide charity that provides a support service to victims of *all* crimes, and the aim of both crime-specific and general crime support organisations is to deliver tailored response plans to enable victims to access relevant support agencies and resources (eg, health, housing, legal advice and so on). However, as with the statutory agencies that work within 'domestic violence' policy frameworks, these organisations operate under the assumption that children are the victims of, rather than the perpetrators of, family violence and abuse. (For example, the guidance documents produced by Victim Support, 2011, and Women's Aid, 2009, both position children as either primary or secondary victims in relation to their service responses.) Given this organisational context, much of what victim support services can offer in response to parent abuse is limited, despite practitioners reporting increased cases of parent abuse, whether through referrals from the police or through

Table 5.2: Statutory frontline service responses to parent abuse (England and Wales)

	Criminal justice	Local authority (LA) social services' children's social care department	Health	Education
Personnel	**Police**: *decision to charge* **Crown Prosecution Service**: *decision to prosecute* **Youth court**: *decision to sentence* **YOS teams**	**Social workers**: *decision to investigate*	**General practitioner, health visitor, nurse, mental health practitioner** ⇧ nominated safeguarding children adviser: *decision to refer*	**Teacher, educational psychologist** ⇧ nominated safeguarding children adviser: *decision to refer*
Assessment[a]	**ASSET report** ⇧ pre-sentence report	LA initial assessment ⇧ core assessment	CAF assessment ⇧ refer to LA social services or ⇧ continue work in health setting	CAF assessment ⇧ refer to LA social services or ⇧ continue work in education setting
Agency responses	Custody or community sentence (eg, Referral Order); possible Parenting Order	Care proceedings (Children Act 1989, section 47) or family support services (section 17)	Child and Adolescent Mental Health Service or other medico-psychiatric support	Educational psychologist, behaviour support team
Conceptualisation of child	Child as *culpable*: **delinquent**	Child as **vulnerable**: *at risk or in need*	Child as having **behavioural/psychiatric/medical problem**	Child as having **learning difficulty/behavioural management problems**
Conceptualisation of parent(s)	Parent(s) as **responsible**, due to *parenting deficit*	Parent(s) as **failure** and/or **deficient**		

Note: [a] All assessments operate according to requirements of the CAF.
Source: Adapted from Hunter et al (2010, p 274)

self-referral (Holt and Retford, 2012). For example, the provision of refuge accommodation, which is commonly offered in cases of IPV, is problematic in cases of adolescent-to-parent abuse because of a mother's legal parental responsibility to her perpetrating child who will then require supervised accommodation. There may also be practical difficulties in accommodating other teenage children – particularly sons – since many refuges have age and gender restriction policies (Baker, 2009). Legal remedies, such as Non-Molestation Orders or Occupation Orders, are also commonly suggested by victim support agencies in cases of IPV. However, such orders are not applicable to perpetrators under 18 years of age because (a) concerns for a child's wellbeing (which such orders might threaten) are likely to take priority in any court decision and (b) they are likely to be unenforceable when used against children (see Hunter and Piper, 2012, for further discussion). Yet despite such limitations, victim support services do usefully respond to parent abuse by offering emotional support, discussing safety measures with parents and providing contacts for behaviour management support, for example (Holt and Retford, 2012).

Parenting organisations' responses

As discussed in Chapter Four, parenting has been increasingly professionalised in the UK over the past 20 years, with huge public investment in parenting programmes, practitioners and resources. While some of this investment has taken shape through targeted and *enforced* support (ie, Parenting Orders), it has also taken shape through voluntary services offering universal parenting support. One example is *Family Lives* (formerly known as *Parentline Plus*), which provides national telephone and web-based support, information leaflets, workshops and courses. Its recent report concerning aggression in children describes its provision of specialist parenting practitioners in health centres and schools, who offer tailored support, either one to one or in a group setting (Parentline Plus, 2010). Family Lives also provides telephone support to parents of teenagers and, as its report documents, it regularly receives a large number of calls concerning parent abuse. Although not specific to cases of parent abuse, an independent evaluation of this service found that 80% of parents felt that their situation had improved in response to the call and 75% of parents said that they would use the service again (Thomas Corum, 2008). Parenting support is also increasingly available online, and a number of support forums discuss problems of parent abuse. My own analysis of how parents use these forums suggests that they are used primarily to enable parents to articulate difficult emotions that may be censored in offline arenas, rather than to provide specific advice and guidance to other parents (Holt, 2011). However, despite this proliferation of both statutory and voluntary parenting support provision, nothing currently exists that is specifically equipped to campaign for, advocate for and respond to the complex issues involved in parent abuse.

Community responses

As discussed in Chapter Two, one important effect of parent abuse is its exacerbation of the social isolation that the parent is already experiencing. This means that potential forms of informal support, through friends, extended families and neighbours, may not be available. Edenborough et al (2008) found that informal social support – having somebody to confide in, having somebody to act as a 'role model' for the young person, meeting parents in similar situations – has helped to alleviate the impact of parent abuse, although it does not appear to stop or reduce the abuse itself. Furthermore, a minority of parents have found support in relatives offering to house their child to give them some relief from the abuse, if only temporarily (Jackson, 2003; Edenborough et al, 2008; Haw, 2010; Holt, 2011). However, the lack of any public recognition of the problem of parent abuse is likely to severely hamper the potential of community responses, particularly within a context where a discourse of parent blame dominates.

Key recommendations for policy makers

This chapter has provided an overview of how frontline services respond to parent abuse and identified how different statutory, voluntary and community organisations are limited in their capabilities to respond effectively. While many practitioners have tried their best to respond appropriately within the parameters set by their organisational policy and practice guidance frameworks, the absence of any formal recognition of the problem of parent abuse has inevitably produced a range of inconsistent ad-hoc responses, which, in many cases, have produced some damaging, perverse outcomes for the families involved. While this chapter has grounded its policy analysis in the UK, the recommendations that follow will no doubt also apply to many other Euro-American contexts where it appears that the same policy silences apply:

1. It is evident that we urgently need to develop **a method for identifying and monitoring cases of parent abuse** that come to the attention of statutory and voluntary/community agencies. This process must start with a **consistent and clear working definition** of parent abuse, as well as an **effective tool for risk assessment**. Burton (2008) raises the point that a lack of consistency in definitions of IPV across legal, statutory and voluntary organisations inhibits and hampers attempts for a coordinated, multi–agency response to IPV: no definition at all makes this impossible in cases of parent abuse.

2. At a national level, 'parent abuse' needs to be recognised as a social problem, with **clear guidance on different organisations' roles and responsibilities** for responding to it. This guidance should include **clear protocol on how to respond,** which, while recognising the priorities of different organisations, should **raise practitioners' awareness of their own potential professional 'blindspots'** that appear to be contributing towards some particularly damaging responses, for example: youth courts issuing sentences that punish the victim and further damage child–parent relations; and social workers failing to recognise how parent abuse can damage parental authority and the ability to parent effectively.

3. **Awareness-raising campaigns** at a universal level are essential, not only for practitioners who come into direct contact with parent abuse (see above), but also for those who may come across it but fail to recognise it, such as housing officers, substance misuse services, benefits agencies, faith groups and youth workers, as well as employers, families, friends and neighbours. In particular, parents need to feel that they are not alone and that a number of forms of support are available for them. Such campaigns will need to consider how parent abuse should be conceptualised, with particular attention paid to how parents and their children are positioned in relation to discourses of responsibility and blame.

4. There are clearly problems with parents being sent on generic 'parenting programmes' organised by their local youth offending service. And while it is promising that a small minority of local youth offending services are now developing specific programmes to respond to parent abuse, many are in their infancy and most remain unevaluated (see Chapter Six). Nevertheless, **a resource for sharing best practice across different sectors**, as well as a **map of what is available regionally**, are essential to enable appropriate referrals to be made. It is also worth highlighting that while youth offending services appear to be at the forefront of developing such programmes, they may not be the most appropriate arena for delivering them.

5. Given the complexity of parent abuse, a range of services need to come together to provide **a multi-agency response**, since the agency that is most appropriate to deal with the perpetrator is unlikely to be the same agency that is most suitable to respond to the victim, or other children in the household. Furthermore, different responses may be required depending on the form and severity of the abuse, and on the specific background and needs of the family. However, one particular service needs to provide **a single point of contact** to follow a case through – otherwise, cases are left to drop. This results in parents feeling lost and practitioners not knowing the outcome of a referral and whether it worked or not, hampering the development of professional knowledge.

Practitioners across the board recognise that a lack of resources (as well as a lack of policy guidance) is preventing them from responding appropriately to parent abuse, and there are fears that a lack of sufficient response both reinforces parents' sense of failure and powerlessness and reinforces the message that such abuse is acceptable (Nixon, 2012). Indeed, research with parents has found that feelings of hopelessness and disempowerment are particularly prevalent in cases where parents have tried a number of formal and informal support options, and where none of them has worked (Edenborough et al, 2008; Haw, 2010; Holt, 2011). To cite one mother's experience: 'everybody was passing the buck' (Doran, 2007, p 69).

Summary

- The problem of parent abuse turns up in the caseloads of frontline practitioners who work in the statutory and voluntary/community sectors, either through parents seeking help directly or via referrals from other frontline services.
- Criminal justice practitioners are only equipped to respond to the problem using tools that are likely to criminalise both parents and young people. There is no clear protocol for police responses to incidents involving parent abuse and juvenile justice interventions available for both parents and young people may be inappropriate and work to exacerbate already-problematic child–family relations.
- Children's social care departments are equipped to respond to problems using interventions that centralise a child who is *at risk of harm*; children who are involved in parent abuse often do not meet the required thresholds to instigate intervention. Adult social care departments are equipped to respond to adults considered 'at risk'

and, using normative constructions of vulnerability, parents are not considered as such.

- Education and healthcare agencies are equipped to respond to the problem using guidance laid down by their LSCB, where referrals to local authority social services departments can be made. No other resources appear to be available to them.
- Voluntary and community organisations, such as Victim Support or parenting support organisations, are not specifically equipped to respond to parent abuse. Furthermore, the potential of informal support networks is hampered by a lack of public recognition of the problem of parent abuse. However, some resources – particularly those that offer emotional support – have been found to be useful.

Notes

[1] MARACs form part of the wider ongoing national domestic violence delivery plan which developed in response to the Home Office (2005) report *Domestic Violence: A National Report.* Their aim is to ensure that victims of domestic violence have access to all relevant statutory and voluntary support services and they include representatives from local police, probation, health, children and adults' safeguarding, schools, social housing, substance misuse services, independent domestic violence advisers and other relevant specialists. Some of the actions made available to a MARAC include sanctuary schemes (which involve making the home secure, installing alarms, changing locks and so on), raising a school's awareness of the need to increase support to children who may have witnessed the violence and providing alternative accommodation for the victimised parent and their children.

[2] The duty of 'positive action' directs police to make an arrest in cases of domestic violence; decisions not to arrest suspects must be justified (Home Office, 2000).

SIX

Working with parent abuse

Introduction

This chapter begins by exploring the help-seeking context of parent abuse, and asks what factors are important when assessing parent abuse prior to intervention work. It then examines a range of intervention programmes that have developed at the local level in response to the problem of parent abuse. It outlines both established group programmes (Breaking the Cycle, Who's in Charge?, Break4Change, SAAIF and Step-Up) and family intervention approaches (systemic family therapy, non-violent resistance and restorative justice conferences). Analysis draws on the theoretical approaches that inform these interventions, the strategies and techniques used within them and the findings produced by evaluation studies. The chapter concludes by identifying the specific features that are central to intervention success and exploring the potential of prevention strategies.

Working with parent abuse: setting the scene

Help-seeking contexts

Intervention work and how its success is measured need to be considered in the context of how parents seek help when experiencing abuse from their children. Mothers report that they have initially sought help from informal sources (friends, family and neighbours) rather than formal support services (Stewart et al, 2006; Howard and Rottem, 2008). However, this informal support has not always been forthcoming, with some mothers reporting that friends and family members have blamed them for the abuse (Howard and Rottem, 2008). There is no existing evidence of any gender differences in help-seeking for parent abuse, although mothers make up the majority of participants in parent abuse intervention support groups. However, we do know that, in cases of intimate partner violence (IPV), men are less likely to seek help from support services and are less likely to report victimisation to the police for fear that such incidents would be seen as 'trivial' (Felson et al, 2002).

It may be that help-seeking behaviours in cases of parent abuse are similarly gendered.

We also know from studies on parent abuse that more specific barriers shape parental help-seeking. For example, mothers who seek help from social support networks have been found to be at increased risk of abuse from their child(ren) (Pagani et al, 2003). Some parents fear that their child will sever the child–parent relationship if they seek help (Paterson et al, 2002) and some parents lie to their child(ren) and other family members about where they are going when seeking help (Howard and Rottem, 2008). Parents may also be afraid of speaking freely in therapeutic encounters for fear of retribution from their children, and those who have had long-term involvement with child protection services may fear sharing information about their family histories for fear of repercussions (Sheehan, 1997). However, research does suggest that parents remain committed to restoring the child–parent relationship and maintaining whatever affection and love remains: Jackson (2003) and Doran (2007) found that the mothers they interviewed did not consider severing the child–parent relationship as an option. Such priorities and motivations may be unique to cases of family abuse that feature adolescent-to-parent abuse and need consideration when working with such families.

Assessment

Prior to intervention, assessment of the family is crucial. In some cases, seemingly physically abusive behaviours may not be 'abusive' at all – Gallagher (2004a) suggests a number of alternative scenarios that should not be included in the category of 'parent abuse'. These include violence borne of defence or retaliation (much like women's violence against men as a response to their own victimisation) and violence borne of an attempt to protect other family members (eg, mother or siblings) from a father's abuse. The assessment of parent abuse will require the identification of a consistent pattern of abusive behaviours *and* an assessment of its impact on other family members. However, given its complexity and the contexts that shape parent abuse, simple 'tick box' inventories that have been used up until now in the research literature (see Box 3.1 in Chapter Three) may not be appropriate in providing a meaningful clinical assessment. Indeed, despite the current dominance of actuarial processes in clinical assessment, detailed qualitative interviews and observations will be necessary prior to the commencement of any intervention work.

Such assessment will need to identify:

- intrapersonal precipitating factors (eg, substance use, mental health issues, learning difficulties);
- interpersonal family processes and dynamics (eg, parenting practices, communication styles);
- family history (including previous experiences of abuse and/or current family stressors);
- structural locations of family members (eg, gender, ethnicity, access to social/economic resources);
- wider cultural issues that might require specialist input (eg, diversities in language, cultural or religious norms).

As discussed in Chapter Three, all of these factors are likely to shape the emergence of parent abuse, as well as the form it takes and the attributions that are made of it, and all will need to be considered in any intervention programme. Analysis of its emergence, stage of trajectory and the 'developmental stage' of each family member involved may also be useful, since the developmental needs of children *and* their parents may shape the requirements of intervention (Wilson, 1996). It may also be useful to explore previous experiences of intervention in light of Sheehan's (1997) observation that the longer abuse persists through previous interventions, the more difficult it is to engage the young person and instil a sense of hope into the therapeutic process.

A suggested template for the assessment of parent abuse for intervention purposes can be found in Appendix A.

Pluralism in intervention work with parent abuse

Different therapeutic techniques in intervention work are underpinned by different theoretical explanations of problem behaviour. For example, *social learning theory*, which explains behaviour through processes of 'modelling' (see Chapter Three), underpins the use of 'behaviour therapy' in treatment to change those behaviours (for example, by the therapist providing the client with examples of 'pro-social' modelling). In practice, however, intervention work with family abuse often draws on a range of theoretical approaches by utilising ideas from social learning theories, cognitive theories, family systems and communications theories while also drawing on wider structural, political and cultural perspectives. Such eclecticism is particularly a feature of groupwork, which often performs a range of functions, such as counselling, education, support and mediation.

Such plurality is vital when working with parent abuse because, as discussed in Chapter Three, current explanatory models remain relatively untested and a range of factors – from mental health problems to cultural norms – are likely to play a role in the commission and maintenance of parent abuse. Therefore, establishing a 'treatment' on the basis of any one theoretical explanation of parent abuse would be inappropriate. Pluralism is also important because of the emotional, behavioural and moral complexities of parent abuse, and responding to these complexities will require different kinds of techniques at different times.

Table 6.1 outlines eight established[1] intervention programmes or approaches that have been developed specifically to work with parent abuse, and these are indeed characterised by a plurality of theoretical approaches and a plurality of functions. As discussed in the previous chapter, in the United Kingdom (as elsewhere) there is no national policy guidance concerning responses to parent abuse, despite practitioners highlighting the need for it. Thus, intervention work that has emerged since the mid-1990s has had to develop at the local level within existing statutory and charity/voluntary sector organisations and usually within existing budgets. Many of these operate as 'group parenting programmes', with some programmes providing simultaneous intervention groups for young people. Other therapeutic approaches operate as 'family programmes', which, while not developed specifically for parent abuse, have been applied successfully to such cases.

Compared to the evaluation data of other family abuse intervention programmes (eg, for IPV and child abuse), the evaluation data regarding the success of intervention programmes for parent abuse is scant and, given its relative infancy, is methodologically limited. That which has been published often uses small, self-selecting samples that may not represent the experiences of all who participate in the interventions, particularly since such intervention work features substantial drop-out rates. Such studies also lack control groups and follow–up data to measure the *long-term effectiveness* of the intervention. Furthermore, some of the studies ask participants about their experiences retrospectively, making it susceptible to post–event confounding variables (including poor memory). At present, we also have no comparison study to evaluate whether group interventions, family interventions or indeed individual interventions are most effective in responding to parent abuse. Nevertheless, there exists sufficient evidence to explore commonalities and differences across the programmes, and the remainder of this chapter identifies what interventions have been developed, what seems to have worked and what common factors can be identified in their success.

Table 6.1: Summary of established parent abuse intervention programmes and approaches

	Programme	Theoretical approach	Aims and techniques	Schedule	Lead agency of delivery	Country	Reference
Group parenting programmes	Breaking the Cycle (1997)	Feminism, family systems theories, attachment theory and theories on trauma and adolescent development	Provides female peer support; addresses safety and practical issues (including legal remedies); skills development (eg. communication, conflict resolution); discusses discourses of gender, violence and motherhood	7 weekly sessions for mothers (plus 1 follow-up 6 weeks later)	Charity sector – child and family welfare	Australia	Paterson et al (2002)
	Who's in Charge? (2006)	Solution-focused brief therapy (SFBT) principles, with educational input	Aims to empower parents by teaching strategies to manage abuse and emotional management skills (to reduce guilt and stress)	8 weekly sessions for parents (plus 1 follow-up 8 weeks later)	Health – youth and family services (includes charity sector)		Gallagher (2004a, 2004b, 2011); O'Connor (2007)
Group parent and young people programmes	Break4Change (2009)		As above for parents; for young people, focuses on skill development (eg. emotional literacy, behaviour strategies) plus 'creative sessions' for young people to reflect on issues	8 weekly sessions for parents + 8 weekly sessions for young people	Criminal justice – youth offending services leading multi-agency team (includes charity sector)	England, UK	Munday (2009)
	SAAIF (1996)	Functional family therapy principles, using multi-agency approach to risk management	Keys aims are to improve communication, to increase insight and awareness, to provide tools for dealing with anger and aggression in oneself and others and to provide an enjoyable experience for parents and their children	Day workshops for families OR 14 weekly sessions for parents + 14 weekly sessions for young people			Priority Research (2009)
	Step Up (1997)	Cognitive-behavioural principles, incorporating ideas from the Duluth Model (making perpetrators accountable and keeping victims safe) within a restorative framework	Challenges attitudes and beliefs; skill development (eg, empathy awareness), using peer support and feedback; cognitive-behavioural strategies (eg, role play and goal setting)	21 weekly sessions for young people + 21 weekly sessions for parents – groups sometimes combine	Criminal justice – court services	USA	Buel (2002), Organisational Research Services (2005), Robinson (2011), Routt and Anderson (2011),

Table 6.1: continued

	Programme	Theoretical approach	Aims and techniques	Schedule	Lead agency of delivery	Country	Reference
Family interventions	Systemic family therapy	eg. Mediation and Family Therapy Service (MATTERS) programme Psychodynamic, narrative therapy, and family systems theories. Also draws on a sociopolitical lens to highlight the role of gender, culture and power in violence	Family therapy sessions that challenge current dynamics and offer conflict resolution skills training. Also offers TARA (Teenage Aggression Responding Assertively) parenting support group	Varies	Health – youth and family therapeutic services	Australia	Sheehan (1997)
	Non-violent resistance (NVR)	Political approaches to non-violence and communications and systems theories	Promotes 'parental presence' through techniques of non-violent resistance and use of reconciliation gestures	5 individual therapy sessions (including meeting with social supports) + 10 telephone support sessions		Israel, UK	Weinblatt and Omer (2008)
	Restorative justice conferences	Political approach that aims to bring agency back to individuals and communities	Encourages discussion and repairing of harm, often via a legally binding 'contract'	Varies	Criminal justice	Australia, Canada	Doran (2007), Daly and Nancarrow (2010)

Group interventions

Group programmes designed specifically for parents experiencing parent abuse began to be developed from the late 1990s, notably in Australia and the United States. Most of these programmes are now trademarked and offer a training and resource package for practitioners. Breaking the Cycle, Who's in Charge?, Break4Change, SAAIF and Step-Up are discussed below.

Breaking the Cycle

Breaking the Cycle was developed in Victoria, Australia by Rosemary Patterson and Helen Luntz, who were based in a youth and family counselling team within an Anglican child and family welfare agency. The programme aimed to build on the success of group programmes for survivors of adult IPV and as such was developed for mothers only. The eight-week programme utilises a therapeutic and educational input, and addresses issues such as adolescent development, communication and conflict resolution skills, and legal and safety options. However, given its feminist therapeutic foundations, this programme also emphasises 'the broader social context [of violence] that takes into account issues of gender, power, entitlement and responsibility' (Paterson et al, 2002, p 92). As such, it is informed by strong constructionist principles in its aims to explore discourses around violence and the social construction of motherhood. A small-scale evaluation of the programme found reduced violence in the home and reduced anxiety and fatigue in mothers, although depression did not reduce. However, the use of post-intervention 'feminist-as-intervention interviews' were useful in identifying what mothers found most helpful about the programme (see Box 6.2 later in this chapter). Programme selection criteria require that the violence is severe enough for mothers to be concerned about the wellbeing of themselves and/or their children, and participation is usually through self-referral.

Who's in Charge?

Who's in Charge?, a group for parents of violent or beyond-control children, was developed by Eddie Gallagher, a social worker and family therapist, in collaboration with local youth and family services and community health service departments in Victoria, Australia. The programme draws on the principles of solution-focused brief therapy (SFBT) in an attempt to address the shortcomings of long-term 'problem-focused' therapeutic approaches, which are often used in adult IPV intervention programmes and which generally suffer from high drop-out rates and poor effectiveness (see Lee et al, 2009). In contrast, SFBT approaches are, as the nomenclature suggests, relatively brief and focus on *solutions to* rather than *causes of* problematic behaviour. By focusing on a client's goals, SFBT approaches aim to (a) bring awareness to situations that most closely represent the client's preferred future and (b) identify strategies that will bring more of those situations into the client's life.

Who's in Charge? attempts to deal with parent abuse by changing parental attitudes and behaviour, and its 10 aims include:

- reducing parental feelings of isolation, guilt, depression and powerlessness;
- increasing awareness of boundaries, emotional support, assertiveness and a sense of hope;
- exploring anger in families and potential strategies for adolescent behaviour change;
- reducing abusive and violent behaviours in families (O'Connor, 2007).

Programme activities include role play, use of videos, group discussions and didactic teaching, and the programme is organised into four parts:

- Part One aims to clarify the nature of abusive behaviour and its (un)acceptability.
- Part Two explores the use of consequences to shape young people's behaviour.
- Part Three explores anger, assertiveness and self-care in parents.
- Part Four is a follow-up session eight weeks after the end of the programme, which aims to consolidate learning and assess the programme's effectiveness (Gallagher, 2011).

An early retrospective questionnaire with eight participants found that the 10 programme aims were achieved at the end of the programme, but some of these aims did not persist over time for all of the parents (notably the improvements in feelings of isolation, guilt, powerlessness and anger) (O'Connor, 2007). This suggested a need for ongoing support following programme intervention and Part Four was subsequently implemented. The course materials have also been adapted to form other group programmes, both in Australia (eg, Who's the Boss?, Out of Bounds) and in England (eg, Break4Change, see below).

Additional resources have also been developed, most notably the use of the Short Message Service (SMS) to reinforce behavioural strategies learned in the Who's the Boss? programme, which a pilot evaluation found to be useful (see Howard et al, 2010).

Break4Change

The feedback from parents who participated in the Who's in Charge? programme suggested a need for a similar programme for young people to attend (O'Connor, 2007). The Break4Change programme in England (UK) attempted to do just this. Break4Change was developed by Brighton and Hove Youth Offending Team in collaboration with a local domestic violence refuge project, the local Targeted Youth Support Service (TYSS) and the local Family Intervention Project. Criteria for participation required violence to be a concern for six months and ongoing engagement with support services, who referred families to the programme. Break4Change used many of the course materials from Gallagher's Who's in Charge? programme to run an eight-week parenting programme. However, it also ran a parallel group for young people who worked on similar themes, including emotional literacy, the nature of violence and abuse (including its impact) and skill development in impulse control, conflict resolution and communication. The aims were to stop the violence and develop more positive relationships between family members. Programme activities for young people included discussions, video and role play, self-reflection activities and 'creative sessions' where a local artists' organisation was commissioned to work with the young people to help them create 'raps' concerning their own behaviour and how to change it (see Box 6.1 for an example). Evaluation identified positive change for both parents and their children (Munday, 2009). Alongside questionnaires, the use of post-programme qualitative interviews enabled a more contextualised analysis of what had changed for the families, as the following quotes illustrate:

> Trying to change things so you are not just responding or defaulting to old habits ... trying to change the way I communicate ... more detached, a bit more objective, trying not to get so caught up with things realising that it's not all down with me, a lot of things she has to learn or work out for herself.... Before I'd help her out or stop her from messing up her life or dropping out of college.... Now I've learnt to hand over some of the responsibilities, pointing

out choices and responsibilities to her and getting a lot less involved. (Parent, England – from Munday, 2009, p 28-9)

I am more in control of my temper. It's kind of made me look at what happens. I now see it as a pattern, that I have some kind of choice in what happens ... so it may not happen as much I suppose ... made me see it more as unacceptable. (Adolescent, England – from Munday, 2009, p 31)

Despite its success, the programme is currently on hold while awaiting further funding.

Box 6.1: Example of a young person's 'rap' from the Break4Change intervention programme

GETTING ON WITH LIFE

First memories, troubles with police, Na I weren't acting like a beast,

Just kept getting in trouble, couldn't stop, Why was I acting like a Lop?

I was confused, everything was a flop, Wrong place and time to deal with a cop,

In and out of care feeling messed up, I was young, I was just a pup (yup)

Now I'm a teen, I wanna grow up, I've been trying, but sometimes I blow up,

I've gotta keep my head down at school, I've gotta stick to them rules,

Now I wanna come out of care, live with my dad, I'm trying to be a more mature lad,

I'm getting on with my life, looking to my goals, Gonna be careful where I stroll.

(Munday, 2009, p 49)

SAAIF (Stopping Aggression and Anti-social Behaviour in Families)

SAAIF was set up in Essex, England (UK) after the local police, the Youth Offending Service, Child and Adolescent Mental Health Services and victim support organisations identified a need for a multi-agency intervention programme to work with families where parent abuse is a feature of family life. The principles of risk management feature strongly in the SAAIF programme, and in recognition of the dynamic quality of abusive relationships in families, the programme continually shares information across agencies and makes regular use of the Structured Assessment of Violence Risk in Youth (SAVRY) (developed by Borum et al, 2003). SAAIF is based on *functional family therapy*, an evidence-based therapeutic approach that was specifically developed for work with adolescent behaviour problems. Functional family therapy is comprehensive in its focus of inquiry and draws on cognitive-behavioural techniques to achieve individual change while also exploring the unique familial and ecological characteristics of each particular family (Alexander and Robbins, 2010). It therefore draws on resources and support from outside the family system and as such aims to identify the role of structural factors in both the maintenance of and the solution to particular family problems. Such a therapeutic foundation makes SAAIF a particularly eclectic programme, and it utilises a range of therapeutic techniques such as role play, cognitive-behavioural strategies (such as the application of 'consequences'), problem solving and skills training (eg, empathy development, listening and communication skills). The programme also features educational content (eg, parenting styles, teenage sexual health, drug awareness). A feature of the programme is the development of a 'parent's toolbox', which parents can continue using once the programme is completed. SAAIF offers both day workshops, which people can self-refer to, and more intensive 14-week programmes for parents and young people, which require referral from a professional. An independent evaluation commissioned in 2009 found that the majority of parents, young people and stakeholders found the programme to be of assistance, with the learning of new communication skills and coping strategies to be of particular benefit (Priority Research, 2009).

Step-Up (Stop, Time out, Evaluate, Prepare, Use skills and Patience)

The Step-Up programme uses a cognitive-behavioural, skills-based approach within a restorative framework. The first Step-Up programme was set up in 1997 by the Department of Judicial Administration and the Prosecuting Attorney's office in King County, Seattle, Washington, US and was designed for court-referred intervention work with 13 to 17-year-olds who have been violent towards parents and/or dating partners. Initially, parents join a separate support group, but often the groups are combined with a few separate sessions built into the programme. Step-Up takes its inspiration from the 'Duluth Model', which was developed in the 1980s in Duluth, Minnesota, US for intervention work with IPV and prioritises making perpetrators accountable and keeping victims safe. The programme encourages young people to recognise their choice to behave abusively and teaches them about healthy relationship interactions. It also aims to highlight the importance of parental authority while challenging young people's sense of entitlement that allows them to challenge this authority (Buel, 2002).

The programme comprises 21 weekly sessions and focuses on the key goals of recognising abusive and non-abusive behaviours, identifying rationales used to excuse abusive behaviours, recognising situations that trigger abusive interactions, learning non-abusive alternative strategies within those situations and empathising with the victim's situation (Buel, 2002; Routt and Anderson, 2011). Programme activities include writing 'responsibility letters' and 'empathy letters' and maintaining an 'abuse journal' and a 'time-out log' to facilitate young people's weekly progress reports to the group, known as 'check-ins'. The 'Power and Control Wheel' is central to the Duluth model in enabling participants to identify abusive and non-abusive behaviours (see Pence and Paymar, 1986), and this aid has been adapted for use in the Step-Up programme (see Figure 6.1).[2] Here, it is used to facilitate discussion during 'check-ins' to enable young people to identify (a) which section of the 'Abuse Wheel' was in operation during a specific abusive interaction that week and (b) which skills need to be put in place to enable the operation of the corresponding section on the 'Respect Wheel'. The parent support programme focuses on safety planning and learning 'response tactics', which may help to avoid the escalation of abusive encounters. The whole group is central in providing positive and negative feedback on the techniques practised during role play, and on each young person's progress overall (Routt and Anderson, 2011).

An early evaluation study found a significant reduction in abusive and violent behaviours in young people and lower recidivism rates at 18 months when compared to a control group (Organisational Research Services, 2005). Evaluation in a further three pilot sites across the US is ongoing. A further development is the *Specialist Juvenile Violence Court*, which was set up in Lucas County, Toledo, Ohio, US in 2007 as part of a wider multi-agency response to youth violence. Here, a judge regularly reviews the progress of the young people who are engaged in the Step-Up family violence programme. A multi-agency meeting is held fortnightly between the judge and relevant staff to discuss each ongoing case, and then families join the courtroom and each young person self-reports on his/her progress since the last court meeting. Overnight detention may be ordered in cases where there has been insufficient progress. The immediacy of this court response sends a strong message to the young person about the unacceptability of both the violence and of not engaging with the intervention programme – something that in itself is seen as a powerful learning exercise for young people (Robinson, 2011).

Figure 6.1: The Abuse and Respect Wheels

Source: Copyright with permission: King County Step-Up Curriculum, G. Routt and L. Anderson, adapted from the Duluth Model, Domestic Abuse Intervention Program.

Family interventions

An alternative to groupwork with parents and/or young people is intervention work with families. Such work has a long pedigree in family therapy and three distinct approaches have been applied to work with parent abuse. These are systemic family therapy, non-violent resistance approaches and restorative justice conferences. These are discussed below.

Systemic family therapy

Systemic family therapy draws on intrafamilial explanations of adolescent-to-parent abuse (see Chapter Three) and focuses on identifying and improving communication patterns between family members. Miccucci (1995) identifies four therapeutic strategies for disrupting what he describes as the 'symptomatic cycles' of parent abuse. First, he highlights the importance of practitioners *supporting parental authority* by insisting that parents must be the decision makers within the therapeutic process (see also Price, 1996). Second, he highlights the practitioner's role in enabling families to attend to *repairing dislocated relationships*. This might be achieved by encouraging family members to express their feelings about themselves and the situation and to listen to each other non-reactively. Third, Miccucci identifies the need for families to *contain conflicts* by recognising how other parties, whether individuals (eg, siblings) or institutions (eg, schools, social services) might serve to escalate the conflict or distract attention away from the initial conflict.[3] Fourth, Miccucci (1995) highlights the importance of *discovering and supporting competence*. This is achieved by encouraging families to recognise the roles and abilities that family members contribute beyond those defined by the problem of parent abuse (eg, 'the aggressor', 'the victim'). In many ways, this strategy has parallels with narrative therapy in its emphasis on the power of re-authoring problematic 'family stories' to enable the emergence of new possibilities in action and understanding (see White and Epston, 1990).

The Mediation and Family Therapy Service (MATTERS) programme developed in Victoria, Australia is one example of a programme that draws on many of these therapeutic strategies in its work with parent abuse. This programme emphasises the need for practitioners to avoid the role of 'expert' when working with families[4] and also the importance of *separating the person from the problem* so that responsibility for change is shared. Such strategies encourage family members to identify their own strengths and resources in finding appropriate solutions, a process that enables family relationships to be repaired (Sheehan, 1997). Sheehan's article is particularly useful in providing therapeutic strategies for engaging resistant young people at the start of intervention. It also discusses safety issues and identifies challenges that can arise in intervention work, such as when other family members are also violent, or how to make the young person accountable for the violence while enabling them to reflect on their motivations for the violence, which may include working through difficult past experiences. Sheehan (1997) advocates the use of *genograms* to explore family histories in intervention work, a technique that has also been used effectively in research work (see Howard and Rottem, 2008). In Sheehan's evaluation of the MATTERS programme, successful outcomes (defined as the cessation of or decrease in violence) were identified in just over half of the 60 families under assessment. Success was associated with cases where violence was less enmeshed in the family's history and where the young people attended at least three sessions (Sheehan, 1997). Criteria for intervention by MATTERS require that the parent(s) has called the police at least once, that the parent(s) has been physically assaulted at least once and that the parent(s) reports feeling afraid of the young person at times. A related eight-week parenting support group (TARA: Teenage Aggression Responding Assertively) is also offered to parents.

Non-violent resistance approaches

Non-violent resistance approaches (NVR) emerged within a sociopolitical context of considering how disadvantaged or marginalised groups fight exploitation and oppression without resorting to violent means. The strategies employed by Gandhi and Martin Luther King during their political struggles are often cited as examples of resistance that can also be practised during family conflicts where dialogue and persuasion may not be enough to facilitate change on their own (Avraham-Krehwinkel and Aldridge, 2010). What is notable about this relatively new approach is its recognition that, as discussed in Chapter Four, cultural changes mean that power relations between parents and children are no longer based on hierarchical parental authority and that parents do not necessarily possess 'power' relative to their children. Thus, interventions that advocate that parents simply regain the power that is 'rightfully theirs' is a problematic strategy.

When applied to cases of parent abuse, NVR requires that parents commit to 'non-violence', and intervention work involves training parents to recognise the signs of abusive interactions and their own role in its escalation. As such, NVR approaches are heavily influenced by intrafamilial explanations of parent abuse and share some common ground with systemic family therapy. Weinblatt and Omer's (2008) concept of 'parental helplessness' (discussed in Chapter Three) is of relevance here, since it produces inappropriate parental responses (whether overly-punitive or overly-permissive), which may serve to exacerbate a child's problematic behaviour. Thus, a key strategy in NVR intervention work is the suggestion of alternative 'resistant' responses that can be practised by parents (Omer, 2001, 2004). The term 'resistant' is important, since it reflects the assumption that while parents cannot 'control' their child and his/her behaviour, they can control their own behaviour (Weinblatt and Omer, 2008).

Parental presence is an important practice in NVR and involves parents personally and tenaciously intervening in the violent or abusive arena (rather than withdrawing from it, which is a strategy commonly described by parents). As such, it aims to 'obstruct the mechanisms of oppression' (Weinblatt and Omer, 2008, p 78). Specific techniques that advocate *parental presence* include the following:

- **The 'sit–in'** – for use inside the family home. Parents quietly sit with the child for up to an hour, announcing that they will wait for a solution from the child.
- **The 'telephone round'** – for use outside the family home. Parents call the child's friends and their child's friends' parents to ask where their child is and to relay the message that they had called.
- **The 'parental visitation'** – also used when the child is outside the home, where parents visit the scene (eg, nightclub, street corner, friend's house). As with the 'sit–in', this technique provides a literal 'parental presence' while at the same time acknowledging that, as parents, they cannot 'make' their child come home. Nevertheless, the technique indicates parents' refusal to submit to their child's wishes.

Another NVR strategy involves promoting the positive aspects of the child–parent relationship. The use of *unconditional* 'reconciliation gestures' (eg, expressing regret at past behaviours, using symbolic gifts, suggesting shared activities) are advocated to enable this. A key principle in NVR is the involvement of a support network of friends and relatives and, initially, NVR counsellors. This network is trained to work with the parent in providing support and love to their child while insisting that the violence and abuse is unacceptable and must stop, and that parents are entitled to resist it. Once face-to-face intervention is complete, NVR intervention work continues with ongoing telephone support.

The NVR programme has been adapted for violence against siblings (Omer et al, 2008) and is unusual in having been evaluated using a randomised controlled trial. This evaluation reported a reduction in 'permissive parenting styles' and in 'parental helplessness'. It also reported a reduction in mothers' reports of child aggressiveness and externalising symptoms, and an increase in mothers' perceptions of social support, although this last change was not evident at follow-up (Weinblatt and Omer, 2008). Furthermore, compared to results frequently reported in more generic parenting programme evaluations, the evaluation reported a very low drop-out rate and no reduction in effectiveness for parents with older children. Such findings suggest that NVR is particularly promising in its attempts to:

- position parent abuse within a sociopolitical context;
- avoid blaming parents and suggesting they can and should 'control' their children;
- promote rigorous evaluation research and offer transparency as to the programme's shortcomings.

Restorative justice conferences

Broadly speaking, the aims of restorative justice are to repair the harm caused by an offence and to make the perpetrator accountable for it. It is underpinned by the assumption that crime is committed against individuals and communities, rather than against 'the state', and therefore reparation should involve victims and their communities (rather than representatives of the state). As such, the methods used to achieve its aims tend to be rather more informal and flexible than other state-sanctioned methods might prescribe. While restorative justice is noted for its conceptual ambiguity and plurality, it has its roots in the civil rights and women's movements of the 1960s, which challenged criminalisation and incarceration practices; in shifts towards citizen participation and victim advocacy in the 1970s; and in a growing recognition of Aboriginal, First Nation and Native American peace-making processes (Daly and Immarigeon, 1998). Restorative justice can be applied to any context where there is conflict, but it is most frequently used in juvenile justice, criminal justice and family welfare and child protection cases. Restorative justice interventions may be offered as a diversion away from the courtroom or as a court-ordered sanction and can be applied to a range of contexts, including children's homes, schools, the secure estate and within the wider community.

A range of specific interventions operate under the umbrella term 'restorative justice', and these include family group conferences, restorative justice conferences, sentencing circles, victim impact panels and other victim-offender mediation practices.

Restorative justice conferences (which are the form of restorative justice most commonly used in response to parent abuse) involve a meeting between a conference facilitator, victim, offender and other community members who may act as supporters. The role of the professional is to facilitate (rather than 'lead') the restorative process and decision making is 'owned' by the participants themselves. Conferences generally begin with the facilitator explaining the process and purpose of the conference and the alleged offence, and then each party voices their story. Following this, all sides agree on resolutions that are acceptable, which may involve a written apology, actions of reparation or restitution (to the victim or community), restrictions on particular behaviours and agreement to participate in further treatment (eg, substance misuse programmes). These agreements become part of a 'contract', which can result in court action if the contract is not complied with (Livingstone et al, 2010). Restorative justice is often thought to be particularly appropriate for young offenders because it is seen to offer a remedial opportunity for moral development (Barton, 2003). Furthermore, the 'shaming' that the process enables, and the subsequent forgiveness it fosters, are seen as integrative rather than alienating, and such benefits are considered to be particularly important for young people who are at a critical stage of their social and identity development (Braithwaite and Braithwaite, 2001).

The use of restorative justice conferences in cases of family violence is often questioned because family violence does not constitute a 'one-off' incident to be discussed and resolved like 'youth offending' is often constructed to be (Stubbs, 2002). However, it has been used in cases of parent abuse. One study (Doran, 2007) examined the experiences of six parents (four mothers and one couple) who had engaged in a restorative justice programme in Nova Scotia, Canada as a result of their child's violence towards them. A second study (Daly and Nancarrow, 2010) analysed three cases of parent abuse (each involving son–mother dyads) in Adelaide, South Australia.[5] In both studies, restorative justice was offered as a diversionary measure following police involvement. Doran (2007) found that, in four out of five cases, the restorative justice process was seen as positive because:

- it provided access to other important services;
- parents felt listened to in a non-judgemental way by practitioners, often for the first time;
- parents felt able to talk with their child in a safe environment about both the violence and other related family issues;
- the community and support system was designed to support the *whole family*, rather than just the child as parents had previously felt to be the case;
- the legally binding contract enforced change, and the presence of authority figures (such as the police) while it was signed underlined its importance.

In many ways, these characteristics, which made the experience so positive, address many of the challenges that face parents who are experiencing abuse from their children, and which have been raised throughout this book:

- the lack of a coordinated system response;
- the social isolation;
- the lack of non-judgemental support from practitioners and the wider community;
- the lack of service engagement with the complex nature of family problems;
- the lack of a safe environment where parents can negotiate with their child;
- the inability to enforce a young person's engagement with change.

And while still involving a police presence, restorative justice circumvents other criminal justice measures, which often criminalise the child and aggravate child–parent relations. However, successful outcomes rely on all of these issues being addressed, and if resources are not available, or if practitioners are not sufficiently trained, then the outcomes may be different (see Daly and Nancarrow, 2010, for examples of less successful outcomes).

Box 6.2: What parents have found to be helpful in interventions for parent abuse

- **Naming the abuse** – Before attending a support group, parents report feeling confused as to whether their experiences really do constitute 'abuse'. Having their experiences validated and defined as abusive and unacceptable comes as a relief to parents and is often the first step in helping them to work through them (Paterson et al, 2002; Monk and Cottrell, 2006; O'Connor, 2007; Munday, 2009).

- **Being listened to and listening to others' experiences** – The articulation of alternative attitudes and ideas opens up possibilities for different ways to think, feel and act. Furthermore, the social support derived from group programmes is useful in helping parents to cope with the abusive behaviours (Paterson et al, 2002; Monk and Cottrell, 2006; O'Connor, 2007; Munday, 2009; Priority Research, 2009).

- **Developing strategies to establish boundaries with young people** – This is partly enabled by parents first establishing in their own minds what is/is not abusive and therefore acceptable (see first point). The consistent implementation of 'consequences', although initially resisted by children, is effective in reducing abuse over time (Monk and Cottrell, 2006; O'Connor, 2007; Munday, 2009; Priority Research, 2009).

- **Developing self-care strategies** – By addressing parents' own physical and emotional needs, parents are in a stronger position to practise new strategies to manage their abusive children (O'Connor, 2007). Particular counselling techniques (such as self-esteem work, communication skills and community networking skills) can help to further this aim when incorporated into intervention programmes (Monk and Cottrell, 2006; Munday, 2009).

- **Education and awareness-raising about the dynamics of parent abuse** – Learning about the role of power, control and anger is helpful both to parents (O'Connor, 2007) and to children and young people (Monk and Cottrell, 2006; Munday, 2009).

Potential prevention strategies

Despite the obvious potential of the group and family intervention programmes discussed in this chapter, working with parent abuse is fraught with complexities and complications. Not least, it requires the consent and engagement of family members and some parents and practitioners have reported that many young people refuse to engage in the programmes (Gallagher, 2004b; Howard and Rottem, 2008). Depending on the nature and theoretical underpinnings of the programme, this may be more or less of a problem. Nevertheless, it is clear that intervention programmes offer only one solution to the problem of parent abuse. A second solution may be the implementation of *prevention* programmes, and this chapter concludes with a brief discussion of what these might look like.

Prevention work in schools

Some of the ideas developed by Break4Change could be developed for work in schools, particularly in light of the success of current work being carried out to prevent domestic abuse and dating violence among adolescents (see, for example, Ellis, 2004; Bell and Stanley, 2006; EVAWC, 2011).[6] Research using community samples with children and young people suggests high levels of acceptance of violence against women (Burman and Cartmel, 2005; Barter et al, 2009) and schools are well placed to work on these attitudes more generally and to raise awareness of parent abuse specifically. As the previous chapter suggested, schools could also play a more proactive role in identifying cases of parent abuse and in responding effectively when support is sought by parents and families. Furthermore, schools themselves need to be aware of the way in which some of their practices might exacerbate parent abuse. For example, we know that school exclusions enable greater opportunities for antisocial behaviour, offending and substance misuse (McAra, 2004; McAra and McVie, 2007). We also know that school exclusions increase stress in parents and young people, and also increase the time young people are forced to spend with their parents, thus increasing the potential for abusive incidents. Cornell and Gelles (1982) identified exclusion from school as a correlative factor in children who assault their parents and schools that exclude children for aggressive behaviour in the classroom should be particularly alert to these risks.

Prevention work in communities

Parents often seek support through friends and family when experiencing abuse and violence from their children, but the social isolation that is both an antecedent to and consequence of parent abuse means that such support can be difficult to find. Furthermore, the culture of blame that surrounds parents when it comes to troublesome and troubling young people means that communities may not necessarily be forthcoming in providing support. Community initiatives therefore have much potential in changing attitudes, increasing knowledge and understanding and mobilising collective action. In relation to tackling domestic violence, community prevention work has been targeted at specific 'at-risk' populations or at specific genders. Successful community work tends to focus on specific aims (eg, enabling the identification of abuse and training in how to respond) and produces a range of strategies and resources (eg, community resource packs, interactive websites and DVDs and community training) – one example being the *Neighbours, Friends and Families* campaign in Ontario, Canada.[7]

Prevention work through media and public campaigns

As with all forms of family abuse, but particularly with adolescent-to-parent abuse, greater public awareness is needed so that parents are not so unprepared if it occurs, as such unpreparedness has been found to worsen its impact and delay attempts to seek help. Media campaigns through television, radio, print media, websites and billboards have all been used to provide information and change those attitudes that tolerate problem behaviours (such as domestic violence). Studies that have evaluated the impact of such campaigns on domestic violence have found that they can increase knowledge and understanding and increase reporting and help-seeking behaviours (Ghez, 2001; Donovan and Vlais, 2005). Particularly effective are campaigns that undertake extensive formative research, which identifies existing attitudes and behaviours (Cismaru and Lavack, 2011). However, there is evidence that such media campaigns may have greater impact on victims than on perpetrators (Keller et al, 2010), suggesting that such an approach needs to be used in combination with other kinds of prevention work.

Summary

- Prior to working with parent abuse, it is important to recognise the contexts of families seeking help, the importance of comprehensive assessment tools and the need for a plurality both in theoretical approaches and in intervention functions.
- A number of group intervention programmes have been developed specifically to work with parent abuse over the past 15 years. They vary in terms of the lead agency, length and schedule of programme, theoretical emphasis and whether they include a young people's group. However, they each feature a range of therapeutic, educational, support and/or mediation functions, each draw on a range of theoretical principles and each include a number of goals.

- Family intervention work has also expanded to work with parent abuse, and three specific approaches have been applied with some success: systemic family therapy, non-violent resistance and restorative justice conferences.
- Evaluation of intervention work is at an early stage, and it has not yet been established which programmes are most effective. However, individual small-scale evaluations have provided information about what parents find most useful. This should act as a useful starting point in the development of a solid research base.
- So far, little work has been carried out to develop prevention strategies in relation to parent abuse. However, school-based work, community initiatives and media and public campaigns all have the potential to raise awareness, change attitudes and improve the identification of and responses to cases of adolescent-to-parent abuse.

Notes

[1] The programmes and approaches discussed are 'established' in the sense that they have been running for a number of years and most have produced some form of documentation and evaluation study. I have deliberately excluded parenting support groups, which deal with more generic 'problem behaviour' in children and young people. However, given the large number of them, many may discuss the problem of parent abuse and include techniques to help parents to manage it.

[2] The ease with which the Power and Control Wheel can be adapted for work with parent abuse tells us something about the similarity of abusive tactics that feature in IPV and parent abuse.

[3] Such damaging processes, referred to as 'triangulation' in the therapeutic literature, might also involve practitioners themselves as they get drawn into the conflict and collude with either the parent or the young person as to who is 'the problem'. The practitioner needs to be aware of such potential risks (Miccucci, 1995).

[4] Cottrell (2001) suggests that this issue is of such importance that parents should organise and run their own support groups without any 'expert' input at all.

[5] See also Morris (2002), which discusses the successful use of a youth justice family group conference in a single case of parent abuse.

[6] For specific examples, see Tender (www.tender.org.uk) and the Astell Project (www.astellproject.org.uk).

[7] See www.neighboursfriendsandfamilies.ca

SEVEN

Adolescent-to-parent abuse: future directions for research, policy and practice

In the Introduction to this book, I talked about the 'scientific authority' that researchers carry when producing knowledge, particularly about provocative issues that can shape people's lives so profoundly. The responsibility of this weighed heavily on me throughout the writing of it, and I am concerned about the risks of particular research findings being misused to develop policies or to reinforce stereotypes that may further disempower, stigmatise and alienate parents, young people and families. I hope that this book has highlighted the complexity of the problem. In particular, I hope that the book has emphasised that neither parents nor their children can be easily categorised into 'victim' or 'perpetrator' roles, nor can they be easily slotted into adversarial positions of 'powerful' versus 'powerless', and the ensuing allocation of blame that often follows. I hope that the book has highlighted how both parents and their children are powerful *and* powerless in all sorts of different ways, in different contexts and at different times, while simultaneously exercising power against considerable personal, emotional, structural and cultural constraints.

Given such complexities, this final chapter aims to provide a brief overview of what steps are now necessary in policy making, practice and research to move the debate on and begin to address the problem of adolescent–to-parent abuse. However, before we do, I would like to explicitly frame this chapter in terms of a key question that implicitly framed every chapter of this book, and which represents a particular challenge to our thinking about this issue: whose responsibility is it?

Whose responsibility?

Perhaps the underlying reason why we have so far struggled to understand and respond appropriately and consistently to parent abuse is because at its heart lies the unresolved issue of responsibility. To allocate responsibility we require a clear dichotomy of 'victim' and 'perpetrator' and in most abusive interactions, whether inside or outside the family, this binary is available to us. However, the 'parent abuse dynamic' produces no such clarity, since it is characterised more by recursion than by a linearity of cause and effect. If we conceptualise parent abuse as 'an incident' (as criminal justice agents have to do), the issue is clear. But a closer exploration of family contexts and histories both shifts and blurs these lines. They shift and blur further when we take into account cultural, legal and political constructions of childhood and parenthood, and the different ways in which children and parents can exercise power in relation to each other.

This dilemma of responsibility at the interpersonal level is reflected in policy dilemmas: in particular, dilemmas over which frontline service (if any) should take responsibility for this emerging social problem. And while both the statutory sector and the voluntary/community sector deliver interventions in this field, the question of who should take responsibility for leading and monitoring in intervention delivery is rarely addressed. While this is an important conceptual question, it also has more practical implications, since we know that outcome success is often shaped by the nature of the organisation that delivers the intervention (Campbell, 1998; Robinson and Hudson, 2011). Yet what I hope is clear from this book is that parent abuse is a health, legal, economic, educational, developmental and human rights issue. As such it is *everyone's problem* and only by working together and pooling the knowledge and resources we have are we going to be able to address it responsibly.

Future directions for policy making

Since the election of the new coalition government in the United Kingdom in May 2010, policy making in England and Wales has quickly taken new directions across all statutory departments. Almost all of these changes will impact on families. For example, changes to welfare benefits mean that poorer families are experiencing real reductions in working tax credits, supported childcare costs, out-of-work benefits and housing benefit. And research suggests that such reductions are likely to have a disproportionate impact on lone-parent households headed by mothers (TUC, 2010). In addition, the Educational Maintenance Allowance, which helps support 16 to 18-year-olds in full-time education, has been withdrawn, tuition fees for young people going into higher education have trebled and the school leaving age is set to rise to 18 years in 2015 (it is currently 16 years in England and Wales). Furthermore, such changes are taking place in a climate of increasing unemployment, particularly for young people aged 18-24 years (House of Commons Library, 2012). As well as increasing stress in families, such changes are also likely to impact on the dynamics of family life by, for example, forcing young people to spend more time with their families at home, stay at home for longer and be economically dependent on their parents. And, however indirectly, this is likely to impact on the commission of and experiences of adolescent-to-parent abuse.

Given that budget cuts appear to be the main driver behind most of these reforms, it would appear that this is not the appropriate political or cultural moment to suggest the development of brand new policies (and brand new budgets) to help address the problem of parent abuse. However, there are ways in which policy makers might address the problem in areas where policy change is already taking place. For example, changes to child protection services are under way following the government's commission of *The Munro review of child protection* in 2011 (Munro, 2011). While the problem of parent abuse received little attention in either the Munro Review or the government's response to it (DfE, 2011), my own response to the proposals identified scope within Munro's 15 recommendations for improving children's social care departments' response to parent abuse. In particular, I highlighted the ways in which Munro's recommendations involving (a) an emphasis on community-based multi-agency working, (b) early intervention and 'early help offers', (c) a shift from a 'compliance culture' to a 'learning culture' and (d) an emphasis on the child's journey, could all meet the frontline challenges presented by parent abuse without requiring drastic policy change or new service budgets (see Holt, 2012b, for further discussion).

There are also other avenues where current policy proposals could be adapted to meet the challenge of parent abuse. The recent Home Office *Call to end violence against women and girls: Action plan* (Home Office, 2011a) failed to acknowledge the problem of adolescent violence towards mothers, despite its claim to eradicate 'any act of gender-based violence' (2011a, p 1). However, many of its 35 listed actions clearly have the potential to address issues that relate to the commission and experience of parent abuse. Examples include the development of a youth prevention campaign to 'encourage teenagers to re-think their views of acceptable violence' (action 2) and the aim to 'explore the prevalence and effects of VAWG [violence against women and girls] on vulnerable groups' (action 9). Action 17 aims to 'run a national campaign to support and help turn around the lives of families with multiple problems' and this also looks like it has lots of potential for developing responses to parent abuse, particularly in its suggestion of providing families with a key worker and improving access to domestic violence services. There has been some concern about the adequacy of health service responses to domestic violence (DH, 2010) and these concerns have also been addressed within this document. This includes actions such as training for health visitors (action 18), working with the National Institute for Health and Clinical Excellence to provide guidance on effective interventions for health professionals (action 30) and introducing specialist training for health professionals who undertake Work Capability Assessments (action 32) – each of which could be expanded to incorporate responses to adolescent-to-parent abuse within their remits. The Action Plan also aims to revise the definition of 'domestic violence' to include victims who are under 18 years (action 77), an aim that was explored further in a subsequent government consultation (Home Office, 2011b). The inclusion of perpetrators under 18 years seems a reasonable suggestion within this remit.

A further potential avenue for change in England and Wales is through the criminal justice system. Although the criminal justice system has taken more steps than most in addressing parent abuse, specifically in terms of the development of local intervention programmes, there are further changes that could be made. The government response (Ministry of Justice, 2011) to the consultation paper *Breaking the cycle: Effective punishment, rehabilitation and sentencing of offenders* (Ministry of Justice, 2010) made a number of suggestions that could be developed to enable a better response to parent abuse. For example, the government response outlines aims to increase the use of restorative justice at all stages of the criminal justice process, particularly for young offenders. As discussed in Chapter Six, restorative justice is one strategy for responding to parent abuse that, if resourced and practised well, may overcome many of the challenges that are presented by the nature of the problem. Within this aim the government also identified the need to improve the advice that sentencers receive about such practices – and clear information and practice guidance should certainly reduce the number of perverse outcomes that have been discussed in this book. One feature of juvenile justice services in England and Wales is that, in contrast to adult systems, intervention programmes are developed and run at the local level by individual Youth Offending Teams and are not standardised or validated nationally. As a result, different statutory agencies, including youth courts, are not necessarily aware of any specific 'parent abuse' programmes offered by their local youth offending service and therefore cannot make appropriate referrals. Unfortunately, the government's aim to make youth offending services 'locally determined and driven' (Ministry of Justice, 2011, p 13) may worsen this problem.

A final note of caution is that any outcome success identified in evaluation studies of interventions should not be used by policy makers and politicians to justify *forcing* families to attend intervention programmes. All of the intervention programmes discussed in Chapter Six took place in a context where participation was voluntary, and research tells us that, in more coercive and punitive contexts, such success is not necessarily repeated (Holt, 2010a, 2010b).

Future directions for practice

> Professionals need to see, hear, and feel the abuse in order
> to truly understand it. (Mother, Australia – from Haw, 2010,
> p 84)

This book has produced a number of consistent messages that practitioners can learn from. One message is the need to be aware of the extent to which parents experiencing parent abuse already feel judged and, as such, the need for practitioners to challenge discourses of 'parental determinism', which can reinforce such feelings. As Chapter Three highlighted, all sorts of factors may 'cause' parent abuse and we can conclude very little with any certainty. Thus, one important practice in our work with parents is to avoid explicitly or implicitly suggesting that the problem of parent abuse is because of the parents, whether through their 'parenting style', quality of attachment, past family traumas or the resources and capital they have (or do not have) access to. While examining these issues during intervention work can certainly be useful (for example, by exploring new communication strategies), it is important for practitioners to present them as possible solutions, not as likely causes that need to be 'undone'. In the Introduction to this book, I talked about the importance of terminology, and this issue is as important for practitioners as it is for researchers. In discussing his intervention work with parents, Gallagher (2004a) emphasises the importance of labelling the behaviour, not the person, and the need to be aware of how particular questions and phrases (such as '*over*protective' and '*over*indulgent') may implicitly reinforce parental determinism and imply that the quality of parenting can be measured in an absolutist, de-contextualised way.

Furthermore, because parent abuse takes place within a hidden, fearful and stigmatised context, a second message concerns the need to increase our knowledge and awareness of its signs and symptoms. Like all family abuses, parent abuse takes culturally specific forms and there is a particular need for awareness of how cultural understandings about what is 'abusive' and what is 'acceptable' (both to tolerate and to disclose) will shape how families seek help. Thus, mothers and fathers need to be able to voice their experiences within a cultural framework that is relevant to them, both during initial assessment and during intervention work. Furthermore, practitioners need to be sensitive to the way that their assumptions and professional background can shape whether and how parents come forward. This involves the need for culturally competent practices that include an understanding of how practitioners' framing of parent abuse might be interpreted by different parents and families.

A third message is that parent abuse is often not the only problem or concern within a family. Chapter One highlighted links between parent abuse and other forms of family abuse, whether previously, contemporaneously or potentially in the future. There is also some evidence of links with youth offending outside the home, problems in school, learning difficulties, substance misuse and mental health problems. Parent abuse appears particularly prevalent in lone-parent families and seems to be targeted towards mothers, who are more likely to be living in households associated with poverty and deprivation, compared to two-parent households. This has a number of implications. First, it is likely that, at present, services engage with different family members at different times in response to different incidents, without ever seeing the wider parallels and overarching contexts. As discussed in Chapter Five, this results in cases being dropped and families being lost, and any potential for identifying parent abuse is missed. A second implication is that, even if an intervention strategy is successful in addressing the parent abuse, other problems and issues may then need addressing to ensure that the parent abuse ends permanently. This might require input from different specialist frontline services, such as mental health services, legal services or school liaison services. Furthermore, the dynamic quality of family life and the continual changes that this entails, not least in terms of age-related changes, means that the appropriateness of any solution will shift. For example, behavioural strategies for work with 13-year-olds may not be appropriate for work with 16-year-olds. The same applies to other potential remedies (eg, removal of a child or parent from the family home). Thus, effective intervention work with parent abuse is likely to be as long term as was the development of the 'parent abuse dynamic' itself, and the need for different solutions in a changing family context needs to be kept in mind when developing intervention strategies.

One final message concerns the strategy of encouraging 'empowerment' in parents, which forms a large part of many intervention programmes (eg, Who's in Charge? and Break4Change). As Chapter Four highlighted, power relations between children and parents need to be considered within a wider context of how structural relations of power operate outside the family home. This requires an understanding of the status, authority and responsibility of parents and their children, relative to each other and in relation to the state. Therefore, intervention programmes must not only tackle the 'everyday' relations of power operating at an interactional level, but also address wider structural transformations of power. This requires a more fundamental consideration of how we construct, organise and institutionalise 'parenthood', 'childhood' and 'adolescence', both within policy and legal discourse and in terms of wider cultural values and ideals.

Future directions for research

The first step in developing our understanding of parent abuse must be to provide a space for parents and their families to articulate their experiences and there is a particular urgency to extend this space to cultures beyond 'normative' Euro-American contexts. While it is a cliché to conclude any academic or research discussion with an appeal for *more research*, I hope that this book has highlighted that this appeal has particular relevance in this particular instance. Yet thinking about how we might develop our research practice in this area requires special creativity. Researching parent abuse, like researching family violence and abuse more generally, requires specific techniques that will enable parents to open up about their experiences. Therefore, perhaps our first research challenge is to find ways to overcome those barriers outlined at the beginning of this book: multiple stigmas, social isolation and parental denial of and disbelief in what is happening. As one example of good research practice, Eckstein (2004) used an 'opening vignette' to introduce the topic to her participants to ensure that their disclosures about the abuse did not appear unpalatable. She also explained to participants that many other parents go through similar experiences and that it is no indication of being a 'bad parent'. She structured her interview schedule to encourage disclosure of the 'whole experience', and used probing questions to encourage participant description of more than just the negative aspects of parent abuse. Other studies have also provided detailed outlines of how they approached this topic area, and I would direct researchers to publications by Doran (2007) and Howard and Rottem (2008) for particularly comprehensive discussions of their methodological and ethical practices.

A related methodological challenge for researchers is the need for participant samples that are longitudinal, large-scale and representative of the wider community. Clearly this is difficult, given the nature of both the target population and the topic area. But hopefully, as recognition of adolescent-to-parent abuse grows, identifying those who are living with it will become easier. This includes children and young people, whose voices about such experiences remain unarticulated. We also need to continue the work already begun on producing quantitative and qualitative data. Robust quantitative data on prevalence is vital to enable policy makers to allocate resources within populations and sub-populations, particularly prevalences within different ethnic groups and social classes where current data are inconclusive.

However, prevalence data only make sense when accompanied by an exploration of *process*. For this, we need more rich and detailed information about:

- the development, maintenance and cessation of parent abuse;
- the ways in which 'risk factors' and 'protective factors' operate for children, parents and families;
- how the commission of, experience of and responses to parent abuse is mediated by intersecting systems of power (such as gender and age);
- how parent abuse is shaped by culturally mediated meanings regarding the nature and acceptability of abuse;
- how power should be exercised within parent–child relationships.

The complexity of parent abuse calls for an analysis that is complex in its approach, and this will require the drawing together of the mutually reinforcing factors at the intrapersonal, interpersonal, family, structural and cultural levels. And just as we need multi-agency teams to tackle parent abuse by pooling their resources and perspectives, so we need multi-research teams that can pool their resources and perspectives derived from relevant individual academic disciplines such as psychology, sociology, anthropology, family studies, cultural studies, politics, history and economics.

Beyond future directions in method and research approach, there are also further research questions that need pursuing. The scope of this book has been necessarily limited to enable a focus on key issues and to provide a comprehensive review of what has been articulated so far. However, I am aware that this may have resulted in some issues being sidelined, in the main because particular aspects remain unarticulated in the research, policy and practice literature that has been reviewed. For example, I am aware that I have focused on, and perhaps over-assumed, particular family formations and in doing so have risked marginalising the experiences of other family forms that make up a family unit. Across all Euro-American cultures, there are many households where grandparents and grandchildren, aunts, uncles, cousins and friends all make up the family unit, and this book has not explored in detail how other family forms shape experiences of, and responses to, parent abuse. Indeed, their absence from the family violence literature more generally is a problem that needs addressing urgently. Furthermore, diversities in how parents are constituted – whether as step-parents, adoptive parents, foster parents, non-resident parents or professional caregivers – are likely to shape experiences of and responses to parent abuse. Again, this is something that requires further articulation in research, policy discussion and practice. For example, we know little of how the role of step-parent is implicated in the exercise of power within (and outside) parent–child relationships, nor how same-sex parenting shapes such processes. We also know little of how legal differences between adoptive parents, foster parents and biological parents shape experiences of and responses to parent abuse. Furthermore, there is increasing evidence of children and young people targeting professional carers within the residential care system (Petrie et al, 2006; Hayden, 2010) but we know little about how such abuses of power are played out in these settings, or of the similarities and departure points in relation to parent abuse. Finally, little has been said about parricide in this book, mainly because research that has explored it suggests that very different dynamics are at play compared with parent abuse (Heide, 1992; Walsh and Krienert, 2009). However, research has so far failed to explore the extent to which parent abuse and parricide are part of a continuum, nor has it explored possible links between child/young person-perpetrated parricide and adult-perpetrated parricide. We also know little about possible links between parent abuse and elder abuse. This makes the need to explore the future contexts of family abuse as important as examining its past.

For parents and families

This book has not been written primarily for parents and families, although of course I hope that they find the content both useful and reassuring. However, a point to end on is the tension between the need for state intervention, via policy-making processes, and the recognition that some families can be made even more vulnerable by these same interventions. The problem of state intervention enabling 'systemic violence' against families already experiencing interpersonal violence has already been identified by researchers, practitioners and campaigners working within the field of intimate partner violence (eg, Martin, 2005). What is missing, as highlighted in Chapter One, is advocacy groups and organisations that can provide the necessary buttress between state and family in cases of adolescent-to-parent abuse. Such groups may offer both a collective organisation to push for policy and institutional reform as well as advocacy for particular families. It may be that such developments may need to start with parents and families themselves, working together with researchers and practitioners.

EIGHT

Resources

Resources for practitioners

- **Alternative Restoratives** (UK)
  www.alternativerestoratives.co.uk/about.htm
  A practitioner-run resource that aims to raise awareness about parent abuse and highlight restorative approaches to intervention. Also organises UK-based training and events for practitioners.

- **Non-Violent Resistance – for practitioners** (UK)
  http://partnershipprojectsuk.com/info-for-pros.html
  A practitioner-run resource providing information and training in non-violent resistance for practitioners who wish to work with families with adolescents who behaving aggressively.

- **Respect** (UK)
  www.respect.uk.net/pages/young-peoples-services.html
  A membership association for domestic violence prevention programmes and integrated support services. Young People's Services is sub-site that offers regular conferences and training for practitioners who are working with young people who use violence in close relationships (including against parents).

- **Sherwood Associates** (UK)
  www.sherwood-associates.co.uk/index.html
  Provides consultancy, training and research in domestic violence, sexual abuse and family violence and offers day-long training courses for practitioners in 'Child to Parent Violence'.

- **Step-up: a counselling programme for teens who are violent at home** (US)
  http://www.kingcounty.gov/courts/step-up.aspx
  Includes curriculum materials and resources for practitioners, and offers training for setting-up own programmes.

- **Youth Justice Board Toolkit: Information Sheet** (UK)
  www.justice.gov.uk/downloads/youth-justice/yjb-toolkits/
  parenting/specialist-issues-child-to-parent-violence.pdf
  An information sheet produced by the Ministry of Justice (England
  and Wales), which outlines definitions, prevalence rates and a
  summary of UK-based and international intervention programmes.

Resources for researchers

- **Eddie Gallagher's Webpages** (Australia)
  www.eddiegallagher.id.au/
  A comprehensive resource offering information for practitioners on
  training and workshops, advice and strategies for parents (including
  details of support services) and research papers and findings for
  researchers.

- **Holes in the Wall** (UK)
  http://holesinthewall.co.uk/
  A blog run by a professional social worker, which provides updates on
  research, practice and policy-making developments – also available
  on Twitter (@HelenBonnick).

- **Parent Abuse Research Network** (UK)
  www.york.ac.uk/law/research/parn/index.htm
  Set up by academics based in the UK, this network is hosted by the
  York Law School and aims to share research developments between
  researchers and practitioners.

Over the years, a number of literature reviews of key research and
findings have been produced. These include reviews by Bobic (2004),
Cottrell and Monk (2004), Robinson et al (2004), Stewart et al (2004),
Kennair and Mellor (2007), Holt (2012a) and Hong et al (2012).

Resources for parents

- **Family Lives (formerly Parentline Plus)** (UK)
  http://familylives.org.uk
  Tel: 0800 800 2222
  Although not specialising in parent abuse, this national charity
  offers support and advice for families needing help for all kinds of
  family issues. Includes parent workshops for managing conflict and
  developing communication skills.

- **Focus Adolescent Services** (US)
  www.focusas.com/Violence.html
  A comprehensive site for parents and families of teenagers who are struggling with all sorts of issues. Offers a sub-site on teen violence, providing information on 'warning signs', advice and strategies, as well as directory for further support and advocacy, including a 'crisis hotline'.

- **Gingerbread 'Family Safe' Project** (UK)
  Tel: 0808 802 0925
  Offers telephone support sessions for lone parents whose children are displaying challenging, violent or aggressive behaviour.

- **Non-Violent Resistance – for parents** (UK)
  http://partnershipprojectsuk.com/info-for-parents.html
  A practitioner-run website that includes a sub-site for parents of adolescents who are behaving aggressively. Includes information and strategies using the non-violent resistance approach.

- **Parent Abuse and Reconciliation Service (PAARS)** (UK)
  www.paars.co.uk/
  Aims to raise public and professional awareness and empower parents and carers and offers both a local support service in the North London area and a national online support service for families living with abusive adolescents.

- **Parentlink** (Australia)
  www.parentlink.act.gov.au/parenting_guides/teens/abuse_to_parents
  A national support website for families, which offers a special webpage for parents experiencing abuse from their children, featuring information, advice and strategies, and further support numbers and weblinks.

- **Queensland Centre for Domestic and Family Violence Research** (Australia)
  www.noviolence.com.au/factsheets.html
  A national organisation that offers a factsheet for parents on adolescent-to-parent abuse, featuring definitions, forms of abuse, experiences, strategies and advice, and further support numbers and weblinks.

- **Walking on Eggshells Resources** (Australia)
  www.flinders.edu.au/ehl/law/law-resources/
  An information booklet and fold-up card offering support and
  advice to parents whose children are behaving violently and abusively.

- **Wish for a Brighter Future** (UK)
  www.wishforabrighterfuture.org.uk
  Provides one-to-one support sessions for families experiencing
  parent-to-adolescent abuse. Sessions are available for both parents
  and young people in the Bristol area. Also runs 13-week 'parent
  abuse' parenting support groups in collaboration with the Single
  Person Action Network (SPAN) and Bristol City Council (see www.
  bristol.gov.uk/node/11603).

- **YUVA** (UK)
  http://dvip.org/yuva-programme.htm
  Tel: 020 7928 2322
  London-based domestic violence support organisation, which has
  recently started offering one-to-one support to young people who
  are violent, and for parents whose children are abusive towards them.
  Also offers an information leaflet.

Adolescent-to-parent abuse: initial assessment

Family names:

Parent(s):..

Key child(ren):...Age: ....

Key child(ren): ....Age: ....

Other family members.. Age: ....

Other family members.. Age: ....

Other family members..Age: ....

Other family members.. Age: ....

1) Intrapersonal precipitating factors (eg, substance use, mental health issues, learning difficulties)

Key child(ren)..

Parent(s)...

Other family members..

2) Interpersonal family processes and dynamics

Parenting practices...

....

Communication styles:..

....

3) Family history

Previous experiences of family abuse...

....

....

Current family stressors..

....

....

4) Structural locations of family members (eg, gender, ethnicity, access to social/ economic resources)

....

....

....

5) Wider cultural issues requiring specialist input (eg, diversities in language, cultural or religious norms)

....

....

6) Trajectory of abuse

Date of emergence...

Forms of abuse observed/reported...

....

....

7) Impact of abuse

Impact on parent(s) ....

Impact on other family members...

....

8) Previous experiences of intervention

Date ....

Description of intervention..

....

9) Other observations ....

....

....

....

....

....

....

....

....

References

Adams, A.E., Sullivan, C.M., Bybee, D. and Greeson, M.R. (2008) 'Development of the scale of economic abuse', *Violence Against Women*, 14 (5), 563-88.

ADSS (Association of Directors of Social Services) (2005) *Safeguarding adults: A National Framework of Standards for good practice and outcomes in adult protection work* [online], London: ADSS, www.adass.org.uk/old/publications/guidance/safeguarding.pdf

Agnew, R. and Huguley, S. (1989) 'Adolescent violence towards parents', *Journal of Marriage and the Family*, 51, 699-711.

Ainsworth, M.D.S. and Bell, S.M. (1970) 'Attachment, exploration, and separation: illustrated by the behavior of one-year-olds in a strange situation', *Child Development*, 41, 49-67.

Ainsworth, M.D.S., Blehar, M.C., Waters, E. and Wall, S. (1978) *Patterns of attachment: A psychological study of the strange situation*, Hillsdale, NJ: Lawrence Erlbaum Associates.

Alexander, J.F. and Robbins, M.S. (2010) 'Functional family therapy: a phase-based and multi-component approach to change', in R.C. Murrihy, A.D. Kidman and T.H. Ollendick (eds) *Clinical handbook of assessing and treating conduct problems in youth* (pp 245-71), London: Springer.

Ambert, A. (1994) 'An international perspective on parenting: social change and social constructs', *Journal of Marriage and the Family*, 56, 529-43.

Anglicare Victoria (2001) *Breaking the cycle – adolescent violence: women's stories of courage and hope*, Victoria, Australia: Anglicare Victoria Meridian Program.

APA (American Psychiatric Association) (1987) *Diagnostic and statistical manual of mental disorders*, 3rd edition, revised (DSM-III-R), Washington, DC: APA.

APA (1994) *Diagnostic and statistical manual of mental disorders*, 4th edition (DSM-IV), Washington, DC: APA.

Archer, J. (2006) 'Cross-cultural differences in physical aggression between partners: a social-role analysis', *Personality and Social Psychology Review*, 10 (2), 133-53.

Avraham-Krehwinkel, C. and Aldridge, D. (2010) *A non-violent resistance approach with children in distress: A guide for parents and professionals*, London: Jessica Kingsley Publishers.

Baker, H. (2009) '"Potentially violent men?": teenage boys, access to refuges and constructions of men, masculinity and violence', *Journal of Social Welfare and Family Law*, 31 (4), 435–50.

Bancroft, L. and Silverman, J. (2002) *The batterer as a parent: Addressing the impact of domestic violence on family dynamics*, Thousand Oaks, CA: Sage Publications.

Bandura, A. (1965) 'Influence of models' reinforcement contingencies on the acquisition of imitative response', *Journal of Personality and Social Psychology*, 1, 589–95.

Bandura, A., Ross, D. and Ross, S. (1961) 'Transmission of aggression through imitation of aggressive models'. *Journal of Abnormal and Social Psychology*, 63, 375–82.

Banyard, V.L. (1997) 'The impact of childhood sexual abuse and family functioning on four dimensions of women's later parenting', *Child Abuse and Neglect*, 21 (11), 1095–107.

Barter, C., McCarry, M., Berridge, D. and Evans, E. (2009) *Partner exploitation and violence in teenage intimate relationships*, London: NSPCC, www.nspcc.org.uk/Inform/research/findings/partner_exploitation_ and_violence_report_wdf70129.pdf

Barton, C.K.B. (2003) *Restorative justice: The empowerment model*, Sydney, Australia: Hawkins Press.

Baumrind, D. (1966) 'Effects of authoritative parental control on child behavior', *Child Development*, 37 (4), 887–907.

Baumrind, D. (1967) 'Child-care practices anteceding three patterns of preschool behavior', *Genetic Psychology Monographs*, 75, 43–88.

Beck, U. (1992) *Risk society: Towards a new modernity*, London: Sage Publications.

Bell, J. and Stanley, N. (2006) 'Learning about domestic violence: young people's responses to a healthy relationships programme', *Sex Education*, 6 (3), 237–50.

Biehal, N. (2012) 'Parent abuse by young people on the edge of care: a child welfare perspective', *Social Policy and Society*, 11 (2), 251–63.

Block, M.R. and Sinnott, J.D. (1979) *Battered elder syndrome: An exploratory study*, College Park, MD: Center on Aging, University of Maryland.

Bobic, N. (2004) *Adolescent violence towards parents* [topic paper], Sydney, NSW: Australian Domestic and Family Violence Clearinghouse, University of New South Wales, www.adfvc.unsw.edu.au/pdf%20 files/adolescent_violence.pdf

Boonzaier, F. (2008) '"If the man says you must sit, then you must sit": the relational construction of woman abuse: gender, subjectivity and violence', *Feminism and Psychology*, 18 (2), 183–206.

Borum, R., Bartel, P. and Forth, A. (2003) *Manual for the structured assessment of violence risk in youth: Version 1.1*, Sarasota, FL: University of South Florida.

Bowlby, J. (1969) *Attachment and loss: Vol. 1: Loss*, New York, NY: Basic Books.

Boxer, P., Gullan, R.L. and Mahoney, A. (2009) 'Adolescents' physical aggression towards parents in a clinically referred sample', *Journal of Clinical Child and Adolescent Psychology*, 38, 106-16.

Braithwaite J. and Braithwaite, V. (2001) 'Revising the theory of reintegrative shaming', in E. Ahmed, N. Harris, J. Braithwaite and V. Braithwaite (eds) *Shame management through reintegration* (pp 33-57), New York, NY: Cambridge University Press.

Brezina, T. (1999) 'Teenage violence toward parents as an adaptation to family strain', *Youth and Society*, 30(4), 416-44.

Brezina, T. (2000) 'Corporal punishment as a cause of teenage violence towards parents: data from a national sample of male adolescents', in G. Litton Fox and M.L. Benson (eds) *Families, crime and criminal justice* (pp 25-44), New York, NY: Elsevier Science.

Bromley, C., Curtice, J. and Seyd, B. (2004) *Is Britain facing a crisis of democracy?*, London: Centre for Research into Elections and Social Trends, Constitution Unit.

Browne, K.D. and Hamilton, C.E. (1998) 'Physical violence between young adults and their parents: associations with a history of child maltreatment', *Journal of Family Violence*, 13, 59-79.

Buel, S.M. (2002) 'Why juvenile courts should address family violence: promising practices to improve intervention outcomes', *Juvenile and Family Court Journal*, 53 (2), 1-16.

Burman, E. (2008) *Deconstructing developmental psychology* (2nd edition), London: Routledge.

Burman, M. and Cartmel, F. (2005) *Young people's attitudes towards gendered violence*, Edinburgh: NHS Scotland, www.healthscotland.com/uploads/documents/GenderedResearch.pdf

Burton, M. (2008) *Legal responses to domestic violence*, Abingdon: Routledge.

Campbell, R. (1998) 'The community response to rape: victims' experiences with the legal, medical, and mental health systems', *American Journal of Community Psychology*, 26 (3), 355-79.

Caplan, P.J. and Hall-McCorquodale, I. (1985a) 'Mother-blaming in major clinical journals', *American Journal of Orthopsychiatry*, 55, 345-53.

Caplan, P.J. and Hall-McCorquodale, I. (1985b) 'The scapegoating of mothers: a call for change', *American Journal of Orthopsychiatry*, 55, 610-13.

Carlson, B.E. (1990) 'Adolescent observers of marital violence', *Journal of Family Violence*, 5 (4), 285-99.

Carlson, B.E. (2000) 'Children exposed to intimate partner violence: research findings and implications for intervention', *Trauma, Violence, and Abuse*, 1 (4), 321-40.

Castañeda, A., Garrido-Fernández, M. and Lanzarote, M. (2012) 'Menores con conducta de maltrato hacia los progenitores: un estudio de personalidad y estilos de socialización' [Juvenile offenders who assault their parents: a study of personality traits and parenting styles], *Revista de Psicologia Social*, 27 (2), 157-67.

Charles, A.V. (1986) 'Physically abused parents', *Journal of Family Violence*, 4, 343-55.

Christie, N. (1986) 'The ideal victim', in E. Fattah (ed) *From crime policy to victim policy*, Basingstoke: Macmillan.

Cismaru, M. and Lavack, A.M. (2011) 'Campaigns targeting perpetrators of intimate partner violence', *Trauma Violence Abuse*, 12 (4), 183-97.

Cleaver, H. and Freeman, P. (1995) *Parental perspectives in cases of suspected child abuse*, London: HMSO.

Cochran, D., Brown, M.E., Adams, S. and Doherty, D. (1994) *Young adolescent batterers*, Boston, MA: Trial Court, Office of the Commissioner of Probation.

Coid, J., Petruckevitch, A., Feder, G., Chung, W., Richardson, J. and Moorey, S. (2001) 'Relation between childhood sexual and physical abuse and risk of revictimisation in women: a cross-sectional survey', *The Lancet*, 358, 450-4.

Coleman, J. (2010) *The nature of adolescence* (4th edition), Abingdon: Routledge.

Cornell, C. and Gelles, R. (1982) 'Adolescent to parent violence', *The Urban and Social Change Review*, 15 (1), 8-14.

Cottrell, B. (2001) *Parent abuse: The abuse of parents by their teenage children*, Ottawa, Canada: Family Violence Prevention Unit, Health Canada.

Cottrell, B. (2005) *When teens abuse their parents*, Halifax, Nova Scotia: Fernwood Publishing.

Cottrell, B. and Monk, P. (2004) 'Adolescent to parent abuse', *Journal of Family Issues*, 25, 1072-95.

Crawford, A. (1997) *The local governance of crime: Appeals to community and partnership*, Oxford: Clarendon Press.

Daly, K. and Immarigeon, R. (1998) 'The past, present, and future of restorative justice: some critical reflections', *The Contemporary Justice Review*, 1 (1), 21-45.

Daly, K. and Nancarrow, H. (2010) 'Restorative justice and youth violence towards parents', in J. Ptacek (ed) *Restorative justice and violence against women* (pp 150-76), Oxford: Oxford University Press.

DCSF (Department for Children, Schools and Families) (2010) *Violence Against Women and Girls (VAWG) Advisory Group final report and recommendations*, London: DCSF.

DeLange, N. and Olivier, M.A.J. (2004) 'Mothers' experiences of aggression in their Tourette's syndrome children', *International Journal for the Advancement of Counselling*, 26 (1), 65-77.

Deptula, D.P. and Cohen, R. (2004) 'Aggressive, rejected and delinquent children and adolescents: a comparison of their friendships', *Aggression and Violent Behavior*, 9, 75-104.

DfE (Department for Education) (2011) *A child-centred system: The government's response to the Munro review of child protection*, London: HMSO.

DH (Department of Health) (2000) *No secrets: The protection of vulnerable adults guidance on the development and implementation of multi-agency policies and procedures*, London: HMSO.

DH (2001) *National Service Framework for Older People*, London: HMSO.

DH (2005) *Action on elder abuse: Report on the project to establish a monitoring and reporting process for adult protection referrals made in accordance with 'No secrets'*, London: DH.

DH (2010) *Responding to violence against women and children – the role of the NHS: The report of the Taskforce on the Health Aspects of Violence Against Women and Children*, London: DH, www.dh.gov.uk/prod_consum_dh/groups/dh_digitalassets/@dh/@en/@ps/documents/digitalasset/dh_113824.pdf

Dobash, R.E. and Dobash, R. (1979) *Violence against wives: A case against the patriarchy*, New York, NY: Free Press.

Donovan, R. and Vlais, R. (2005) *VicHealth review of communication components of social marketing/public education campaigns focused on violence against women*, Melbourne, Australia: Victorian Health Promotion Foundation.

Donzelot, J. (1979) *The policing of families*, London: Hutchinson.

Doran, J.E. (2007) 'Restorative justice and family violence: youth-to-parent abuse', Mount Saint Vincent University, Halifax, Canada, unpublished MA.

Downey, L. (1997) 'Adolescent violence: a systemic and feminist perspective', *Australian and New Zealand Journal of Family Therapy*, 18 (2), 70-9.

Du Bois, R.H. (1998) 'Battered parents: psychiatric syndrome or social phenomenon?', in A.Z. Schwarzberg (ed) *The adolescent in turmoil* (pp 124-33), Westport, CT: Paeger Trade.

Eastman, M. (1984) *Old age abuse*, London: Age Concern England.

Eckstein, N.J. (2002) 'Adolescent-to-parent abuse: a communicative analysis of conflict processes present in the verbal, physical, or emotional abuse of parents', *ETD collection for University of Nebraska – Lincoln*, paper AAI3045512, http://digitalcommons.unl.edu/dissertations/AAI3045512

Eckstein, N.J. (2004) 'Emergent issues in families experiencing adolescent-to-parent abuse', *Western Journal of Communication*, 68 (4), 365-88.

Edenborough, M.D., Jackson, D., Mannix, J. and Wilkes, L. (2008) 'Living in the red zone: the experience of child-to-mother violence', *Child and Family Social Work*, 13, 464-73.

Edenborough, M.D., Wilkes, L.M., Jackson, D. and Mannix, J. (2011) 'Development and validation of the Child-to-Mother Violence Scale', *Nurse Researcher*, 18 (2), 63-76.

Elliott, G.C., Cunningham, S.M., Colangelo, M. and Gelles, R.J. (2011) 'Perceived mattering to the family and physical violence within the family by adolescents', *Journal of Family Issues*, 32 (8), 1007-29.

Ellis, J. (2004) *Preventing violence against women and girls: A study of educational programmes for children and young people*, London: WOMANKIND Worldwide.

Estevez, E. and Gongora, J.N. (2009) 'Adolescent aggression towards parents: factors associated and intervention proposals', in C. Quin and S. Tawse (eds) *Handbook of aggressive behavior research* (pp 143-64), Hauppauge, NY: Nova Science Publishers.

Evans, D. and Warren-Sohlberg, L. (1988) 'A pattern analysis of adolescent abusive behaviour towards parents', *Journal of Adolescent Research*, 3 (2), 201-16.

EVAWC (End Violence Against Women Coalition) (2011) *A different world is possible: Promising practices to prevent violence against women and girls* [online], London: EVAWC, www.endviolenceagainstwomen.org.uk/data/files/promising_practices_report.pdf

Fagot, B.A. and Kavanagh, K. (1990) 'The prediction of antisocial behaviour from avoidant attachment classification', *Child Development*, 61, 864-73.

Farrington, D.P., Loeber, R. and Ttofi, M.M. (2012) 'Risk and protective factors for offending', in B.C. Welsh and D.P. Farrington (eds) *The Oxford handbook of crime prevention* (pp 46-69), Oxford: Oxford University Press.

Felson, R.B., Messner, S.F., Hoskin, A.W. and Deane, G. (2002) 'Reasons for reporting and not reporting domestic violence to the police', *Criminology*, 40 (3), 617-48.

Ferguson, H. (1996) 'The protection of children in time: child protection and the lives and deaths of children in child abuse cases in socio-historical perspective', *Child and Family Social Work*, 1 (3), 205-17.

Finkelhor, D. (1983) 'Common features of family abuse', in D. Finkelhor, R.J. Gelles, G.T. Hotaling and M.A. Straus (eds) *The dark side of families: Current family violence research* (pp 17-28), London: Sage Publications.

Finkelhor, D., Turner, H. and Ormrod, R. (2006) 'Kid's stuff: the nature and impact of peer and sibling violence on younger and older children', *Child Abuse and Neglect*, 30 (12), 1401-21.

Finzi, R., Ram, A., Har-Even, D., Shnit, D. and Weizman, A. (2001) 'Attachment styles and aggression in physically abused and neglected children', *Journal of Youth and Adolescence*, 30 (6), 769-86.

Follingstad, D.R., Rutledge, L.L., Berg, B.J., Hause, E.S. and Polek, D.S. (1990) 'The role of emotional abuse in physically abusive relationships', *Journal of Family Violence*, 5, 107-20.

Foucault, M. (1975) *Discipline and punish: The birth of the prison*, London: Penguin.

Foucault, M. (1976) *The history of sexuality. Volume 1: An introduction*, London: Penguin.

Foucault, M. (1980) 'Truth and power', in C. Gordon (ed) *Michel Foucault: Power/knowledge: Selected interviews and other writings 1972–1977* (pp 109-33), Brighton: Harvester Press.

Frizzell, A.W. (1998) 'Biting the hand that feeds? The social construction of adolescent violence toward parents as a social problem', unpublished Master's thesis, University of New Brunswick, Canada.

Furedi, F. (2009) *Socialisation as behaviour management and the ascendancy of expert authority (The Kohnstam Lecture)*, Amsterdam, the Netherlands: Amsterdam University Press.

Gallagher, E. (2004a) 'Parents victimized by their children', *Australian and New Zealand Journal of Family Therapy*, 25, 1-12.

Gallagher, E. (2004b) 'Youths who victimize their parents', *Australian and New Zealand Journal of Family Therapy*, 25, 94-105.

Gallagher, E. (2011) *The who's in charge? Group* [online], http://web.aanet.com.au/eddiegallagher/violence%20to%20parents.html

Galvani, S. (2010) *Supporting families affected by substance use and domestic violence: Research report*, London: Adfam, www.adfam.org.uk/docs/dv_report.pdf

Gangoli, G. and Rew, M. (2011) 'Mothers-in-law against daughters-in-law: domestic violence and legal discourses around mother-in-law violence against daughters-in-law in India', *Women's Studies International Forum*, 34 (5), 420-9.

Gebo, E. (2007) 'A family affair? The Juvenile Court and family violence cases', *Journal of Family Violence*, 22 (7), 501-9.

Gelles, R.J. and Straus, M.A. (1979) 'Determinants of violence in the family: toward a theoretical integration', in W.R. Burr, F. Reuben Hill, I. Nye and I.L. Reiss (eds) *Contemporary theories about the family*, New York, NY: Free Press.

Ghanizadeh, A. and Jafari, P. (2010) 'Risk factors of abuse of parents by their ADHD children', *European Child and Adolescent Psychiatry*, 19 (1), 75-81.

Ghez, M. (2001) 'Getting the message out: using media to change social norms on abuse', in C. Renzetti, J. Edleson and R. Kennedy Bergen (eds) *Sourcebook on violence against women*, London: Sage Publications.

Giddens, A. (1991) *Modernity and self-identity: Self and society in the late modern age*, Cambridge: Polity Press.

Gillies, V. (2005) 'Meeting parents' needs? Discourses of "support" and "inclusion" in family policy', *Critical Social Policy*, 25 (1), 70-90.

Goldson, B. and Jamieson, J. (2002) 'Youth crime, the "parenting deficit" and state intervention: a contextual critique', *Youth Justice*, 2 (2), 92-9.

Goody, E.N. (1982) *Parenthood and social reproduction: Fostering and occupational roles in West Africa*, New York, NY: Cambridge University Press.

Griffin, C. (1993) *Representations of youth*, Cambridge: Polity Press.

Haber, M.G. and Toro, P.A. (2009) 'Parent–adolescent violence and later behavioral health problems among homeless and housed youth', *American Journal of Orthopsychiatry*, 79 (3), 305-18.

Hakim, J. (2011) 'The school of hard knocks (interview by Catherine Campbell)', *The Psychologist*, 24 (7), 512-15.

Harbin, H.T. and Madden, D.J. (1979) 'Battered parents: a new syndrome', *American Journal of Psychiatry*, 136, 1288-91.

Hardy, M.S. (2001) 'Physical aggression and sexual behavior among siblings: a retrospective study', *Journal of Family Violence*, 16 (3), 255-68.

Harris, L.J. (2006) 'An empirical study of parental responsibility laws: sending messages, but what kind and to whom?', *Utah Law Review*, 5-34.

Hartz, D. (1995) 'Comparative conflict resolution patterns among parent–teen dyads of four ethnic groups in Hawaii', *Child Abuse and Neglect*, 19 (6), 681-9.

Hassouneh-Phillips, D. and Curry, M.A. (2002) 'Abuse of women with disabilities: state of the science', *Rehabilitation Counselling Bulletin*, 45 (2), 96-104.

Haw, A. (2010) *Parenting over violence: Understanding and empowering mothers affected by adolescent violence in the home*, Perth, Australia: Patricia Giles Centre.

Hayden, C. (2010) 'Offending behaviour in care: is children's residential care a "criminogenic" environment?', *Child and Family Social Work*, 13 (4), 461-72.

Hayes, E. (2006) 'Is media coverage of parenting creating less emotionally healthy families?', in *Proceedings of Parent-Child 2006: Happy families?*, London: National Family and Parenting Institute.

Heide, K.M. (1992) *Why kids kill parents: Child abuse and adolescent homicide*, Columbus, OH: Ohio State University Press.

Hendrick, H. (1997), 'Constructions and reconstructions of British childhood: an interpretive survey 1800 to the present', in J. Allison and A. Prout (eds) *Constructing and reconstructing childhood* (2nd edition), London: Falmer Press.

Hester, M. and Eriksson, M. (2001) 'Violent men as good-enough fathers? A look at England and Sweden', *Violence against Women*, 7 (7), 779-98.

Hester, M., Westmarland, N., Gangoli, G., Wilkinson, M., O'Kelly, C., Kent, A. and Diamond, A. (2006) *Domestic violence perpetrators: Identifying needs to inform early intervention*, Bristol: University of Bristol in association with the Northern Rock Foundation and the Home Office.

Hester, M., Pearson, C., and Harwin, N., with Abrahams, H. (2007) *Making an impact: Children and domestic violence* (2nd edition), London: Jessica Kingsley Publishers.

Holden, G. and Ritchie, K. (1991) 'Linking extreme marital discord, child rearing and child behaviour problems: evidence from battered women', *Child Development*, 62 (2), 311-27.

Holt, A. (2008) 'Room for resistance? Parenting Orders, disciplinary power and the construction of the "bad parent"', in P. Squires (ed) *ASBO nation: The criminalisation of nuisance* (pp 103-22), Bristol: The Policy Press.

Holt, A. (2009) 'Parent abuse: some reflections on the adequacy of a youth justice response', *Internet Journal of Criminology*, 1-11, www.internetjournalofcriminology.com/Holt_Parent_Abuse_Nov_09.pdf

Holt, A. (2010a) 'Disciplining "problem parents" in the youth court: between regulation and resistance', *Social Policy and Society*, 9 (1), 89-99.

Holt, A. (2010b) 'Managing "spoiled identities": parents' experiences of compulsory parenting support programmes', *Children & Society*, 24 (5), 413-23.

Holt, A. (2011) '"The terrorist in my home": teenagers' violence towards parents – constructions of parent experiences in public online message boards', *Child and Family Social Work*, 16 (4), 454-63.

Holt, A. (2012a) 'Researching parent abuse: a critical review of the methods', *Social Policy and Society*, 11(2), 289-98.

Holt, A. (2012b) 'Adolescent-to-parent abuse and frontline service responses: does Munro matter?', in M. Blyth and E. Solomon (eds) *Effective safeguarding for children and young people: Responding to the Munro Review* (pp 91-106), Bristol: The Policy Press.

Holt, A. and Retford, S. (2012) 'Practitioner accounts of responding to parent abuse – a case study in ad hoc delivery, perverse outcomes and a policy silence', *Child and Family Social Work*, available on *Early View*, doi: 10.1111/j.1365-2206.2012.00860.x

Holt, M.G. (1993) 'Elder abuse in Britain: Meeting the challenge in the 1990s', *Journal of Elder Abuse and Neglect*, 5 (1), 33-40.

Home Office (1990) *Domestic violence*, Home Office Circular 1990/60, London: Home Office.

Home Office (2000) *Domestic violence*, Home Office Circular 19/2000, London: Home Office.

Home Office (2005) *Domestic violence: A national report*, London: Home Office.

Home Office (2006) *National Domestic Violence Delivery Plan: Progress Report 2005/06*, London: Home Office.

Home Office (2011a) *Call to end violence against women and girls: Action plan*, London: Home Office, www.homeoffice.gov.uk/publications/crime/call-end-violence-women-girls/vawg-action-plan?view=Binary

Home Office (2011b) *Cross-government definition of domestic violence: A consultation*, www.homeoffice.gov.uk/publications/about-us/consultations/definition-domestic-violence/dv-definition-consultation?view=Binary

Home Office (2012) *Homicides, firearm offences and intimate violence 2010/11: Supplementary volume 2 to crime in England and Wales 2010/11*, London: Home Office, www.homeoffice.gov.uk/publications/science-research-statistics/research-statistics/crime-research/hosb0212/hosb0212?view=Binary

Hong, J.S., Kral, M.J., Espelage, D.L. and Allen-Meares, P. (2012) 'The social ecology of adolescent-initiated parent abuse: a review of the literature', *Child Psychiatry and Human Development*, 43 (3), 431-54.

Honjo, S.W. (1988) 'Family violence in Japan—a compilation of data from the Department of Psychiatry, Nagoya University Hospital', *Psychiatry and Clinical Neurosciences*, 42 (1), 5-10.

hooks, b. (1984) *Feminist theory: From margin to centre*, Boston, MA: South End Press.

House of Commons Library (2012) *Youth unemployment statistics*, SN/5871, London: House of Commons, www.parliament.uk/briefing-papers/SN05871

Howard, J. and Rottem, N. (2008) *It all starts at home: Male adolescent violence to mothers*, St Kilda, Australia: Inner Couth Community Health Service Inc and Child Abuse Research Australia, Monash University.

Howard. J., Friend, D., Parker, T., and Streker, G. (2010) 'Use of SMS to support parents who experience violence from their adolescents', *Australian Journal of Primary Health*, 16 (2), 187–91.

Humphreys, C. and Mullender, A. (2004) *Children and domestic violence: A research overview of the impact on children*, Totnes: Research in Practice.

Hunter, C. and Piper, C. (2012) 'Parent abuse: can law be the answer?', *Social Policy and Society*, 11 (2), 217-27.

Hunter, C., Nixon, J. and Parr, S. (2010) 'Mother abuse: a matter of youth justice, child welfare or domestic violence?', *Journal of Law and Society*, 37 (2), 264-84.

Ibabe, I. and Jaureguizar, J. (2010) 'Child-to-parent violence: profile of abusive adolescents and their families', *Journal of Criminal Justice*, 38 (4), 616-24.

Inamura, H. (1980) *Kateinai boryoku: Nihongata oyakokankei no byori* [*Filial violence: Pathology in the parent–child relationship in Japan*], Tokyo, Japan: Shinyosha.

Itzin, C., Taket, A. and Barter-Godfrey, S. (2010) *Domestic and sexual violence and abuse: Tackling the health and mental health effects*, Abingdon: Routledge.

Jablonski, J. (2007) *Characteristics of parenting associated with adolescent to parent aggression*, Philadelphia, PA: Chestnut Hill College.

Jackson, D. (2003) 'Broadening constructions of family violence: mothers' perspectives of aggression from their children', *Child and Family Social Work*, 8 (4), 321-9.

Jackson, D. and Mannix, J. (2004) 'Giving voice to the burden of blame: a feminist study of mothers' experiences of mother blaming', *International Journal of Nursing Practice*, 10, 150-8.

James, A., Jenks, C. and Prout, A. (1998) *Theorising childhood*, Oxford: Polity Press.

James, A.L. and James, A. (2001) 'Tightening the net: children, community and control', *British Journal of Sociology*, 52 (2), 211-28.

Jenks, C. (ed) (1982) *The sociology of childhood: Essential readings*, London: Batsford Academic and Educational.

Kalmus, D. (1984) 'The intergenerational transmission of violence in the family', *Journal of Marriage and the Family*, 46, 11-19.

Kazdin, A.E. (1998) *Parent Abuse Inventory*, New Haven, CT: Yale Child Conduct Clinic.

Keller, S.N., Wilkinson, T. and Otjen, A.J. (2010) 'Unintended effects of a domestic violence campaign', *Journal of Advertising*, 39 (4), 53-68.

Kempe, C.H., Silverman, H., Steele, B., Droegemueller, W. and Silver, H. (1962) 'The battered child syndrome', *Journal of the American Medical Association*, 181, 17-24.

Kennair, N. and Mellor, D. (2007) 'Parent abuse: a review', *Child Psychiatry and Human* Development, 38, 203-19.

Kennedy, T.D., Edmonds, W.A., Dann, K.T.J. and Burnett, K.F. (2010) 'The clinical and adaptive features of young offenders with histories of child–parent violence', *Journal of Family Violence*, 25(5), 509-20.

Kethineni, S. (2004) 'Youth-on-parent violence in a central Illinois county', *Youth Violence and Juvenile Justice*, 2 (4), 374-94.

Kettrey, H. and Emery, B. (2006) 'The discourse of sibling violence', *Journal of Family Violence*, 21, 407-16.

Kitzinger, J. (2010) 'Transformations of public and private knowledge: audience reception, feminism and the experience of childhood sexual abuse', in J. Haaken and P. Reavey (eds) *Memory matters: Contexts for understanding sexual abuse recollections* (pp 63-104), London: Routledge.

Kitzmann, K.M., Gaylord, N.K., Holt, A.R. and Kenny, E.D. (2003) 'Child witnesses to domestic violence: a meta-analytic review', *Journal of Consulting and Clinical Psychology*, 71 (2), 339-52.

Kotchick, B.A. and Forehand, R. (2002) 'Putting parenting in perspective: a discussion of the contextual factors that shape parenting practices', *Journal of Child and Family Studies*, 11 (3), 255-69.

Kozu, J. (1999) 'Domestic violence in Japan', *American Psychologist*, 54 (1), 50-4.

Kratcoski, P.C. (1985) 'Youth violence directed toward significant others', *Journal of Adolescence*, 8, 145-57.

Krienert, J.L. and Walsh, J.A. (2011) 'My brother's keeper: a contemporary examination of reported sibling violence using national level data, 2000-2005', *Journal of Family Violence*, 26 (5), 331-42.

Kumagai, F. (1981) 'Filial violence: a peculiar parent–child relationship in the Japanese family today', *Journal of Comparative Family Studies*, 3, 337-49.

Langhinrichsen-Rohling, J. and Neidig, P. (1995) 'Violent backgrounds of economically disadvantaged youth: risk factors for perpetrating violence?', *Journal of Family Violence*, 10 (4), 379-97.

LaPierre, S. (2008) 'Mothering in the context of domestic violence: the pervasiveness of a deficit model of mothering', *Child and Family Social Work*, 13, 454-63.

Laporte, L., Jiang, D., Pepler, D.J. and Chamberland, C. (2009) 'The relationship between adolescents' experience of family violence and dating violence', *Youth and Society*, 43 (1), 3-27.

Laurent, A. and Derry, A. (1999) 'Violence of French adolescents toward their parents: characteristics and contexts', *Journal of Adolescent Health*, 25 (1), 21-6.

Lee, M.Y., Uken, A. and Sebold, J. (2009) 'Accountability for change: solution-focused treatment of domestic violence offenders', in P.Lehmann and C.A. Simmons (eds) *Strengths-based batterer intervention: A new paradigm in ending family violence* (pp 55-85), New York, NY: Springer.

Lesko, N. (1996) 'Past, present and future conceptions of adolescence', *Educational Theory*, 46 (4), 453-72.

Levendosky, A.A., Lynch, S.M. and Graham-Bermann, S.A. (2000) 'Mothers' perceptions of the impact of woman abuse on their parenting', *Violence Against Women*, 6 (3), 247-71.

Lindfield, S. (2001) *Responses to questionnaire: Parenting work in the youth justice context*, Brighton: Trust for the Study of Adolescence.

Lister, R. (2008) 'Investing in children and childhood: a new welfare policy paradigm and its implications', in L. Arnlaug and C. Saraceno (eds) *Childhood: Changing contexts* (pp 383-408) *(Comparative Social Research, Volume 25)*, Bingley: Emerald Group Publishing.

Livingston, L.R. (1986) 'Children's violence to single mothers', *Journal of Sociology and Social Welfare*, 13, 920-33.

Livingstone, N., Macdonald, G. and Carr, N. (2010) 'Restorative justice conferencing for reducing recidivism in young offenders' (Protocol), *Cochrane Database of Systematic Reviews*, issue 12, article no.: CD008898, doi: 10.1002/14651858.CD008898

London SCB (Safeguarding Children Board) (2008) *Safeguarding children abused through domestic violence* [online], London: London SCB, www.londonscb.gov.uk/domestic_violence/

London SCB (2009) *Safeguarding children affected by gang activity and/or serious youth violence for child practitioners* [online], London: London SCB, www.londonscb.gov.uk

London SCB (2010) *London child protection procedures* [online], London: London SCB, www.londonscb.gov.uk/procedures

McAra, L. (2004) *Truancy, school exclusion and substance misuse*, Edinburgh: Centre for Law and Society, www.law.ed.ac.uk/cls/esytc/findings/digest4.pdf

McAra, L. and McVie, S. (2007) *Criminal justice transition*, Edinburgh: Centre for Law and Society, www.law.ed.ac.uk/file_download/publications/3_676_criminaljusticetransitions.pdf

McCloskey, L.A. and Lichter, E.L. (2003) 'The contribution of marital violence to adolescent aggression across different relationships', *Journal of Interpersonal Violence*, 18 (4), 390-412.

McMahon, A. (2004) 'Parental restitution: soft target for rough justice', in R. Hil and G. Tait (eds) *Hard lessons: Reflections on governance in late modernity* (pp 115-30), Aldershot: Ashgate.

Madriz, E. (1997) 'Images of criminals and victims: a study on women's fear and social control', *Gender and Society*, 11, 342-56.

Mann, K. and Roseneil, S. (1994) 'Some mothers do 'ave 'em: backlash and the gender politics of the underclass debate', *Journal of Gender Studies*, 3 (3), 317-31.

Martin, P.Y. (2005) *Rape work: Victims, gender and emotions in organization and community context*, London Routledge.

Micucci, J.A. (1995) 'Adolescents who assault their parents: a family systems approach to treatment', *Psychotherapy: Theory, Research, Practice, and Training*, 32 (1), 154-61.

Miller, T. (2005) *Making sense of motherhood: A narrative approach*, Cambridge: Cambridge University Press.

Ministry of Justice (2010) *Breaking the cycle: Effective punishment, rehabilitation and sentencing of offenders*, London: HMSO.

Ministry of Justice (2011) *Breaking the cycle: Government response*, London: HMSO.

Mirrlees-Black, C., Mayhew, P. and Percy, A. (1996) *The 1996 British Crime Survey: England and Wales*, London: HMSO.

Misch, P., Benjamin, L. and Barnes, D. (2011) 'Teenage intra-familial aggression against parent(s) – a mental health perspective', paper presented at the 2011 Respect National Conference: 'You Just Don't Get it! Young People's Violence in Close Relationships', The Wellcome Collection Conference Centre, London, 18 February.

Mitchell, E.B. (2006) 'The violent adolescent: a study of violence transmission across generations', doctoral dissertation, retrieved from ProQuest Dissertations and Theses, accession order no AAT 3236043.

Monk, P. and Cottrell, B. (2006) 'Responding to adolescent-to-parent abuse: a qualitative analysis of change factors', *Canadian Social Work*, 8 (1), 1-12.

Monks, C.P., Smith, P.K., Naylor, P., Barter, C., Ireland, J.L. and Coyne, I. (2009) 'Bullying in different contexts: commonalities, differences and the role of theory', *Aggression and Violent Behavior*, 14, 146-56.

Morris, A. (2002) 'Children and family violence: restorative messages from New Zealand', in H. Strang and J. Braithwaite (eds) *Restorative justice and family violence* (pp 89-107), New York, NY: Cambridge University Press.

Muehlenhard, C.L., Powch, I.G., Phelps, J.L. and Giusti, L.M. (1992) 'Definitions of rape: scientific and political implications', *Journal of Social Issues*, 48 (1), 23-44.

Munday, A. (2009) 'Break4Change: does a holistic intervention effect change in the level of abuse perpetrated by young people towards their parents/carers?', unpublished BA (Hons) Professional Studies in Learning and Development dissertation, University of Sussex.

Munro, E (2011) *The Munro Review of child protection: Final report – a child-centred system*, London: HMSO.

Naylor, P.B., Petch, L. and Williams, J.V. (2011) 'Sibling abuse and bullying in childhood and adolescence: knowns and unknowns', in C. Barter and D. Berridge (eds) *Children behaving badly? Peer violence between children and young people* (pp 47-58), Chichester: Wiley.

Nixon, J. (2012) 'Practitioners constructions of parent abuse', *Social Policy and Society*, 11 (2), 229-39.

Nock, M.K. and Kazdin, A.E. (2002) 'Parent-directed physical aggression by clinic-referred youths', *Journal of Clinical Child Psychology*, 31, 193-205.

Noll, J.G., Trickett, P.K., Harris, W.W. and Putnam, F.W. (2009) 'The cumulative burden borne by offspring whose mothers were sexually abused as children: descriptive results from a multigenerational study', *Journal of Interpersonal Violence*, 24 (3), 424-49.

NSPCC (2011) *Child abuse and neglect in the UK today*, London: NSPCC, www.nspcc.org.uk/Inform/research/findings/child_abuse_neglect_research_PDF_wdf84181.pdf

Nugent, Y. (2011) 'The abuse of parents by their adolescent children', paper presented at the 'Fifth National Practitioners Seminar Addressing Young People's Use of Violence in Close Relationships', Respect National Conference, Nottingham, 5 October, www.respect.uk.net/data/files/loughborough_university_pdf.pdf

O'Connor, R. (2007) *Who's in charge? A group for parents of violent or beyond control children*, Adelaide, Australia: Southern Junction Community Services.

O'Keefe, M., Hills, A., Doyle, M., McCreadie, C., Scholes, S., Constantine, R., Tinker, A., Manthorpe, J., Biggs, S. and Erens, B. (2007) *UK study of abuse and neglect of older people: Prevalence survey report* [online], London: National Centre for Social Research and King's College London, www.elderabuse.org.uk/AEA%20Services/Useful%20downloads/Prevalence/Prevalence%20Report-Full.pdf

O'Leary, K.D., Malone, J. and Tyree, A (2004) 'Physical aggression in early marriage: prerelationship and relationship effects', *Journal of Consulting and Clinical Psychology*, 62 (3), 594–602.

Omer, H. (2001) 'Helping parents deal with children's acute disciplinary problems without escalation: the principle of nonviolent resistance', *Family Process*, 40 (1), 53–66.

Omer, H. (2004) *Non-violent resistance: A new approach to violent and self-destructive children*, Cambridge: Cambridge University Press.

Omer, H., Schorr-Sapir, I. and Weinblatt, U. (2008) 'Non-violent resistance and violence against siblings', *Journal of Family Therapy*, 30, 450–64.

Organisational Research Services (2005) *King County Step-Up program evaluation*, Seattle, WA: Organisational Research Services.

Pagani, L., Larocque, D., Vitaro, F. and Tremblay, R.E. (2003) 'Verbal and physical abuse toward mothers: the role of family configuration, environment, and coping strategies', *Journal of Youth and Adolescence*, 32 (3), 215–22.

Pagani, L., Tremblay, R.E., Nagin, D., Zoccolillo, M., Vitaro, F. and McDuff, P. (2004) 'Risk factor models for adolescent verbal and physical aggression toward mothers', *International Journal of Behavioral Development*, 28 (6), 528–37.

Pagani, L., Tremblay, R.E., Nagin, D., Zoccolillo, M., Vitaro, F. and McDuff, P. (2009) 'Risk factor models for adolescent verbal and physical aggression toward fathers', *Journal of Family Violence*, 24 (3), 173–82.

Pagelow, M.D. (1982) *Woman batterings: Victims and their experiences*, Beverly Hills, CA: Sage Publications.

Parentline Plus (2008) 'You can't say go and sit on the naughty step because they turn round and say make me', *Aggressive behaviour in children: Parents' experiences and needs* [online], http://plptesting.tribalhosted.co.uk/default.aspx?page=viewarticle&module=articles-view&id=309

Parentline Plus (2009) *Parentline Plus helps lift the lid on parents coping with abuse from their children* [online], http://familylives.org.uk/press-pr/statements/parents-coping-abuse-their-children

Parentline Plus (2010) *When family life hurts: Family experience of aggression in children*, London: Parentline Plus.

Parton, N. (2007) 'Protecting children: a socio-historical analysis', in K. Wilson and A. James (eds) *Child protection handbook* (3rd edition) (pp 9-30), Oxford: Elsevier.

Parton, N. (2011) 'Child protection and safeguarding in England: changing and competing conceptions of risk and their implications for social work', *British Journal of Social Work*, 41, 854-75.

Paterson, R., Luntz, H., Perlesz, A. and Cotton, S. (2002) 'Adolescent violence towards parents: maintaining family connections when the going gets tough', *Australian and New Zealand Journal of Family Therapy*, 23, 90-100.

Paulson, M.J., Coombs, R.H. and Landsverk, J. (1990) 'Youth who physically assault their parents', *Journal of Family Violence*, 5, 121-33.

Pearce, D. (1978) 'The feminization of poverty: women, work and welfare', *Urban and Social Change Review*, 11, 28-36.

Peek, C.W., Fischer, J.L. and Kidwell, J.S. (1985) 'Teenage violence toward parents: a neglected dimension of family violence', *Journal of Marriage and the Family*, 47 (4), 1051-8.

Pelletier, D. and Coutu, S. (1992) 'Substance abuse and family violence in adolescents', *Canada's Mental Health*, 40 (2), 6-12.

Pence, E. and Paymar, M. (1986) *Power and control: Tactics of men who batter*, Duluth, MN: Minnesota Program Development.

Penhale, B. (2008) 'Elder abuse in the United Kingdom', *Journal of Elder Abuse and Neglect*, 20 (2), 151-68.

Perera, H. (2006) 'Parent battering and the psychiatric and family correlates in children and adolescents', *Sri Lanka Journal of Child Health*, 35, 128-32.

Petrie, P., Boddy, J., Cameron, C., Wigfall, V. and Simon, A. (2006) *Working with children in care: European perspectives*, Maidenhead: Open University Press.

Phillips, D.A., Phillips, K.H., Grupp, K. and Trigg, L. (2009) 'Sibling violence silenced: rivalry, competition, wrestling, playing, roughhousing, benign', *Advances in Nursing Science*, 32 (2), E1-E16.

Phoenix, A. and Woollett, A. (1991) 'Motherhood: social construction, politics and psychology', in A. Phoenix, A. Woollett and E. Lloyd (eds) *Motherhood: Meanings, practices and ideologies*, London: Sage Publications.

Pinchbeck, I. and Hewitt, M. (1969) *Children in English society*, London: Routledge & Kegan Paul.

Pretorius, R. (1992) 'Parents as victims of abuse by rebellious children and the role of Tourette's syndrome as a causal factor', *Maatskaplike Werk (Social Work)*, 28 (2), 7-13.

Price, J.A. (1996) *Power and compassion: Working with difficult adolescents and abused parents*, New York, NY: Guilford Press.

Priority Research (2009) *Evaluation of SAAIF (Stopping Aggression and Antisocial Behaviour in Families)*, Sheffield: Priority Research/ North Essex Partnership NHS Foundation Trust, www. theministryofparenting.com/wp-content/uploads/2012/02/1109-SAAIF-evaluation-Report.pdf

Qvortrup, J. (1994) 'Childhood matters: an introduction', in J. Qvortrup, M. Bardy, G. Sgritta and H. Wintersberger (eds) *Childhood matters: Social theory, practice and politics* (pp 1-24), Aldershot: Avebury Press.

Raj, A., Sabaewal, S., Decker, M.R., Nair, S., Jethva, M., Krishnan, S., Donra, B., Saggurti, N. and Silverman, J.G. (2011) 'Abuse from in-laws during pregnancy and post-partum: qualitative and quantitative findings from low-income mothers of infants in Mumbai, India', *Maternal and Child Health Journal*, 15 (6), 700-12.

Reece, H. (2009) 'The degradation of parental responsibility', in R. Probert, S. Gilmore and J. Herring (eds) *Responsible parents and parental responsibility* (pp 85-102), Oxford: Hart Publishing.

Renken, B., Egeland, B., Marvinney, D., Mangelsdorf, S. and Sroufe, L.A. (1989) 'Early childhood antecedents of aggression and passive-withdrawal in early elementary school', *Journal of Personality*, 57 (2), 257-81.

Rich, A. (1976) *Of woman born: Motherhood as experience and institution*, New York, NY: W.W. Norton.

Robinson, A. and Hudson, K. (2011) 'Different yet complementary: two approaches to supporting victims of sexual violence in the UK', *Criminology and Criminal Justice*, 11 (5), 515-33.

Robinson, L. (2011) *Interventions and restorative responses to address teen violence against parents*, Report for the Winston Churchill Memorial Trust, www.alternativerestoratives.co.uk/docs/WCT_REPORT.pdf

Robinson, P.W., Davidson, L.J. and Drebot, M.E. (2004) 'Parent abuse on the rise: a historical review', *American Association of Behavioral Social Science*, 58-67.

Rogoff, B. (2003) *The cultural nature of human development*, Oxford: Oxford University Press.

Romero, F., Melero, A., Canovas, C. and Antolin, M. (2005) *La violencia de los jovenes en la familia: Una aproximacion a los menores denunciados por sus padres* [*Youth violence in the family: An approach to children reported by their parents*], Barcelona: Generalitat of Catalunya.

Rose, N. (1989) *Governing the soul*, London: Routledge.

Routt, G. and Anderson, L. (2011) 'Adolescent violence towards parents', *Journal of Aggression, Maltreatment and Trauma*, 20 (1), 1-19.

Sabina, C. and Straus, M.A. (2008) 'Polyvictimization by dating partners and mental health among U.S. college students', *Violence and Victims*, 23 (6), 667-82.

Samaan, R.A. (2000) 'The influences of race, ethnicity, and poverty on the mental health of children', *Journal of Health Care for the Poor and Underserved*, 11 (1), 100-10.

Segal, U.A. (1999) 'Family violence: a focus on India', *Aggression and Violent Behaviour*, 4 (2), 213-31.

Sheehan, M. (1997) 'Adolescent violence – strategies, outcomes and dilemmas in working with young people and their families', *Australian and New Zealand Journal of Family Therapy*, 18 (2), 80-91.

Simonelli, A.C., Mullis, T., Ellio, A.N. and Pierce, T.W. (2002) 'Abuse by siblings and subsequent experiences of violence within the dating relationship', *Journal of Interpersonal Violence*, 17 (2), 103-21.

Simpson, T.L. and Miller, W.R. (2002) 'Concomitance between childhood sexual and physical abuse and substance use problems: a review', *Clinical Psychology Review*, 22 (1), 27-77.

Sims, E.N., Dodd, V.J. N. and Tejeda, M.J. (2008) 'The relationship between severity of violence in the home and dating violence', *Journal of Forensic Nursing*, 4 (4), 166-73.

Skuja, K. and Halford, K.W. (2004) 'Repeating the errors of our parents? Parental violence in men's family of origin and conflict management in dating couples', *Journal of Interpersonal Violence*, 19 (6), 623-38.

Snyder, H.N. and McCurley, C. (2008) 'Domestic assaults by juvenile offenders', *Juvenile Justice Bulletin*, Washington, DC: Office of Justice Programs.

Snyder, H.N. and Sickmund, M (1999) *Juvenile offenders and victims: 1999 national report*, Pittsburgh, PA: National Center for Juvenile Justice, https://www.ncjrs.gov/html/ojjdp/nationalreport99/toc.html

Southwell, P.L. (2008) 'The effect of political alienation on voter turnout 1964-2000', *Journal of Political and Military Sociology*, 36 (1), 131-45.

Spillane-Grieco, E. (2000) 'From parent verbal abuse to teenage physical aggression?', *Child and Adolescent Social Work Journal*, 17 (6), 411-30.

Sroufe, L.A., Carlson, E.A., Levy, A.K. and Egeland, B. (1999) 'Implications of attachment theory for developmental psychopathology', *Development and Psychopathology*, 11, 1-13.

SSI (Social Services Inspectorate) (1992) *Confronting elder abuse*, London: HMSO.

SSI (1993) *No longer afraid: The safeguard of older people in domestic settings*, London: HMSO.

Stanko, E.A. (2003) *The meanings of violence*, London: Routledge.

Stanley, N., Cleaver, H. and Hart, D. (2009) 'The impact of domestic violence, parental mental health problems, substance misuse and learning disability on parenting capacity', in J. Horwath (ed) *The child's world: The comprehensive guide to assessing children in need* (2nd edition), London: Jessica Kingsley Publishers.

Stephenson, M., Brown, S. and Giller, H. (2011) *Effective practice in youth justice*, Abingdon: Routledge.

Stewart, M., Burns, A. and Leonard, R. (2007) 'Dark side of the mothering role: abuse of mothers by adolescent and adult children', *Sex Roles*, 56 (3-4), 183-91.

Stewart, M., Jackson, D., Mannix, J., Wilkes, L. and Lines, K. (2004) 'Child to mother violence: what does the literature tell us?', *Advances in Contemporary Nursing*, 18 (1/2), 199-210.

Stewart, M., Wilkes, L.M. and Mannix, J. (2006) 'Child-to-mother violence: a pilot study', *Contemporary Nurse: A Journal for the Australian Nursing Profession*, 21 (2), 297-310.

Strathern, M. (1997) 'Gender: division or comparison?', in K. Hetherington and R. Munro (eds) *Ideas of difference: Social spaces and the labour of division* (pp 42-63), Oxford: Blackwell.

Strathern, M. (2005) *Kinship, law and the unexpected: Relatives are always a surprise*, Cambridge: Cambridge University Press.

Strathern, M. (2011) 'What is a parent?', *Journal of Ethnographic Theory*, 1 (1), 245-78.

Straus, M.A. (1979) 'Measuring intrafamily conflict and violence: the Conflict Tactics Scales (CTS)', *Journal of Marriage and the Family*, 41 (1), 75-88.

Straus, M.A., Gelles, R.J. and Steinmetz, S.K. (1980) *Behind closed doors: Violence in the American family*, New York, NY: Doubleday.

Straus, M.A., Hamby, S.L., Boney McCoy, S. and Sugarman, D.B. (1996) 'The revised Conflict Tactics Scales (CTS2): development and preliminary psychometric data', *Journal of Family Issues*, 17, 283-316.

Strom, K.J., Warner, T.D., Tichavsky, L. and Zahn, M.A. (2010) 'Policing juveniles: domestic violence arrest policies, gender, and police response to child–parent violence', *Crime and Delinquency*, OnlineFirst: doi: 10.1177/0011128710376293

Stubbs, J. (2002) 'Domestic violence and women's safety: feminist challenges to restorative justice', in H. Strang and J. Braithwaite (eds) *Restorative justice and family violence* (pp 42-61), Cambridge: Cambridge University Press.

Sullivan, P.M. and Knutson, J.F. (2000) 'Maltreatment and disabilities: a population based epidemiological study', *Child Abuse and Neglect*, 24 (10), 1257-73.

Tew, J. and Nixon, J. (2010) 'Parent abuse: opening up a discussion of a complex instance of family power relations', *Social Policy and Society*, 9 (4), 579-89.

Thomas Corum (2008) *Evaluation of the individual telephone service*, London: Parentline Plus.

Tidefors, I., Arvidsson, H., Ingevaldson, S. and Larsson, M. (2010) 'Sibling incest: a literature review and a clinical study', *Journal of Sexual Aggression*, 16 (3), 347-60.

Tomlin, S. (1989) *Abuse of elderly people: An unnecessary and preventable problem*, London: British Geriatrics Society.

TUC (Trades Union Congress) (2010) *The gender impact of the cuts: A TUC cuts briefing*, London: TUC, www.tuc.org.uk/extras/genderimpactofthecuts.pdf

Turner, H.A., Finkelhor, D. and Ormrod, R. (2010) 'Poly-victimization in a national sample of children and youth', *American Journal of Preventive Medicine*, 38 (3), 323-30.

Uekert, B., Sagatun-Edwards, I., Crowe, A., Peters, T., Cheesman, F. and Kameda, D. (2006) *Juvenile domestic and family violence: The effects of court-based intervention programs on recidivism*, Washington, DC: US Department of Justice, https://www.ncjrs.gov/pdffiles1/nij/grants/216614.pdf

Ullman, A. and Straus, M.A. (2003) 'Violence by children against mothers in relation to violence between parents and corporal punishment by parents', *Journal of Comparative Family Studies*, 34 (1), 41-60.

UN (United Nations) (1989) *Convention on the rights of the child*, Geneva: Office of the High Commissioner for Human Rights.

UN (1993) *Declaration on the elimination of violence against women*, Geneva: UN General Assembly, www.un.org/documents/ga/res/48/a48r104.htm

Victim Support (2011) *Domestic violence: Information from Victim Support*, London: Victim Support, www.victimsupport.org/Help%20for%20victims/Different%20types%20of%20crime/Domestic%20violence

Walker, L.E. (1978) 'Battered women and learned helplessness', *Victimology*, 2, 525-34.

Wallbank, J. (2001) *Reconstructing motherhood(s)*, London: Prentice-Hall.

Walsh, J.A. and Krienert, J.L. (2007) 'Child–parent violence: an empirical analysis of offender, victim, and event characteristics in a national sample of reported incidents', *Journal of Family Violence*, 22 (7), 563-74.

Walsh, J.A. and Krienert, J.L. (2009) 'A decade of child-initiated family violence comparative analysis of child–parent violence and parricide examining offender, victim, and event characteristics in a national sample of reported incidents, 1995-2005', *Journal of Interpersonal Violence*, 24 (9), 1450-77.

Weinblatt, U. and Omer, H. (2008) 'Nonviolent resistance: a treatment for parents of children with acute behaviour problems', *Journal of Marital and Family Therapy*, 34 (1), 75-92.

White, E. and Epston, D. (1990) *Narrative means to therapeutic ends*, New York, NY: Norton.

White, S., Wastell, D., Peckover, S., Hall, C. and Broadhurst, K. (2009) 'Managing risk in a high blame environment: tales from the "front door" in contemporary children's social care', in *Risk and public services* (pp 12-14), London and Oxford: Economic and Social Research Council.

Wiehe, V.R. (1997) *Sibling abuse: Hidden physical, emotional and sexual trauma* (2nd edition), Thousand Oaks, CA: Sage Publications.

Wilcox, P. (2012) 'Is parent abuse a form of domestic violence?', *Social Policy and Society*, 12 (2), 277-88.

Wilson, J. (1996) 'Physical abuse of parents by adolescent children', in D.M. Busby (ed) *The impact of violence on the family: Treatment approaches for therapists and other professionals* (pp 101-23), Boston, MA: Allyn & Bacon.

Winnicott, D. (1953) 'Transitional objects and transitional phenomena', *International Journal of Psychoanalysis*, 34, 89-97.

Women's Aid (2009) *The survivor's handbook*, London: Women's Aid Federation of England.

Yllo, K. (1988) 'Political and methodological debates in wife abuse research', in K. Yllo and M. Bograd (eds) *Feminist perspectives on wife abuse*, Newbury Park, CA: Sage Publications.

Youth Justice Board/Ministry of Justice (2011) *Youth justice statistics 2009/10 England and Wales: Statistics bullettin* [online], www.justice. gov.uk/publications/docs/yjb-annual-workload-data-0910.pdf

Zelizer, V. (1985) *Pricing the priceless child*, New York, NY: Basic Books.

Index

Note: The following abbreviations have been used – *f* = figure; *n* = note; *t* = table

A

absent parents 33, 52, 63, 74, 92, 94
abuse: definition 16
'abuse journal' 130
Abuse and Respect Wheels 131*f*
Action for Children 18*t*
Action on Elder Abuse 18*t*, 22
Adams, A.E. 39
ADHD *see* attention deficit
  hyperactivity disorder
'adolescent-to-adolescent dating
  violence' 35*n*
adolescent-to-parent abuse/violence
  see parent abuse
adolescents
  as perpetrators of violence against
    women 21
  social status 90–2
  'status ambiguity' 91, 92
adoptive parents 151
ADSS *see* Association of Directors of
  Social Services
adult social care responses 110
advocacy organisations 18*t*, 20, 21,
  152
age: perpetrators 30–1, 33, 34, 97
age of consent 83
agency discourses 91
agentic parent 106
Agnew, R. 41
Ainsworth, M.D.S. 65–6
Alternative Restoratives (UK) 153
ambivalent-insecure 66
American Journal of Psychiatry 9
Anderson, L. 10–11, 101
anger 126
Anti-Social Behaviour Order (ASBO)
  105
anxiety: parental 49–50, 54

'appropriate victim' 64
ASBO (Anti-Social Behaviour Order)
  105
'asking patterns' 46, 60
assessment: intervention work
  111–12, 120–1, 140, 157–8
Association of Directors of Social
  Services (ADSS) 22, 110
Astell Project (prevention group)
  142*n*
'at risk' individuals 20, 61, 107, 109,
  110, 117–18, 140
'attachment theory' 65–6, 123*t*
attention deficit hyperactivity disorder
  (ADHD) 59, 73
Australia 6, 8, 13*n*, 27, 123*t*, 124*t*,
  125–7, 136
authoritarian/authoritative style
  parenting styles 67–8
authority *see* parental authority
avoidance strategies 48
avoidant-insecure 66
awareness-raising campaigns 116, 138,
  139, 140, 142*n*

B

'backing off' 64
Bandura, A. 62
Barnardo's 18*t*, 20
'battered baby syndrome' 20
*Battered elder syndrome: An exploratory
  study* (Block and Sinnott) 21
'battered parent syndrome' 9, 21, 26
Baumrind, D. 66–7, 97*n*
behaviour therapists 100*t*, 121
behavioural traits/deficits 61–2
*Behind closed doors: Violence in the
  American family* (Straus) 9
betrayal 50, 54

'beyond parental control' 108
biological parents 151
blame 10, 50, 54, 58, 64, 70, 75, 81,
    135, 139, 147
  mothers 82, 94–5, 119
Block, M.R. 21
Bobic, N. 154
'Bobo doll' (laboratory experiments)
    62
Bowlby, J. 65–6
Break4Change 123*t*, 127–8, 139
Breaking the Cycle 123*t*, 125
*Breaking the cycle: Effective punishment,
    rehabilitation and sentencing of
    offenders* (Ministry of Justice) 146
Brezina, T. 63
Brighton and Hove Youth Offending
    Team 127
British Crime Survey 28
Broken Rainbow 21
Browne, K.D. 28
Buel, S.M. 103
Burton, M. 116

C

CAF (Common Assessment
    Framework) 111
*Call to end violence against women and
    girls: Action plan* (Home Office) 21,
    145–6
CAMHS *see* Child and Adolescent
    Mental Health
Canada 6, 23, 27, 104, 124*t*, 136
Care Orders 108
'category codes' 102
CEOP *see* Child Exploitation and
    Online Protection Centre
cessation of parent abuse 47–9, 150
Charles, A.V. 67
child abuse 2, 4, 43, 64, 87, 90, 102,
    108, 109
  as type of family abuse 17, 18*t*,
    19–20, 24, 25, 33, 34, 35*n*
Child and Adolescent Mental Health
    (CAMHS) 100*t*, 128
Child Exploitation and Online
    Protection Centre (CEOP) 18*t*, 20
child labour 83
child neglect 19
child protection 19, 145
Child-to-Mother Violence Scale
    (CMVS) 6, 60–1

'child-to-parent violence' *see* parent
    abuse
childhood
  'becoming' 83, 91
  discourse of 'innocence' 83, 84
  power and 85–92
  social status 90–2
'childrearing': feminist approach 80,
    97*n*
'childrearing style' *see* parenting style
children 96–7
  in need of protection 92
  parenthood/childhood and power
    85–92
  as perpetrators of violence against
    women 21
  reshaping of parents, state and 82–5
  social construction of child–parent
    relationship 79–82
Children Act (1989) (UK) 83, 108
children's rights 82–5, 87, 89–90
children's social care services 107–9
child–parent bond 80–1
'clinical samples' 5–6
clinical 'syndrome' 59
CMVS *see* Child-to-Mother Violence
    Scale
cognitive traits/deficits 61–2
cognitive-behavioural programmes
    106, 123*t*, 128–9, 130, 131*f*
Common Assessment Framework
    (CAF) 111
common-sense understandings 58, 64,
    65, 75–6, 81, 86, 92, 95
community
  impact on life of 51–3
  prevention work in 139–40
  responses to abuse 115
community sector 99, 117, 144
'complementary escalation' 67–8
'compliance culture' 145
conduct disorder 73
Conflict Tactics Scale (CTS) 60, 77*n*
constructionism 125
'contract': restorative justice 136, 137
control: exercise of 1–2
Convention on the rights of the child
    (United Nations) 23, 83, 90
coping strategies 47–8, 54, 68, 75
Cornell, C. 139
Cottrell, B. 10, 57, 63, 71, 104, 141*n*,
    154

counselling 53, 138
'creative sessions': intervention work 127
criminal justice services 5, 10, 12, 13*n*, 29, 72–3, 146
  intervention programmes 123*t*, 124*t*
  responses to abuse 100*t*, 101–110, 113*t*, 117
Criminal Law Amendment Act (1885) 83
criminal responsibility 84, 97*n*
'criminalisation of social policy' 100, 101
CTS *see* Conflict Tactics Scale
'cultural authority' 2
cultural background 33–4, 44, 121, 147, 150
'culture of silence' 10–11
'cycle of violence' theory 25, 109, 132

D

damaging property 39–40, 54*n*
'dating violence' 20, 24, 25, 34, 35*n*, 129
daughters: prevalence amongst 29–30, 64
Declaration on the elimination of violence against women (United Nations) 23
'delinquency' discourse 101, 103
denial 49, 149
denigration of parenting abilities 38–9, 42
Department of Health (DH) 22
Department of Judicial Administration (Seattle, US) 129
Derry, A. 27
'deserving victim' 10
despair 50–1, 54
determined child 106
deterrence 105
developmental psychology 80–1
deviancy discourses 91
DH (Department of Health) 22
disability 17, 88, 110
disbelief: parental 44, 46, 49, 149
discipline 47, 48, 54*n*, 138
'discourse of determinism' 25
Domestic and Family Violence Research, Queensland Centre for (Australia) 155–6
Domestic Violence: A National Report (Home Office) 118*n*

domestic violence
  courts 103
  definition of 146
  support groups 112
Domestic Violence Helpline, National 21
Donzelot, J. 84
Doran, J.E. 120, 136–7, 149
Du Bois, R.H. 26
Duluth Model 123*t*, 129, 130, 131*f*

E

Eckstein, N.J. 44, 45*f*, 46, 47, 64, 70, 90, 104, 149
economic abuse 3, 16, 17, 39–41, 104
economic power 87
Eddie Gallagher's Webpages 154
Edenborough, M.D. 6, 75, 115
education and educational services 71, 83, 100*t*, 139, 142*n*, 144
  behavioural problems at school 32, 33, 34, 148
  responses to abuse 111–12, 113*t*, 118*n*
Educational Maintenance Allowance 144
elder abuse 2–3, 17, 18*t*, 21–2, 23, 33, 34, 102, 110, 151
Elder Abuse, International Network for the Prevention of 22
Elder Abuse, National Committee for the Prevention of 22
Elementary Education Act (1870) 83
Elliott, G.C. 61
emotional abuse 3, 16, 20, 35*n*, 38, 42–3, 44, 45*f*, 47, 70
emotional impacts 49–51
emotionalisation 80–1
'empathy letters' 130
employment: parental 53
epidemiological surveys 5–6, 12, 26–7
ethnicity 31–2, 34, 71–2, 76, 83
European Court of Human Rights 84
evaluation data 122, 135, 141
'everyday teenage behaviour' 38
explanations
  interpersonal 57–8, 62–5, 121, 143–4
  intrafamilial 58, 68–71, 76, 121
  intrapersonal explanations 58–62
extended family members 53

F

factors: identifying 57–8, 150
Factory Act (1933) 83
'failing parent' 89
families
  different forms of 151
  governance of 84–5
  as source of support 100*t*, 115, 134, 139–40
family abuse
  different forms of 15–17, 18*t*
  emergence as a 'social problem' 19–24
  impact on life of 1–2, 51–3
  intrafamilial explanations 58, 68–71, 76, 121
  relationship between different forms of 24–5, 148
family group conferences 136, 141*n*
family intervention work 132–8, 151–2, 127, 141
Family Lives (formerly Parentline Plus) 28, 100*t*, 111, 114, 154
'family programmes' 122
family systems theory 68-71, 123*t*
Family Violence Research, Queensland Centre for Domestic and (Australia) 155–6
Family Violence Survey, National (US) 6, 9, 22, 27
fathers and fatherhood 64, 79
  absence of 33, 52–3, 94
  lone parents 95
  occupation 32
  prevalence amongst 28–9
  responsibility/blame 94–5
  'ultimate authority' 94
fear 49, 54, 101–2, 120
femininity 92–4, 123*t*
feminism 20, 21, 80, 96, 123*t*, 126
'feminist-as-intervention interviews' 125
Ferguson, H. 19
'fighting back' 87
filial violence 33, 35*n*
financial abuse *see* economic abuse
Finkelhor, D. 9, 85
Focus Adolescent Services (US) 155
foster parents 151
Foucault, M. 86
France 27, 59

friends: informal support 114, 134, 139–40
Frizzell, A.W. 3
frontline services 7, 99, 115–17, 144, 148
  see also under individual services
functional family therapy 123*t*, 128–9

G

Gallagher, E. 67, 123*t*, 125–7, 147, 154
gang involvement 32, 34
Gebo, E. 29, 30
Gelles, R. 139
Gelles, R.J. 15–16
gender 4, 64, 66, 75, 76, 81, 83, 97
  family abuse 18*t*
  parents 28–9, 74
  parents and power 92–6
  perpetrators 23, 25, 28–30, 31, 33, 34
  seeking help 119–20
generational transmission of violence 11, 25, 62–5
genograms 133
Germany (Republic of) 26
Gingerbread 'Family Safe' Project (UK) 155
'good enough mothering' 65
'good parenthood' 51, 95
Goody, E.N. 81
governance of family life 84–5
grief/loss 50, 51, 54
group intervention work 121, 122, 124*t*, 125–30, 138, 140
guilt 51, 126

H

Hakim, J. 96
Hamilton, C.E. 28
Harbin, H.T. 9, 21, 67
harm caused 16–17, 18*t*, 124*t*
Hartz, D. 31
Hawaii 31
Health, Department of (DH) 22
health problems 53
health visitors 100*t*, 146
healthcare services 100*t*, 111–12, 113, 123*t*, 124*t*, 146
help-seeking 108–9, 119–20, 140
helplessness *see* parental helplessness
'hierarchy of abuse' 70

Hispanic adolescents 32
Holes in the Wall (UK) 154
home curfew 105
Home Office 21, 118*n*, 145–6
homelessness 72
'honeymoon period' 48
hooks, b. 80
hopelessness 50–1, 107, 117
House of Commons Select
    Committee on Violence in
    Marriage (1974) 20
Howard, J. 72, 149
Huguley, S. 41
Human Rights Act (1998) 110

I

'ideals' of violence 92–4
impact of parent abuse 18*t*, 38, 49–53,
    54
'in need' children 109
'inconsistent parenting' 67
Incredible Years (behavioural
    programme) 106
India 33–4
individualisation 80–1
institutionalised discrimination 102
inter-parental violence 64
intergenerational transmission 11, 25,
    62–5
'internal working model' 65
International Network for the
    Prevention of Elder Abuse 22
interpersonal factors 57–8, 62–5, 121,
    143–4
intervention work 6, 8, 11, 13, 31,
    55*n*, 58, 142*n*, 144, 145, 146
    assessment 111–12, 120–1, 140,
        157–8
    criminal justice services 123*t*, 124*t*
    evaluation data 122, 135, 141
    family interventions 132–8
    future directions for practice 147–51
    group interventions 121, 122, 124*t*,
        125–30, 138, 140
    help-seeking contexts 108–9,
        119–20, 140
    perpetrators 103, 105, 129–30
    pluralism in 121–2, 140
    prevention strategies 138–40, 141,
        145

as 'punishment' for 'bad parenting'
    106
youth offending services 101, 105–7
Intimate Partner Violence (IPV) 2,
    20–1, 24, 25, 48, 68, 73–4, 93, 102,
    109, 152
    abusive tactics 38, 39, 42, 141*n*
    emergence of 20–1
    family abuse and 17, 18*t*, 33, 34
    group interventions 125, 126, 129
    support services 112, 114, 116, 119
intrafamilial factors 58, 68–71, 76, 121
intrapersonal factors 57, 58–62, 76
Israel 34, 124*t*

J

Jackson, D. 44, 120
Japan 33, 34
Judicial Administration, Department
    of (Seattle, US) 129
judicial responses 103–4
Justice, Ministry of 146
Juvenile Batterer's Intervention
    Program (US) 103
juvenile courts 104, 130, 146
Juvenile Delinquency Protection
    Orders (US) 103

K

Kitzinger, J. 4
knowledge: parental 88–9
Kozu, J. 33

L

Laurent, A. 27
learned helplessness 93–4
'learning culture' 145
learning difficulties 32
legal power 89–90
lesbian, gay, bisexual and transgender
    (LGBT) 21
Lesko, N. 91
local authority services 107, 113*t*
Local Children's Safeguarding Board
    (LSCB) 111–12, 117
London Children's Safeguarding
    Board (London CSB) 111
lone parents 29, 50, 74, 92, 95, 144,
    148, 155
loss/grief 50, 51, 54

LSCB (Local Children's Safeguarding Board) 111–12
Luntz, Helen 125

M

Madden, D.J. 9, 21, 67
maintenance: parent abuse 47–9, 150
'man of the house' 94
management: parent abuse 47–9
MARAC *see* Multi-Agency Risk Assessment Conference
masculinity 92–4
mattering 61
Mediation and Family Therapy Service (MATTERS) programme 124*t*, 132–3, 141*n*
medical discourses 91
Men's Advice Line 21
mental health problems
  parents 53, 88, 93
  perpetrators 32, 34, 57, 58–9, 72, 73, 76, 148
mental health services 100*t*, 111
Micucci, J.A. 69, 70, 132
Ministry of Justice (England and Wales) 146, 154
minority ethnic families 31, 71–2
Mirrlees-Black, C. 28
'modelling' 62–3, 121
Monk, P. 57, 63, 154
'mothering continuum' 80
mothers and motherhood 1, 52–3, 64, 79, 87, 92–3, 148
  awareness of onset 44
  group intervention 125
  help-seeking contexts 119–20
  lone parents 29, 92, 95, 144, 148
  physical power and 87
  prevalence of abuse amongst 27, 28–9
  responsibility/blame 94–5
  sense of unnaturalness in abuse 82
multi-agency response 117, 123*t*, 128, 130, 145
Multi-Agency Risk Assessment Conference (MARAC) 102, 118*n*
multi-research teams 150
Munro review of child protection, The (2011) 145

N

'naming' the problem 4, 5, 138, 147
narrative therapy 132
National Committee for the Prevention of Elder Abuse 22
National Domestic Violence Helpline 21
National Family Violence Survey (US) 6, 9, 22, 27
National Health Service and Community Care Act (1990) 22
National Institute for Health and Clinical Excellence (NICE) 146
National Society for the Prevention of Cruelty to Children (NSPCC) 18*t*, 19, 20
National Survey of Youth (US) 6, 26–7
nationality 33–4
negative reinforcement 62, 63
neglect 16–17
Neighbours, Friends and Families campaign (Canada) 140, 142*n*
'nested ecological model' 57
NICE (National Institute for Health and Clinical Excellence) 146
Nixon, J. 108
No secrets: The protection of vulnerable adults (Department of Health) 22
Non-Molestation Orders 114
non-violent resistance (NVR) approaches 124*t*, 133–5
Non-Violent Resistance (UK) 153, 155
'not-mattering' 61
NSPCC *see* National Society for the Prevention of Cruelty to Children
nurturing 81, 82

O

obsessive-compulsive disorder (OCD) 59
Occupation Orders 114
Omer, H. 67, 134
online support forums 114
onset of parent abuse 31, 44, 45*f*, 46, 74, 150
'opening vignette': researchers 149
operant conditioning 62–3
'oppositional symptoms' 59
'overly-permissive parenting' 9

P

PAARS (Parent Abuse and Reconciliation Service) (UK) 155
Pagani, L. 29, 33
parent abuse dynamic 85, 96, 107, 108
  case characteristics 32–3, 34, 42
  compared to other family abuse 18*t*
  culture of silence 10–11
  definition 1–3, 12, 13*n*, 54*n*
  development of 38, 39, 43–4, 45*f*, 46–9, 70, 148
  forms of 37–43, 54
  historic background 9–11
  prevalence patterns 5–6, 7, 18*t*, 26–34, 150
  problems with terminology 3–4, 12
  research problems 4–7
  situating within infrastructures of family abuse 23–4
Parent Abuse and Reconciliation Service (PAARS) (UK) 155
Parent Abuse Research Network (UK) 154
Parent-Directed Aggression Inventory 60
parental authority 39, 47, 70, 81, 82, 85, 90, 91, 116, 129, 132, 133
'parental determinism' 147
parental helplessness 2, 67, 93–4, 134, 135
'parental presence' 124*t*, 134
parental responsibility (legal) 82–5, 95, 104, 107, 114
parental roles 81–2
'parental visitation' technique 134
parenthood
  defining parameters of 79–80
  as a 'labour of love' 80–1
  power and 85–92
  social status of 90–2
'parentification' 67
'parenting deficit' 106, 107
'parenting expertise' 90–1
Parenting Orders 95, 104, 106, 114
parenting organisations/resources 7, 10, 114–15, 116, 117
parenting practices 57, 65–8, 72, 81, 147
Parentline Plus *see* Family Lives
Parentlink (Australia) 155
parents 28–9, 49–50, 53, 54, 96–7, 151–2

age during abuse 31
diversity in constitution 151
ethnicity, religiosity and social class 31–2
gendering and power 92–6
nationality and culture 33–4, 44, 121, 147, 150
parenthood/childhood and power 85–92
'quality of attachment' 65–6, 68, 147
reshaping of children, state and 82–5
resources 88–9, 154–6
social construction of child–parent relationship 79–82
social isolation 4, 5, 10, 53, 71–3, 88, 115, 126, 137, 149
sources of support sought by 100*t*
understanding of causes of parent abuse 73–6, 147
victimisation of perpetrators by 63
as victims 10, 93, 95
'parent's toolbox' 128–9
parricide 3, 13*n*, 151
Paterson, R. 55*n*
'pathological parenting' 68
Patterson, Rosemary 125
Paulson, M.J. 32
'peacemaking' 87
peer groups: perpetrators and 57, 71–3, 74, 76
'peer' victimisation 23
permissive parenting 66, 67–8, 135
perpetrators
  age 30–1, 33, 34
  ethnicity, religiosity and social class 31–2
  explanations for abuse 74–5
  gender 23, 25, 28–30, 31, 33, 34
  intervention work 103, 105, 129–30
  nationality and culture 33–4
  psychopathologies 6–7, 9, 13, 58–61
  victim protection and 102, 114, 118*n*
  victimisation by violent parent 63
personal life: impact on 51–3
personality traits/deficits 61–2
physical abuse 5, 6, 16, 41–2, 44, 45*f*, 46, 47, 60, 70, 120
physical power 88
pluralism: in intervention work 121–2, 140
police services 100*t*, 101–3

policy making 144–7
political approach 124*t*
political power 87
polyvictimisation 17, 34, 43, 51
'positive action' policies 103, 118*n*
positive reinforcement 62
post-traumatic stress disorder (PTSD)
    59, 63
poverty 57, 71, 72, 87, 148
Power and compassion: Working with
    difficult adolescents and abused parents
    (Price) 9, 81, 90
'Power and Control Wheel' 130, 131*f*,
    141*n*
power relations 2, 8, 57, 76, 83, 96–7,
    133, 143, 148–9, 150
    gendered imbalances 74
    gendering and parenthood 92–6
    parenthood/childhood and 85–92
    parenting styles 67
    reshaping of children, parents and
        state 82–5
    social construction of child–parent
        relationship 79–82
powerlessness 90, 94, 96–7, 107, 126,
    143
practitioners: resources 153–4
prevalence patterns 5–6, 7, 18*t*, 26–34,
    150
prevention strategies 138–40, 141,
    145
Price, J.A. 9, 81, 90
process of abuse 150
psychoanalytic perspective 63
psychological determinism 81
psychopathological perspective 6–7, 9,
    13, 58–61
psychosis 73
PTSD *see* post-traumatic stress
    disorder
Public Protection Investigation Unit
    (UK) 102
punishment 62

Q

'quality of attachment' 65–6, 68, 147
Quebec Longitudinal Study of
    Kindergarten Children (Canada)
    6, 27
Queensland Centre for Domestic
    and Family Violence Research
    (Australia) 155–6

R

re-victimisation 25, 65
'reciprocal escalation' 67
'reciprocality': child–parent
    relationship 51
Refuge 18*t*, 21
refuge accommodation 114, 127
rehabilitation 105
religiosity 31–2
remorse 48
reparation 105
repeat victimisations 17, 34
'requesting patterns' 46, 60
research: future directions 149–51
researchers: resources 154
resentment 50, 51, 54, 74
residential care system 151
'resistant' responses 134
resources: parental 88–9, 154–6
Respect (UK) 153
'Respect Wheel' 130, 131*f*
'response tactics' 130
responsibility: for abuse 13*n*, 40–1,
    50, 51, 58, 75, 83, 94–5, 104, 107,
    143–4
'responsibility letters' 130
'responsive parenting' 65
restorative justice 124*t*, 135–8, 146
Rich, A. 80
rights: children's 82–5, 87, 89–90
risk assessment/management 116,
    128, 150
Rose, N. 80–1
Rottem, N. 72, 149
Routt, G. 10–11, 101

S

SAAIF *see* Stopping Aggression and
    Anti-social Behaviour in Families
'sacralization of the child' 80
Safeguarding adults (Association of
    Directors of Social Services) 110
Safeguarding children abused through
    domestic violence (London SCB) 111
Safeguarding children affected by gang
    activity and/or serious youth violence
    for child practitioners (London
    Children's Safeguarding Board)
    111
'safeguarding responsibilities' 20, 107
sanctions 47, 48, 54*n*, 138

Save the Children 18*t*, 20
SAVRY (Structured Assessment of Violence Risk in Youth) 128–9
schizophrenia 73
school exclusions 139
schools *see* education and educational services
'scientific authority' 3, 57, 58, 73, 77*n*, 80, 143
secondary victimisation 24–5, 35*n*
secure attachment 66
Segal, U.A. 33
self-care strategies 138
sentencing circles 136
seriousness: different kinds of abuse 44, 49
sexual abuse 16, 20, 39, 43
sexuality: parental 39
SFBT *see* solution-focused brief therapy
shame 2, 50, 61, 89, 136
Sheehan, M. 121, 133
Sherwood Associates (UK) 153
Short Message Service (SMS) 127
sibling abuse 2, 17, 18*t*, 22–3, 25, 34, 51–2, 108–9, 135
'silent treatment' 42
Single Person Action Network (SPAN) 156
Sinnott, J.D. 21
'sit-in' technique 134
size differential 41–2
social class 31–2, 34, 76, 83
social deprivation 71–3
social isolation 4, 5, 10, 53, 71–3, 88, 115, 126, 137, 149
social learning theory 62–5, 121
'social problems' 9, 10, 13
social science discourses 91
social services 100*t*, 107, 108, 113*t*, 117
Social Services Inspectorate (SSI) 22
sociocultural explanations 58
sociopolitical approach 124*t*, 133, 135
solution-focused brief therapy (SFBT) 123*t*, 125–7
sons
  physical power and 87, 88, 92
  prevalence amongst 29–30, 64
Spain 30–1
SPAN (Single Person Action Network) 156

Specialist Juvenile Violence Court (US) 130
sponsoring: role of parent in 81, 82
Sri Lanka 59
SSI (Social Services Inspectorate) 22
state responsibilities 18*t*, 20, 84–5, 96, 108, 151
step-parents 94, 151
Step-Up *see* Stop, Time out, Evaluate, Prepare, Use skills and Patience
Stewart, M. 48–9, 75
Stop, Time out, Evaluate, Prepare, Use skills and Patience (Step-Up) 123*t*, 129–30, 153
Stopping Aggression and Anti-social Behaviour in Families (SAAIF) 123*t*, 128–9
'strange situation' 65, 66, 80
Strathern, M. 79
Straus, M.A. 9, 15–16, 64
structural factors 58, 71–3, 76, 121
Structured Assessment of Violence Risk in Youth (SAVRY) 128–9
substance abuse 32, 33, 34, 57, 58, 60, 72, 73, 76, 148
Supernanny (television programme) 10, 90
Supervision Orders 108
swearing *see* verbal abuse
systemic family therapy 124*t*, 132–3, 134

T

Targeted Youth Support Service (TYSS) 127
Teenage Aggression Responding Assertively (TARA) 124*t*, 133
telephone support services 114, 134
Tender (prevention group) 142*n*
terminology: problems with 3–4, 12
therapeutic discourses 91
threats 42, 43, 89, 90, 101
'tick box' inventories 120
'time-out logs' 130
Tourette's syndrome 59
'transformative' television programmes 10, 90
'triangulation' 141*n*
Triple P (behavioural programme) 106
TYSS (Targeted Youth Support Service) 127

U

Ullman, A. 64
'unconditional love' 51
unconditional 'reconciliation gestures'
    134
unemployment 144–5
United Kingdom 8, 17, 18t, 21–2,
    28, 83
United Nations 23, 83, 90
United States 6, 8, 13n, 23, 59, 101,
    103, 104, 123t, 125
  parenting practices 65–6, 67
  prevalence of abuse 26–7, 28, 29,
    32, 34

V

VAWG (violence against women and
    girls) 145
verbal abuse 3, 37–9, 42, 43, 44, 45f,
    46, 47, 70
victim impact panels 136
victim protection 102, 114, 118n
Victim Support (charity) 112, 117
victim support services 112, 114, 128
violence 4, 15–16, 24
  'abnormality' and 62
  cultural normalisation of 93
  'cycle of violence' theory 25
  'ideals' of 92–4
  legislation 20–1
violence against women and girls
    (VAWG) 145
Violence in Marriage, House of
    Commons Select Committee
    (1974) 20
Violent Behaviour Questionnaire 60
voluntary sector 19, 20, 21, 99, 100t,
    117, 122, 123t, 144
  responses to abuse 112, 114–15

W

'wait until your father gets home'
    narrative 94
Walker, L.E. 93
'walking on eggshells' 49
Walking on Eggshells Resources
    (Australia) 156
weapons; use of 29
Weinblatt, U. 67, 134
welfare benefits 144

When teens abuse their parents (Cottrell)
    10
Who's the Boss? programme 127
Who's in Charge? 123t, 125–7
Wiehe, V.R. 23
Wilcox, P. 109
Winnicott, D. 65
Wish for a Brighter Future (UK) 156
Women's Aid 18t, 21, 112
Work Capability Assessments 146

Y

York Law School 154
Youth Justice Board Toolkit:
    Information Sheet (Ministry of
    Justice) 154
Youth, National Survey of (US) 6,
    26–7
youth offending 72–3, 83, 107, 136,
    148
  services 101, 105–7, 116, 123t, 127,
    128, 146
Youth in Transition (YIT) (US) 6,
    26–7
Youthful Offenders Act (1854) 83
YUVA (UK) 156

Z

Zelizer, V. 80